Life on the Invisible Line

John Bouchard

Order this book online at www.trafford.com
or email orders@trafford.com

Most Trafford titles are also available at major online book retailers.

Printed in the United States of America.

ISBN: 978-1-4907-2044-9 (sc)
ISBN: 978-1-4907-2045-6 (e)

Library of Congress Control Number: 2013921936

Trafford rev. 11/26/2013

www.trafford.com

North America & international
toll-free: 1 888 232 4444 (USA & Canada)
fax: 812 355 4082

Introduction

I was trained at Saganaga Lake, Ontario, a remote but popular wilderness lake destination for thousands of outdoor enthusiasts. Saganaga Lake lived up to its name: Lake of many Islands. Saganaga is comprised of coloured rocks and red pine with visible etchings of history; ancient Indian rock paintings; a place where nesting copper pots along with muskets can be found deep in its' waters. Somewhere midway beneath Saganaga's waves, an invisible line zigzags east to west, defining the border between the US and Canada. At the western end of the lake, running south to north, a line on a map indicates Quetico Provincial Park. For wildlife officers on both sides of the invisible line, enforcement and jurisdiction are especially important. A minor incident has potential for international embarrassment. In time, both sides learned to work together, for they shared mutual accord: a concern for people, wildlife, and nature.

I spent eighteen years in the Land of the Voyageurs. The tree line along Saganaga Lake is forever etched in my mind. Like jagged inky tape, it unreels from time to time in my mind, taking me from place to place and eventually back to home base. It's like traveling in a dream with eyes wide open. I can hear the drone of the outboard and see the silvery wake curving to disappear behind islands. I look ahead, then behind, rounding Windy Point. Waves tell me my navigation is right. Dickie's Rock remains where it always should be, submerged, left of the line of travel. The warmth of a propane light glides past me. Then I realize that all that I see is stationary, and it is I who is moving.

All life is a story, humans put them on paper. I needed some encouragement to bring this project to fruition. Any credit or blame must be shared by 4 teachers and a former principal. Like these stories they too come from both sides of the border. Carla Arneson, Art teacher, and Meagan Heiman, English teacher, hail from Ely Minnesota and were my early encouragers. Carole Ouimet, my daughter, is a French teacher from Vancouver Canada, who persevered through much of the data entry and kept the dream alive when I was ready to give up. From Thunder Bay, Phyllis Dalgleish, my computer Guru and teacher, turned the dream into reality. I've given the last word to Harold Alanen, retired principal, as writer of my biography. One might wonder what brought all of us together. The answer is simple: wilderness. I am thankful for all of them.

John Bouchard

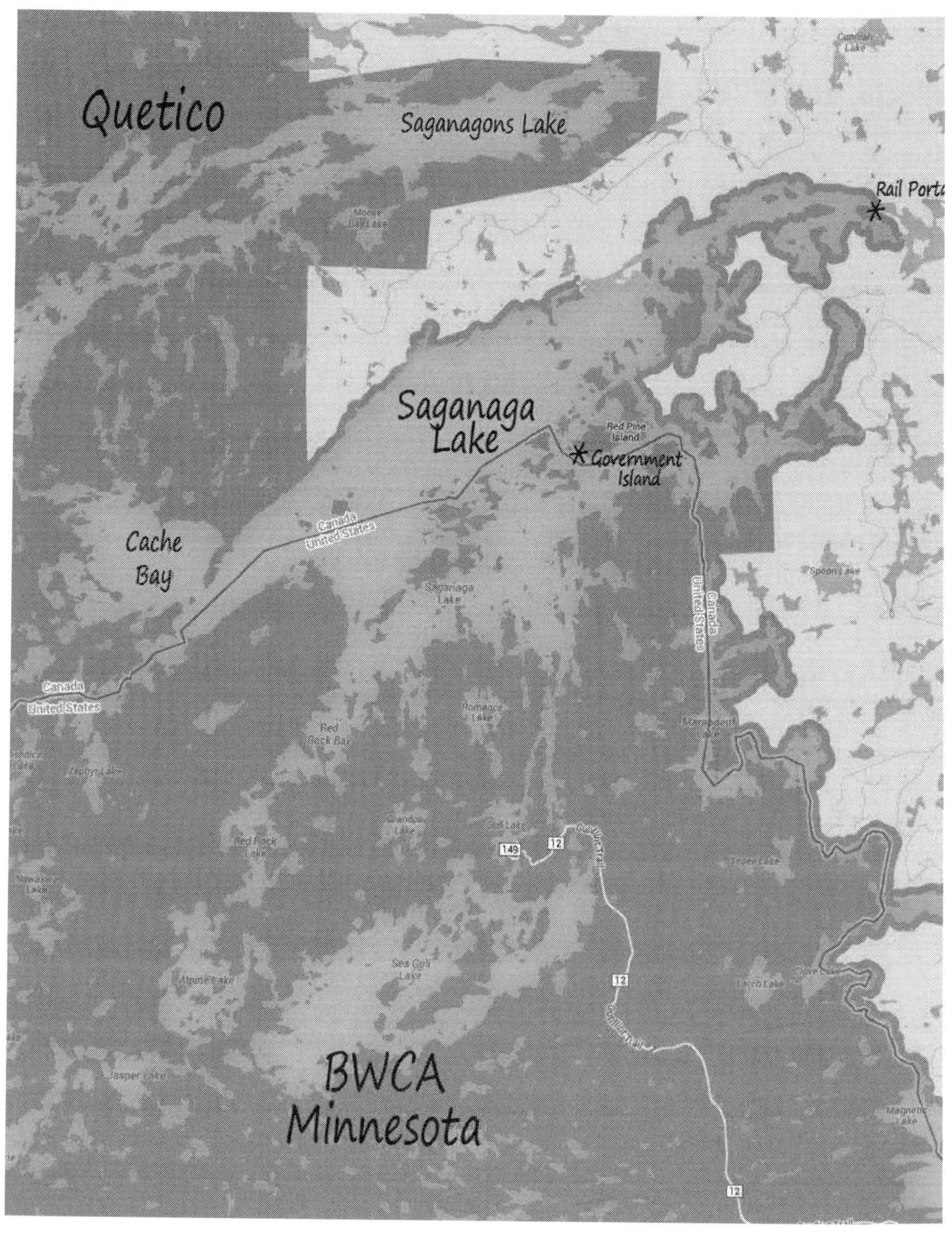
Quetico
Saganagons Lake
Rail Porta
Saganaga Lake
Government Island
Cache Bay
BWCA
Minnesota

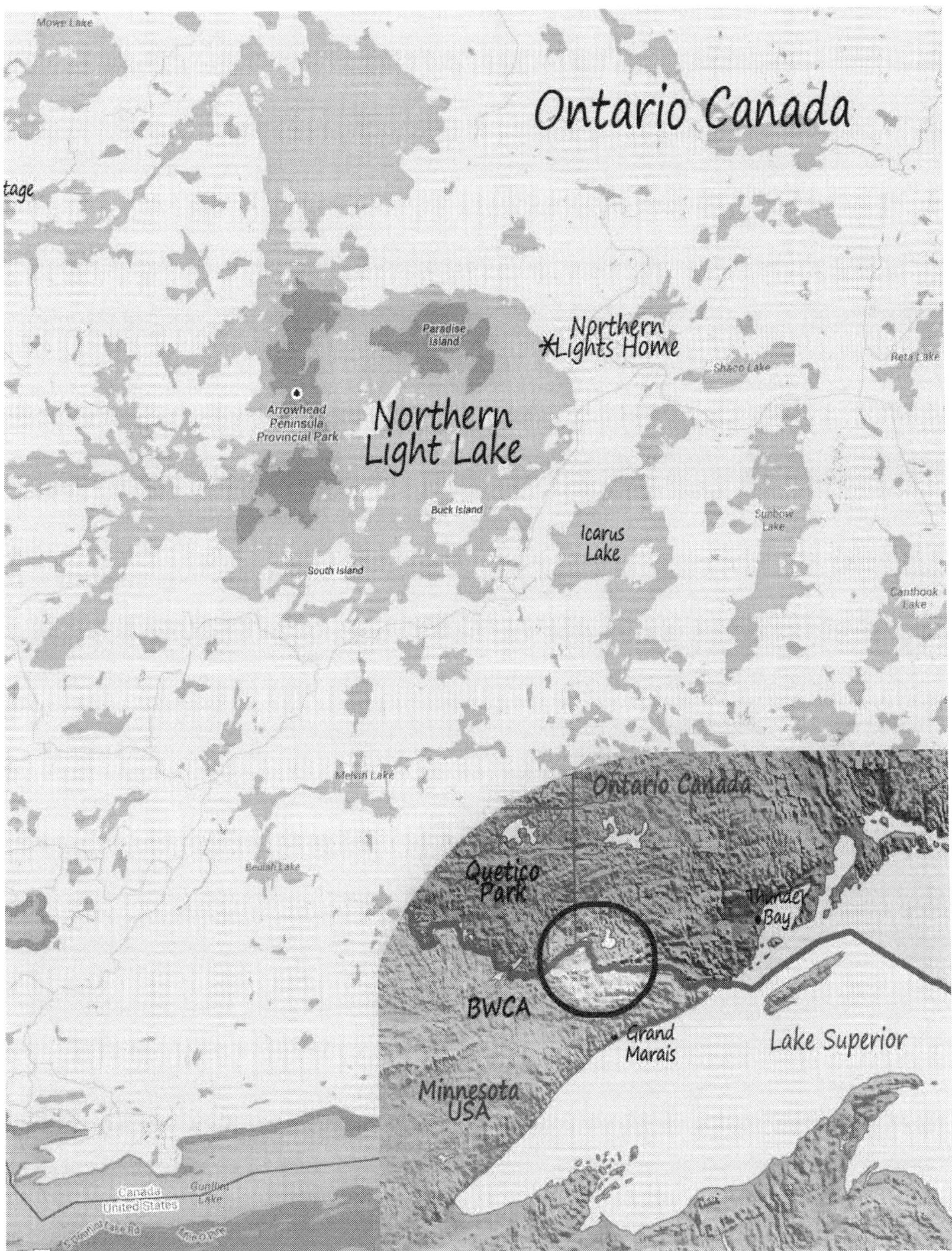

Mowe Lake
Ontario Canada
tage
Paradise Island
Northern
*Lights Home
Shaco Lake
Reta Lake
Arrowhead Peninsula Provincial Park
Northern
Light Lake
Buck Island
Icarus
Lake
Sunbow Lake
South Island
Canthook Lake
Melvin Lake
Beulah Lake
Canada
United States
Gunflint Lake
Ontario Canada
Quetico
Park
Thunder
Bay
BWCA
Grand
Marais
Lake Superior
Minnesota
USA

Contents

The Early Years

Wilderness Mail Delivery

As the train went by, my mother caught the hoop with our mail attached.

Double Jeopardy on the Trapline

In 1963 and 1964 Eve and I lived our winters at an abandoned railroad hamlet called Petry; trapline 139.

Roadmaster Borski Came to talk to Eve!

It all started with a visit days before. Borsky the road master spoke to Eve. "Missus, yous tells you husband he's be KILL-ETT! Stay off railroad track!"

The day before I had managed to jump the track into a ravine. My skidoo made it through the rock cut in time. I looked up as a freight train whizzed by with a rail crew shaking their fists at me. I had already decided this was a dangerous convenience that I'd have to give up. Borsky had turned up the heat by telling on me to Eve. As a result of this, Borsky bore a resemblance to Boris Karloff, an actor who starred in Frankenstein movies. He had dark circles under his eyes, perhaps because of the black soot from a long career of railroading. He held the title of Road Master along this

stretch of track, and if he resembled a raccoon it made no difference, he was the boss! Whatever I thought, from now on I would travel the Petry River. Back in '64, I had no idea that one day I would teach snowmobile and ATV safety courses.

After my 22 caliber accident years before, I never thought I was invincible. I revelled in my independence, a sense of freedom I'd never understood before. With no regrets I exchanged a sign design job for a life on the trap line. The toughest part is the first winter in any trapping area, building pole bridges across rivers where currents flow. The sheer adventure of seeing lakes never before seen brought me never ending enthusiasm. In the spring I obtained better maps, a decision that ultimately rang the doorbell of opportunity for work and a career with Lands and Forests. From tower man, I became a park ranger, deputy warden, and ended up as a conservation officer. Because of experiences learned in my past regarding matters of safety, I was hard on people when conducting hunter safety tests, especially when it came to properly handling firearms. I felt eminently qualified having experienced what a gun could do when in the hands of drunken or careless people. It no longer mattered to me that I'd had an accident; what mattered most was that I had survived. I wanted others to have a safe outcome when handling weapons.

Nine years after my accident, I was on the Petry River trapping and learning my trails. I relished my life in nature. Borsky was right. I soon established new trails along the bogs that followed the edge of the river. One day I stopped my skidoo to study the slip, hop, and slide of an otter's tracks that lead across the river. At first his home appeared to be a hole in the river bank, a great place to set a 330 Conibear humane trap I thought. I caught a glimpse of the otter in the shadows.

Anxious to know, I took the plunge. It was a hole in the river with thin ice and a fair current flowing on a river bend. Sand gathered so it wasn't deeper than my upper chest. My hands coiled out without my will and gripped the brush hard. To my surprise, a large piece of ice pancaked and ran off with the flow. For a brief moment I observed about six inches of air formed under the ice. The ice itself was nothing more than a suspended bridge, with little or no support above flowing water. This ice could collapse at any given moment. The river level had already dropped by the end of February. Wet as I was, I knew I could make it home, if my 9 HP skidoo started. The sun was high and the March wind was warm and early. I was glad that this day wasn't like January, when the section crew had told me that the temperature had dipped to fifty degrees below zero.

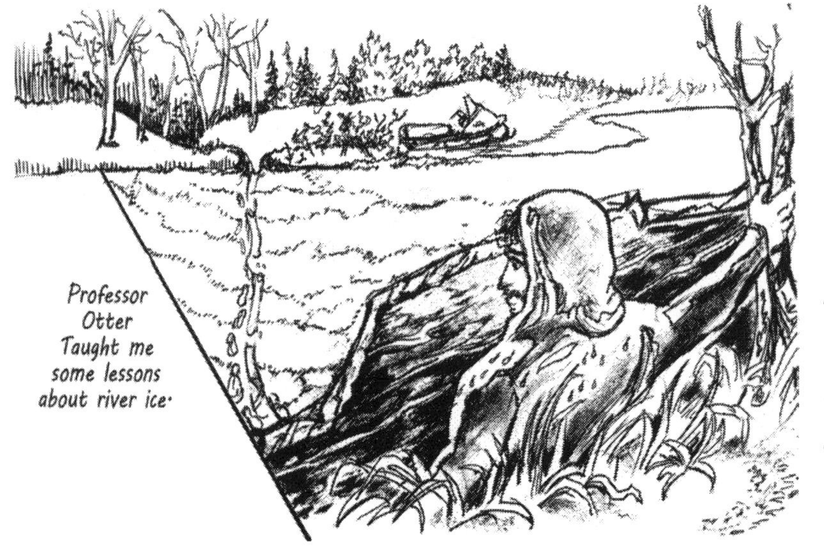

Professor Otter Taught me some lessons about river ice.

I was glad to hear my single cylinder putting and bogey wheels turning. I wouldn't have to strip off my clothes and build a fire in the naked blue elements. I didn't have to haywire a broken rubber track to get home. I knew that in thirty-five minutes I'd be sitting by a wood stove with coffee and wearing dry clothes. Eve would be showing me linoleum block prints, colorful designs on paper that she had created and now hung on a clothesline drying.

I would have liked to have thanked Professor Otter but I never saw him again. I learned to never follow an otter to the edge of a river. It could be hazardous to your health, especially in the winter, because an otter can put you on thin ice.

Beef on a Mitt

John Hook taught me that a tire tube harness on snowshoes was safer if you ever broke through the ice, a single tension knot pulled, allowed for quick release. "Swimming with snowshoes is not good," he said.

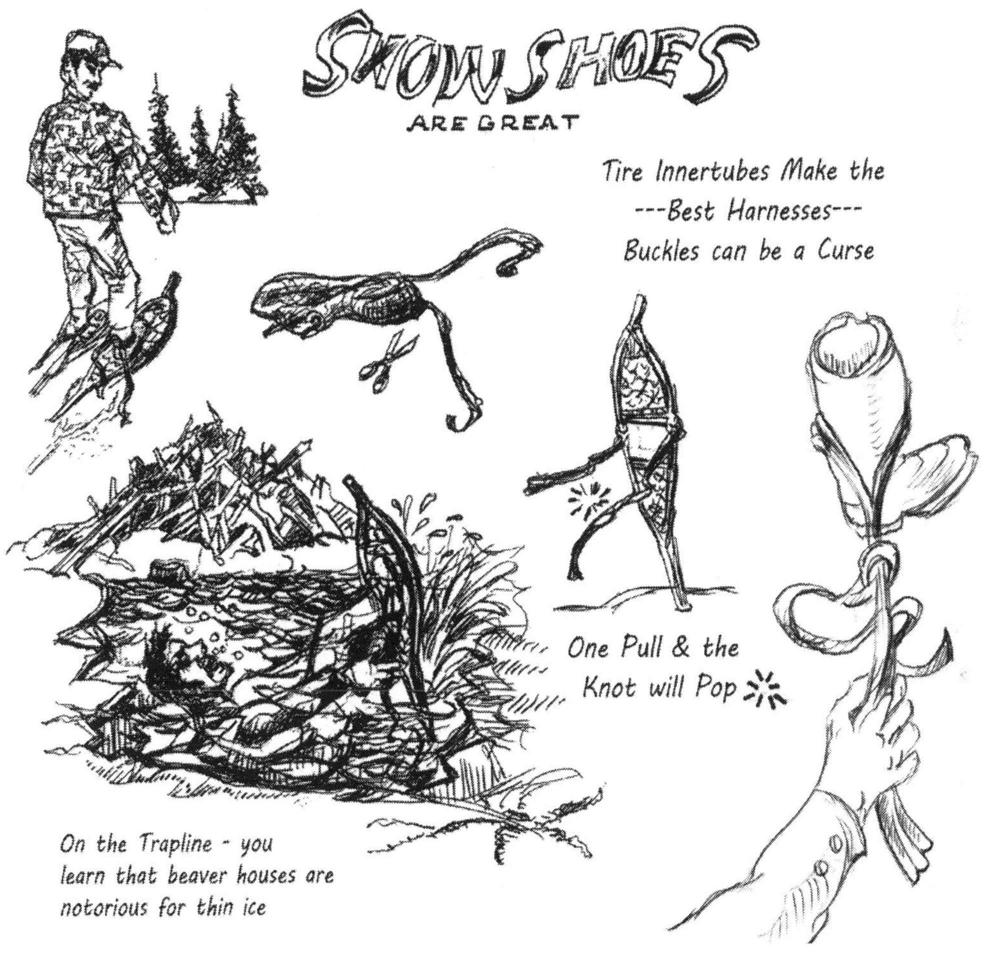

I learned that with a single rubber knot, tension would hold snowshoes on for walking, and that a tug on either of the two tethers caused a quick release.

As his student I had a great teacher; his specialty was under ice trapping. In order to learn I offered to be his apprentice. We had adjoining traplines. His line was eleven miles northwest at Quern, and mine was east at Petry, Ontario. Since he was about to retire, I was his gopher. He enjoyed my role and our relationship. His health declined as his age inclined. As the months passed things had become routine. In the morning we'd trap and have lunch in the open air cafe surrounded by deep snow. During an open fire lunch break John's words startled me. "You be eat for fat. I be eat for lean." He handed me my beef on a mitt and explained he had an ulcer problem. I stared at two chunks of beef. There was no need to explain. Instead he stated, " Fat be good for you to fight cold."

Inwardly I was amused. By spring I recognized a great trapper, teacher, and master. He was very fussy, even about the shape of nature's poplar branches, and how they'd fit exactly around under ice trap sets. If they were not precise, he would send me back to cut and gather more.

It's strange how by chance so many of us meet. Hook had a nice cabin, including fantastic walleye fishing on a point on Selwyn Lake which he wanted to sell· One spring he sold to my mom and stepdad· Well into their 50s, they sold what they had and arrived by rail on a flatcar loaded with tools· Their temporary new home was Hook's cabin situated on a beautiful point of land·

Meanwhile that spring, Eveline and I returned to my job as a tower man· We later learned that having sold their farm, my parents now had to start from scratch· At nearby Quorn they purchased abandoned railroad buildings, dismantled them and even saved the shingles, and carried beams and all materials around a rapids· Then from the materials they built a raft· All things floated to Hook's point at Selwyn Lake· From those early efforts, a viable business developed called Selwyn Lake Camps· From start to finish, I know that by the light of coal oil lamps, cribbage was played for more than twenty-four winters before they retired; a proud accomplishment·

Theirs was a Herculean feat at any age· Her husband always said that she could make something from nothing, and they did· Timing is everything· In the 60s, it was still possible for others to have similar opportunities· At Wawang Lake, a young ranger quit his job and made himself a resort· As of 2008 starting "from scratch" no longer applies· Lake land is rare; remoteness is even more precious·

Mom's lessons about survival started at an early age, going back to the 1940s· Single moms never had it easy· Back then life could be nearly impossible· The war, tokens, food rationing··· added to every dilemma· Mom had to have tenacious will, humour, and grit. My brother Syd was seven and I was eight. One day our mom said, "We're going on a hike". We climbed high up Grouse Mountain at Vancouver BC. Nearing dark she hushed any notion of home or bed. Reading our bewildered looks she said, "We're camping out." Soon she fashioned a dome out of entwined willows. "Now give me your raincoats." She created a bed from those, we ate some munchies and slept all night.

Later, when Christmas came, my mom could not afford a tree. Instead she decorated a chair with presents underneath. It turned out to be one of the best Christmases ever! She could build, cook, can, and sew. She even built a hay wagon! She'd say, "This is the way you do it Stupe!" She was invariably right. She showed how to chink a log cabin to keep the cold out. I guess some of it rubbed off...

In my formative years my resume might have read: I know how to separate milk, observe antelope when riding to school on horseback, felt the sting of towering dust storms in the prairies, delivered papers for the Sun in British Columbia, stooked wheat, checked traps in muskrat houses in the sloughs and fields of Manitoba, picked tobacco at Tillsonburg, Ontario, rollerskated in Toronto... Looking back life had incredible variety. Early life for the three of us was both urban and rural. The lakes and forests came much later. My mother, brother and I were nomadic until our teens. From Toronto to Vancouver and in between, we had traversed east to west many times. My brother Syd became a Peace Keeper in the Canadian Army. I chose forestry and became a wildlife officer. Thanks Mom!

Secrets of the Trapline

Anyone can beat the winter blahs· Survival is key to all that we do in life· With more than 40 years trapline experience secrets must be revealed to benefit mankind· Warning: Do not try these techniques at home or in the city·

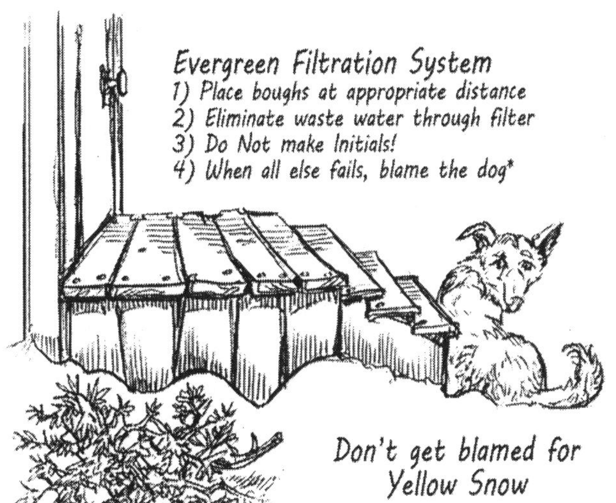

Priorities?

Eve and I were married August 18, 1961. As we moved from being renters to owners, our first property was our trap shack. 1968 offered opportunity. We purchased a lake lot at Northern Light Lake. A triad shaped A-frame would take time to build. We spent our first winter in the 12' by 12' insulated portion of the A-frame. We joked that if we could survive the winter, we could survive anything. Our TV consisted of a slanted window, where we could see stars between frosted shapes.

Every day Eve would walk half a mile to a nearby resort to visit Ida Richardson. The winter population at Northern Light Lake was roughly six.

The main portion of our A-frame was unheated and unfinished; none the less I would accomplish what work I could. I worked on the loft which was 12 feet high. Our dream home had to be completed. One frosty morning, climbing the ladder to the top, the ladder slipped. My leg was trapped in the top rung. The ladder and I hit the floor with a loud thump! My weight had bent the aluminum around my felt covered boot. I rejoiced that my ankle was not broken. I remember cursing every loving nail I had pounded in the house, as I lay moaning on the floor.

I heard the crunch of Eve's footsteps. She had returned! I moaned even louder hoping to feel some healing sympathy. Moments later, wide eyes looked down on me. In her Dutch-Indonesian accent she asked, "Yohnie, what happened?" I pointed up gasping, "I fell from the top". I waited for more sympathy as I extracted my ankle. The borrowed ladder from Customs looked like a silver pretzel. I thought, "Poor Eve, she is suffering over my pain". Her chin was trembling.

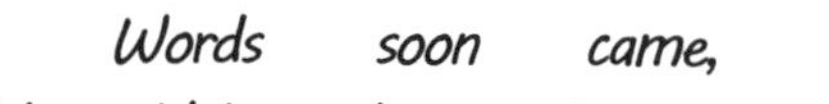

Words soon came, "Yohnie, Yohnie, do you think we will have to pay Customs for the ladder?"

Lynx

It was not unusual for the neighbors at Northern Light Lake to meet on the road for Sunday walks. Eveline was popular and today she was unusually excited and animated because a lynx was in our yard. "It's near the shed and is after the moose head that Yonny put on the roof!" she exclaimed, wide eyed and out of breath. The three men bust out in a big guffaw. They liked Eveline with her Dutch Indonesian accent, but they still teased her unmercifully.

"Come on Eve," one said. "Tell us the truth. You saw a giant rabbit."

"Come see!" Eve said frantically.

"No Eve we believe you," Ed said. He winked at this friends. "Aye?"

"Sure," the others said jokingly. "We believe you. You saw a giant rabbit with big whiskers!"

"We're going for coffee," Ed said. "Come on Eve, we'll buy."

"No!" Eve said. "I'm worried about the dog, but if you see Yonny tell him to come home."

Eve went home to find Gypsy running circles around the shed barking wildly. As the lynx jumped down it quickly fell into a hostile position. The lynx wanted the moose head and it instantly became a standoff. Eve, fearing for the dog, ran into the house and grabbed a 16-gauge shotgun. She fired one well placed shot and the lynx crumpled. She scooped up the lynx and headed back toward the road and the resort. Her timing could not have been more perfect! Coming over a sand hill, Ed and the boys were returning from coffee. "See!" Eve proudly proclaimed. "I did see a lynx."

AN HOUR LATER EVELINE CAME DOWN THE TRAIL CARRYING A LYNX!

The men stared, mouths agape as though they saw a mirage.

"Can we touch it Eve?" Ed asked. They reached out their hands. "We've never seen a lynx this close before!"

They were dumbstruck at the unique tufted pencil-like extensions on the lynx's ears.

"You shot it in the yard Eve?" asked Ed.

"Yes over by the shed," Eve said. "I was afraid that it might get the dog. I have to give it to Frank and Helen because it is their trap line. So if you happen to see Frank please tell him for me."

"I've never heard of anyone shooting a lynx before. It's hard to believe. It is rare to even see one." Bob told Ed.

"Yeah, it's hard to believe that Eve did it!" Ed said.

"I told you but you laughed at me," Eve said with a big grin.

"Oh Eve, people only tease people they like," Ed said. "Of course we believed you!"

A reporter from Thunder Bay contacted Eve to verify the story. Soon hundreds believed Eve as the article appeared in the paper a few days later.

"My Personal Forensics"

Eve missed the windows. Good Shot!

When I returned from patrol I was astounded. She had shot a lynx! She even missed all the stacked windows needed to complete our A-frame home that we were in the process of building on Northern Light Lake.

Eve and I agreed that in life it's sweet to overcome any prejudice or adversity whether in fun or in seriousness. The greatest triumph is not that you convince others, but find belief in yourself.

Lynx Plentiful In Area; Lady Trapper Bags One

Reprinted with permission from the Thunder Bay Chronicle-Journal

EVE BOUCHARD

By BOB ECKHOLM
Staff Writer

A lady trapper from Northern Light Lake shot a lynx under strange circumstances recently.

On Saturday, Feb. 10, Eve Bouchard was walking with her dog toward a neighbor's house a half-mile from her own residence. As she approached the house, the dog began to bark furiously and the cause of his excitement was found to be a large lynx standing in the neighbor's yard.

The neighbors happened to be out fishing so Mrs. Bouchard proceeded to Jock Richardson's camp about 1½ miles away. She related the story to a group of fishermen at the lodge who kidded her about the incident and apparently took it with a grain of salt.

She subsequently returned to her own home on the shore of Northern Light Lake and just as she approached thepremises her dog began barking again. Investigating she found a lynx nosing around a number of frozen moose heads near a shed.

While the dog kept the lynx occupied, Mrs. Bouchard sneaked into her house by the back door and loaded a 16-gauge shotgun. Her first shot which she fired from an open window missed the big cat, but a second volley caught the animal between the eyes.

Mrs. Bouchard's husband John said he didn't know whether the lynx was the same one seen at the neighbor's but he did say there was an abundance of lynx in the Northern Light Lake area this winter.

Mrs. Bouchard takes an avid interest in the out-of-doors and operates a trapline from time to time. Northern Light Lake is located about 70 miles west of Thunder Bay.

Saganaga Lake Impresses

Saganaga Lake has beauty and historical significance. The explorer La Vérendrye mapped and passed this way. It is of little known historical significance that for generations families have lived in the area. Lives passed, ongoing and relatively unknown, continued in the very shadows of the City of Thunder Bay. The Powells understood a jewel of nature when they found it, as did the Richardsons, Madsens, Bensons and Ambrose, including other names that followed. If anyone asked, "Who are the modern voyageurs?" my answer would be, "The Americans". My impression was that the Americans have a keener appreciation of what we fail to see, or take for granted. Saganaga even came to the attention of world famous photographer Yousuf Karsh, who came to take Jock's picture for the New Yorker Magazine. As recently as 2007, former officers, Customs and Wildlife, reflect that their Saganaga experience was the best they remember.

Jock Richardson

How Was the Border Line Decided?

Old stories coincide with memories along the invisible line between Minnesota and Ontario. Once you track the line, all the boundary markers zig zag; one island in, another out. Curious twists seem to be drawn by a contortionist.

It's not hard to envision. Old tales at Saganaga Lake claim that officials and surveyors of old roamed the lake. Both sides imbibed in bourbon and scotch and played poker for positions as to how the international boundary would be established between Canada and the United States. Following the sovereign line of each land of domain seems to give merit to the story.

"Yes," one might have said. "I think yes."

The spectre of mischief and men by an oil lamp with pencils and maps could well have been played late into the night, while beavers gnawed bark and went about their business building dams and claiming their turf without any respect to what men's plans decided· Beavers don't give a hoot·(Owls do!)

Truth?

"Hoo· Hoo·"

Why the boundary was so devised raises more questions than answers; however, it is always intriguing to follow the boundary line by boat· The line can be straight on course and then veer off at a great angle, grabbing a small island leaving another, and suddenly veer inexplicably out to the greater water like a roller coaster on its side· Should you look back, your vision connects that the line could have easier been drawn straight· Someone had aces in his hand, or made a good bluff when the pot was small· When they finally slept and woke in the morning, heads aching, they couldn't change a thing· They had no eraser· Is it anyone's guess?

I came to believe the story because it makes sense at times when the weaves and staggering of the invisible boundary line cause me to wonder: How did it get so crooked? It's a curious matter for inhabitants on both sides of the border· They are affected by different laws and rules on each side of Lake Saganaga·

The lake draws many people· Fire is the fear which both sides face in common· When fires happen, and they happen far too often through carelessness, its uniqueness is lost· The life of the red pine is devastated and with it so too are the lives of people long settled who are burned out and forced to live elsewhere· There's more to fire than hectares, timber *and lost economies. Natural fires are being far too often assisted by carelessness. The imbalance is very evident along the border country. Those who argue that fires are good for renewal might as well believe that bombs are also good for renewal. After all, after bombs, tornadoes, earthquakes—all devastation (except for Chernobyl), we often see renewal.*

So help me, I can't accept that disaster is good for trees, animals or people. Could it be that I lack sophistication? I believe that the old ways of regular boat patrols carrying fire pumps was the best means for quick response and fire suppression.

Training Day

As soon as the pontoons of the float plane touched the waters of Saganaga I knew this is where I wanted to be. P.J. Nunan and his dog Smokey showed me how to access the Ranger Station on Government Island. There was no key, you just climbed in through the side window.

He showed me around Government Island before his plane took off.

Then Peter said "Good Luck Deputy, try to make do with the old patrol equipment until your new boat and motor arrive in a couple of weeks. Try and blend in and not look too conspicuous."

The Day I Almost Quit Before I Started Spring 1967

My time as deputy at Saganaga Lake began in the fall after my second summer as a fire lookout and forest ranger. My seasonal contract for $11 per day was almost over; I was offered an extension of three weeks to assist Keith, a seasoned wildlife officer. We came back from extended patrols on various lakes with a stunning array of firearms we had seized.

Soon after that my wife, Eveline and I, with Put-Put our cat, headed north to our trap line for the winter. I was surprised to be called into the office of Al Elsey, the supervisor of the Fish and Wildlife District of Thunder Bay. It was rumoured, that this biologist and seasoned field officer, took the point of an illegal spear during a poaching event years ago.

"We happen to have a seasonal paid position for a deputy conservation officer at Saganaga Lake," he explained." It's a contract position. My sources tell me you did well with Keith. Do you think you could handle it, international border and all?"

Did I think I could handle it? Yes indeed!

On my first day on the job, I was alone. It was open season for walleye at Horsetail Rapids. Never had I seen so many boats and anglers congregating.

Armed with only fishing regulations, I patrolled the lake in my boat passed friendly folks who were waving, nodding, smiling, and shouting greetings. "Not a bad start," I thought. I smiled and nodded back. Someone on a boat offered coffee, but I politely declined. Not good for image, I thought. Could be misunderstood. Not only was I in my dream job but I was also in control.

Then someone asked, "Are you the new warden who got thrown in the lake last night?" Heads turned and nodded, and the boaters moved their boats closer, gathering in a circle around me.

"The news is all over the lake, on our side ... a giant of a guy ... steelworker from Chicago ... police are looking for him ... took exception to being checked before season opener ... shook the warden like a rag doll ... not far from here ... a portage or so up the Maraboeuf River ... late last night ... the warden was pounded on and thrown in the river." They told me that the warden, bruised but not badly injured, managed to get to the sheriff and that the steelworker was to be extradited to face charges at Grand Marais.

I managed the day with a few minor violations: no license, too many lines... I headed back to Government Island, hoping my wife hadn't heard the story and worried that there was more to enforcement than met the eye. A week or so later I met Earl Nelms. "Yes, it was me," he admitted, "the US Warden." He went on to explain, "I'm not exactly a small guy. Had a lot of training in the service before I joined wildlife enforcement," he said. He showed me his bruises. "My pappy always said if you look hard enough, you will find someone who can whup you." He smiled. "Dad was right."

Later, as I understand, extradition did take place and the mighty steel worker settled issues in a way not to his liking in the courts of Minnesota.

Earl was a colourful man who was lost in a plane crash a few years later. He inspired me in 1967, and his memory remains today. There are no borders where wildlife concerns are met.

One Life for Another

It would be hard to find anyone who came from a more diverse cultural background than my wife Eveline Tinkelenberg did. She was born of Dutch and Indonesian parents on a small island, Tan Jung Pandean Billiton, in the land of the Komodo dragons. Once known as Batavia under Dutch Indies control, Indonesia experienced turmoil when its founding president Sukarno took power in the early 50s. Anyone with Dutch names or heritage sought safety elsewhere, mainly in Holland and North America. Eve came to Canada and lived half her life at Saganaga and Northern Lights lakes. Eve's two brothers and her father survived Japanese concentration camps and were forced to labour on the River Kwai in Burma. Later her father, an inspector of narcotics in Jakarta, died in an explosion.

Eve came from a family that enjoyed music. Her brother Pieter had a band, and her niece Jose Tinkelenberg was a lead singer in a band that had platinum and gold records in Europe. Eve liked Hawaiian music, and she was known for her Indonesian candle dancing. Eve enjoyed teaching some of the local native girls how to dance. Stationed on Government Island I was blessed to have an Island girl as my wife.

Eveline Bouchard, a true island girl. She was born on an island in Indonesia before coming to Government Island on Saganaga.

Like Father, Like Daughter

In the 1970s, Customs began to notice a drug trend. At Ontario border stations drugs were being found in diaper boxes, hair, sleeping bags, even on babies...

The Royal Canadian Mounted Police process court and enforcement for Canadian Customs. The police search men as Customs can; however, the searching of women is another matter. Women search women. Eveline became Chief Inspector of Narcotics on females at Saganaga Lake.

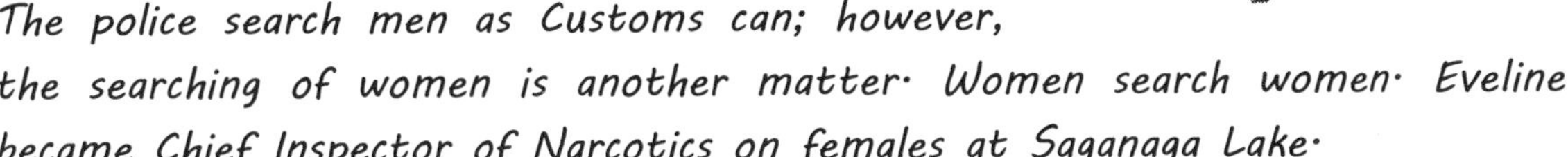

Without revealing her Dutch Indonesian search secret to others, Eve found drugs without ever touching the women, however I knew her secret. She'd have the women place their hands on their heads and do the "can-can" dance. Today we see people in exercise programs on television utilizing the same technique; jump and kick, kick and jump, a-hup, a-hup; jump and kick, kick and jump, a-hup, a-hup.

As a conservation officer's wife, Eve contributed directly to enforcement. From time to time, she choreographed a few young women before the courts as requested.

Eveline:
1967 - 1985
at Saganaga Lake
station on
Government Island.

Wives who love nature are a great asset.

1968: Toying with Fate?

During the Nam years; was it luck or fate that I met George Grooms of Minneapolis? He owned Animal Fair, a company that created stuffed animal toys.

At an impromptu cartoon fest at Lowel Blake's cabin, Grooms said he'd hire me if I moved to the States. Surely he's joking I thought. Apparently not!

I began the process with US Immigration. With a seasonal lay-off looming and no clear signs of becoming a permanent wildlife officer on the horizon, a winter on the trap line could rest. Fate had intervened.

"Are people nuts?" I thought as I drove down the highway heading to Chanhassen, Minnesota. Travelling at seventy or eighty miles an hour, I felt like a kamikaze pilot from Japan who had been stranded for years and didn't know that the war had ended. Somehow, fate seemed less reliable. By mid-winter my designs were in the market. JC Penney's and other large chains were buying and selling Benny the Bear, Ozzy the Otter, and Bucky the Beaver. Grooms, my boss, was happy. Three hundred plus sewing machines were going strong. More factories were opening in Florida and Japan. By spring, my claustrophobia and longing for the outdoors was nearly out of control. I could not bear to live my life in a cubicle for the next thirty years.

Bucky was homesick for his roots, we both returned to the North

There is no rehab for anyone addicted to the outdoors. I made a lot of friends in the States and received a lot of support when going to the States. While there was some disappointment in leaving, most people understood and encouraged me to pursue my own dream. I returned to Saganaga Lake, Ontario, as a deputy warden and trapper. This apprenticeship was a long one.

In 1985 I gave up the trap line to become a full time warden/conservation officer. Ironically, I had to leave Saganaga Lake and move north to Nakina. It was fate that my career ended at Upsala in '94. I retired with lots of memories.

Looking back to 1964 . . . I had no plans at that time when I went to the Lands and Forests office. The reason was only to obtain some good updated maps for a recently acquired trapping area. Then I met Chief Ranger George Murray.

Without much thought, words came out as I was leaving. "Are there any jobs?"

"Yes," he said. "if you can handle heights. We have one position for a tower man. Eleven dollars per day."

"No problem with heights," I lied.

"Okay," he said. "The job's yours."

The first climb was tough. I was terrified as I climbed the last twenty-five feet to the little trapdoor entrance which seemed to be in outer space.

Native Rangers provided good advice, "Put your packsack on in front so it doesn't get caught on the hoops going up."

Somehow I made it into the tower. By the end of the summer I could scale the tower on the outside, climbing the hoops.

The moral of this story is that the sky's the limit. Once you reach the top, no matter how high, persevere. Follow experienced advice. Keep going as long as it takes, and eventually you'll make it.

In life we go through many hoops, but the view is worth it especially when looking back. When I first saw Saganaga, I wanted to be there. Goal achieved. 1967-1985. Time well spent.

My Apparition

I remember a morning's early light at the trap shack. It was a March morning and the snow was more like glare ice from the early spring daily melt and re-freeze cycle; the season for trapping was just about over. Travel was best done early in the morning and late in the evening, taking care to avoid rocky shoals where the sun melted the ice. After splashing my face with water, I looked out the window, south toward Horsetail Rapids. I had to rub my eyes. No, it wasn't my imagination but I simply couldn't put together what I was seeing. A small tan deer? No, the legs and feet were wrong, more like a stray Great Dane with a light muzzle. Maybe it was a lost dog from last fall that got away from hunters. That didn't make much sense wither. I had never seen a hunter using Boxers or Danes to hunt bear. I should have gone outside in bare feet but by the time I got the felt liners back into my boots and my boots on the creature was gone. A deer on glare ice could not have disappeared so fast. I would be spread eagled and floundering in these conditions. Many a wolf found easy prey this way. I tried to confirm the tracks, but thin ice at the Falls prevented exploration, and the icy conditions hid any other evidence of my visitor.

I decided to go about my business; I had miles to go to get home to Northern Light Lake. I decided to shrug matters off and get things closed up at the trap shack. Before I headed out Dicky Powell came by and we had a chat. I told him about the Great Dane and he confirmed that he had never seen one in the area either. I went out toward Saganagons Lake and picked up my last Conibear traps, stopped in at the Deschampes Bay, stored the traps and closed up for the season. With my sleigh loaded I would say goodbye to my Saganaga friends until open water in May. I stopped at Irv & Tempest's place, Art Madsen's and then the Chippewa Inn. Dicky had gone to the end of the trail to get local mail and newspapers. It was a risky business, the ice was not the best this season.

At Northern Lights Eveline was glad I made it, no slush or snowmachine problems. She had my favorite dinner of sweet and sour Walleye waiting for me when I arrived. She asked if I had heard the news. I asked what news? She had heard on the CB radio from Saganaga that the paper said mountain lions, cougars had been sighted in Minnesota. There were several reports of sightings along the border, had I heard that? I wanted to say that I had not heard the news but maybe I saw

what made the news· Being a bit of a doubting Thomas I was used to dealing with evidence and in this case I had none· I thought best to let sleeping dogs lie· Eveline said, "Some say cougars can be dangerous"· I thought maybe if cornered· I opted to allay worry, to have a king's life in enforcement or trapping a worried wife can be detrimental· Soon Eve was asleep, tired and weary as I was· I spent the night in fitfull sleep· Haunting my mind were juxtapositioning, superimposing images of the creature I saw today with ones I had seen many years ago running across the Banff Springs Golf Course in Alberta· All I can say is the news never mentioned any sightings of big Boxers or any Great Danes· My trap shack was situated no more than half a mile from Minnesota's border· Even now, I still wonder what I saw that morning·

The Birth of Old Ugly

It all began in May of 1970, miles into the Falls Chain deep in Quetico Park. Kirk Reid and I joined to do an interior patrol. We portaged each falls safely. On the high-water mark below Koko Falls, we spotted a battered canoe with a gaping hole. It was an old mishap, so we claimed it as our own.

By the time we reached Kawnipi Lake we were wet and cold. We'd been out for days. A late season snow squall and cold rain had caught us. We hung our wet clothes and slung a plastic sheet near the fire to speed-dry our wool long johns. As we caught walleyes with crude hand lines, the fire burnt the legs of our long john underwear, but at least they were dry. Finally, it was time to journey back to Cache Bay Ranger station. Pam and Paul Money came to greet us.

"What happened?" Pam called out.

"Nothing," I said.

"Nothing?" They pointed to the wreck, half submerged, that we were towing and constantly emptying out.

"Oh that?" Kirk smiled proudly. "We found it tethered on Koko Falls."

"You mean to say you made all those portages with that piece of junk?"

We nodded.

"We like it," I said. "It's like you guys, all bent out of shape."

"But the end is crushed," Pam said.

"It'll have a square stern," Ken countered.

"But it's ugly," Paul said.

"That's what we'll name it," I said. "Old Ugly. After you."

"Once we fix it," Kirk said.

"We?" Pam and Paul shook their heads.

Soon with a lot of hacksawing, the canoe was cut in half. More pounding, pulling, and pushing with jacks reduced it from seventeen feet to about fifteen and a half feet in length. It had an upward snout. The front rider barely touched the water. A camouflage paint job helped hide scars and added to its element of surprise. Balanced and quite seaworthy, it was responsive to a three horsepower motor. It never leaked.

Old Ugly performed many patrols and shocked and amused many anglers on Saganaga Lake until it retired on Trap Line Lake between Saganaga and Northern Lights Lake in 1984. I gave it my highest regard for it had served fish and wildlife admirably.

Within the Ministry of Natural Resources, only a few select members of fish and wildlife have memories of Old Ugly and its performance beyond the call of duty. Fish and wildlife gained an invaluable secret weapon against those forces that sought to plunder the fish and wildlife resources of Ontario.

I cannot imagine the fear in the souls of poachers as Old Ugly roared out of hidden reaches, the sun at her back, bow held high.

In the early mid-eighties, Paul Shebourne from Macalister University in St. Paul, Minnesota, sent his usual thank you letter. This one was special. The letterhead read World Press. It became a valuable face-saver.

For several years, a dozen or more young journalists from all over the world would take a canoe trip up to Saganaga Lake. This sparked interest, especially for Eveline who was from Indonesia. We met people from Eveline's native Indonesia and other faraway places such as Zaire, Poland, and Uruguay. In the late fall they had camped at Eve's trap shack site on an open point of land, and we took to visiting with them in the early evenings.

One year the journalists didn't want to leave Canada without seeing a beaver, so each evening I took four at time to a beaver house in Powell Bay. We sat motionless near the feed bed, and listened for the sound of beaver feeding; which sounds like two small rocks clicking; an unusual sound. A feed bed is a stockpile of branches, mostly poplar that beavers feed on. Branches cut from trees along shorelines are floated in proximity to a beaver house, pushed down and anchored into the mud. Virtually a Deli below the winter's ice, enough to last the winter. Beavers swim out under the ice and gnaw off a morsel to eat in the comfort of their house. A good sign of a healthy colony is when freshly peeled sticks are observed under the ice.

Hearing a loud snap in the nearby woods, I gave the shh-sign and we waited. I knew it was too early in the fall to see moose, but I thought what the heck. Cupping my hands, I let out a few low grunts. Soon the bushes were moving slowly, and remarkably, a massive bull came out. He could not have been better choreographed. Near the water's edge, he turned ever so slowly, showing his gold-bronze rack for all to see. This bull not only impressed the journalists, who were hardly breathing with eyes wide open, but he also seemed to impress himself. The moose and we stared at each other for a few tense moments, and then he turned around back into the brush.

At camp that night, the journalists began telling the others, "He called 'Moose-ee, come to us,' and he come to us. He big! I scared! So close!"

The more I listened to them the more I felt like Tarzan of the North.

When word got out about my moose-calling abilities I caught heck from the guys in the office. "Hey guys, listen to this," said Berny, coordinator of Fish and Wildlife. "JB's trying to say he called a moose. I imagine this early in the fall he needed help and couldn't call 'Sooey! Sooey! Oink, oink!' for lunch." The others laughed.

There was no point hanging around the office that day. Besides, I had one hundred and twenty or so miles to go; almost fifty by truck and then west with the sun in my eyes for twenty-two miles on Northern Light Lake before hitting the rail portage and paddling another nine miles to the station on Government Island on Big Saganaga Lake·

Back home, Eveline soothed my wounded pride with a fantastic sweet and sour walleye and an exotic salad with peanut butter sauce· In bed later that night I said, "Even if I'd sworn on a Bible, Berny would have laughed even louder·"

Eve smiled· "Look at things this way, Yonny," she said, using my pet name· "You made someone happy today·"

I covered my head with a pillow and fell asleep·

Vengeance came about two weeks later· Charlotte Powell, our mail lady, boated in with a letter from Paul Shebourne and the words World Press stamped in front· Letter in hand, I strutted into Berny's office later that same day·

"Hi," I said· "How's it going?"

Berny didn't lift his head· "Crazy as usual, opening moose season," he said· "Phone ringing off the hook· Desk filled with complaints·" Then he looked up, and he saw the paper in my hand· "What do you have for me? More complaints?"

"Nah," I said· "This time it's good news·"

"What news?"

"Apparently the World Press recognizes my moose-calling ability·" I handed him Paul's letter·

He read it while I beamed· Smiling he finally spoke· "You'd better be moving along," he said· "You'll be late for court, JB"

WORLD PRESS INSTITUTE
MACALESTER COLLEGE

John and Eve Bouchard
P.O. Box 6
RR 2
Nolalu, Onàario
Canada POT-2-KO

August 9, 1979

Dear John and Eve:

Believe it or not, another year has come and gone. The 79-80 WPI Fellows arrive in St. Paul to begin a new year on September 10th. I have just spoken with Rich Humphrey of Wilderness Waters Outfitters in Grand Marais about arranging our annual camping trip to Lake Saganaga. We plan to be on the lake Saturday, September 22 through Monday, September 24.

We would love to use your land again as a camp site. More importantly, John, we would be grateful if you could join us for part of our stay and take some of the Fellows in search of wildlife. Last year's journalists will never forget your moose calling, especially its successful results!

Let me know if you will be with us. I look forward to seeing you both.

Regards,

Paul

Paul V. Sherburne
Program Director

PVS:bb

P.S. I'm enclosing a list of the current Fellows. Sorry, Eve, no Indonesians!

St. Paul, Minnesota 55105 (612) 647-6360

POWELL BAY

SEPT. 78 I used a TEMPEST (POWELL) BENSON CALL — J. Bouchard

Cache Bay -Snippets of History

Once I met a kindly couple. The man was upset when he'd found that everything was gone from an ancient Native American grave site, on a small rock island located near the channel entrance to Silver Falls. Supposedly he was the child of a Native American chief. While facts in time often turn to lore, stories indicated that pottery and arrowheads found on Kawnipi Lake suggested that a large Native American settlement once existed on the lake. Stories stated that the white man's disease, smallpox, wiped it out. Rock paintings at Cache Bay show two figures, a large and small figure (suggesting youth). One figure has a top knot; the other has more like a feather, which suggests two people met for an occasion at Cache Bay. Visions were to make peace: One chief offering his son to the other as a show of good faith during their meeting, although all is open to interpretation and conjecture. The significance is that a child appears in a rock painting at Cache Bay. Other stories claim the high rocks were perfect for ambush on the way to Silver Falls. More than one diver has died below the falls attempting to find artifacts.

My drawing is from memory, only intended to depict what one interpreter saw; variations of headdress on a smaller figure and a warrior in the background. Whatever the story, the gravesite is gone. 1967.

The Cast of Characters

John, Eveline and Sasha at Government Island

A Very Brief Who's Who

In my early years at Northern Light Lake and Saganaga, spring and fall were quiet lonely times. In late November, when the ice started to form, the island residents were unable to travel until it became thick enough to make it safe for snowshoes and snowmobiles. This could take two to three months. In the spring, the reverse would happen, the wait for the ice to break up and allow movement by boat. Since there were no telephone lines in the area, Irv proposed we all get CB radios. Just after dark each evening the chatter would begin. We adopted strange names since you never knew who was listening.

Art Madsen (aka Lonewolf) trapped on the north shore of Saganaga Lake and caught the most wolves of anyone in the area. He was the only trapper I ever knew who wore a long trench coat when trapping. Art Trapped well into his 80's. Irv and Art were old friends that had prankster rivalry in their blood. Their days were spent scheming and plotting ways to outdo one another.

John & Eve Bouchard
Waboose & Wapiti (CB Names)

Irv and Tempest Benson went by the handle Beaver Castor. Irv had multiple talents. He was a gunsmith, welder, iron sculptor and true innovator but he put his greatest efforts into his humour. Irv was known for the elaborate pranks he planned and executed, but even the everyday things like his snow machine showed his sense of humour with its special name.

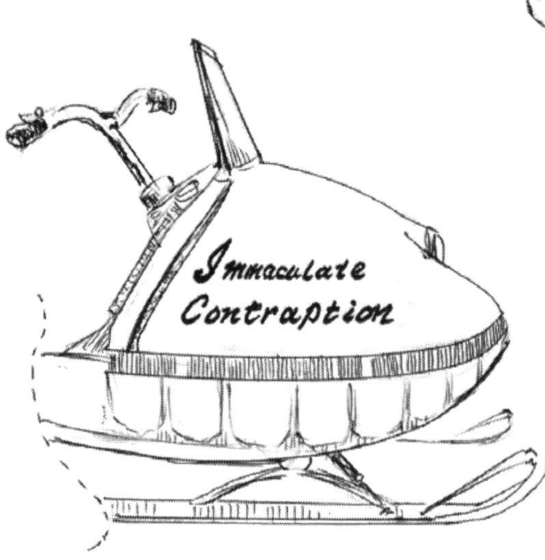

Irv and Buster: Some Stories Are Mine Because I Know about Them

At Saganaga Lake, Irv and Tempest had their own traplines. Each had a dog team and would tend to different areas in the vast north woods. They met bi-weekly at a central cabin location to share the adventures they had had. When he was without Tempest, Irv shared his bed with Buster, his lead sled dog. A ritual developed. Irv, exhausted, would fall fast asleep while Buster would nestle closer as the dying embers in the wood stove made the night chillier. Soon Buster's cold wet nose would find the center of Irv's back or neck, sending a shock down his spine. A sub-conscious ritual, nothing was said as Buster accepted an elbow to his head. It was merely a matter of space and consequence.

When Tempest was due, Irv would finish skinning the animals he had trapped, cut wood, tidy the cabin, fill the coal lamps, and wait for her arrival. They'd have much to talk about; news from their respective trapping areas. Irv was very confident in Tempest's woods-wisdom and ways, always saying she had taught him everything. I can attest to her skills. In my years of hunting and trapping, I never shot a moose without her name on it. She taught me how to call a moose. Tempest had strong roots in her Chippewa-Ojibwa ancestry.

As the sun made its ascent one cold winter afternoon, Tempest arrived back at the cabin, her dogs chatting excitedly with Irv's pack. She hung her mitts to dry high above the stove. They ate stew along with Irv's favorite, Ritz crackers, and drank tea. Later, they crawled under the thick quilt on their bed and soon were fast asleep. The backdrop of stars in the night sky seemed wider than ever that night, and the full moon moved as if to meet the heavy smoke that rose straight up the chimney of the woodstove. Occasional pops followed by long hissing sounds hinted that Irv had thrown in some spruce. Suddenly, a louder pop was heard. Tempest bolted upright, her eyes blinking.

"What'd you do that for?" she said.

"What'd I do what for?" Irv asked.

"You know," she said. "Don't play innocent with me."

"What?"

"You hit me with your elbow when I was sleeping." She rubbed her shoulder in a circular motion. "Let's hear your chicken explanation why. I want a straight answer."

"Ah," Irv said. "I musta thought you were Buster." He made things worse by telling Tempest she had a cold nose.

"What do you mean I have a cold nose?" Tempest was now fully awake.

Buster was quite happy sleeping on the floor.

He didn't understand Irv either.

Don and Thora

In 1967, Cache Bay Quetico Ranger Station was manned by Don and Thora McClure, Fire Tower Ranger "men" of long standing with Lands and Forests. I had heard how Don was once found on the tower floor with walls blown away during a fierce lightning storm. He wasn't sure how long he was unconscious.

"Luckily," he said, "I didn't roll over the edge and drop to the ground."

Don and Thora were extremely friendly Rangers, they welcomed everyone.

To aid visitors coming to the station, shiny tin lids were tied to cedar trees. They spun like wings on a lynx trap to attract the eyes' attention and help people find their way.

Benny & Ollie

Benny Ambrose lived on the south shore of Ottertrack Lake and was known as a friendly loner, trapper and prospector with bronze hands as tough as knots. Ben was strong and stocky, hardship was a joke, he belonged in the forest as much as a tree, and he only left Ottertrack briefly and out of necessity. Today was important, it was plywood day. Ben left his house early. After portaging into Saganaga he headed east some 18 miles then swung south to the Gunflint Trail. Two hours more by truck and he would meet Ollie in Grand Marais. Ben and Ollie would return together with a boat load of goods covered by a few sheets of plywood.

As a courtesy Ben would stop in at Government Island, say hello, shake and break a few hands, and be on his way. As a U.S. resident Ben was not required to pay any duties or taxes but he stopped to avoid Customs any confusion. A boat going by with a load might be seen as someone entering or transporting goods illegally causing officers a chase for naught. Ben, usually alone, might be recognized from a distance but today with the full load and Ollie along, he made the stop.

Ollie longed for a few days of solitude, away from the heady pace of Grand Marais, the gulls around the Blue Water Café, the rolling waves of Lake Superior and the tourists who came from busier places to get away from it all. Ollie would help Ben with portaging all his goods and a few projects in the quiet tranquility of Ottertrack Lake. In his mind he anticipated the night and silence, the stars above and maybe even a glimpse of the Northern Lights, rather than the transport trucks roaring by with headlights on. In contrast to Ben, Ollie was of Nordic heritage and much smaller, although he prided himself on his power.

As the two friends left Government Island heading west everything was going well. The channel was calm with little wind although they were protected by many islands. As they headed into the open part of the lake at least the bow would be pointed directly into the prevailing westerly winds. With the extra weight of all the supplies the boat was riding low, adding some stability. Ben looked to the sky for advice, everything was in the timing. Dark clouds of deep blue were on the western horizon, the trick was going to be getting across the open water. Progress was slow because of all the weight in the boat; it was a race to beat the invisible wind. "Oh blessed and cursed is the wind, it alone brings the storm, it alone clears the sky!" Ben made good progress through the chop of white capped waves but with about a mile to go to the lee shore the howls and sprays picked up. Ben told Ollie to hold things down but the next thing he saw was Ollie taking off clutching a sheet of plywood. He soared like a great eagle for a brief time but soon dove into the lake like an Osprey. A great gust had done its best.

Once Ollie and the plywood were retrieved, both agreed that wet plywood was not good, but how to dry it out? Trying to dry it by the stove at camp might work, but drying too fast might cause it to warp and separate. They decided it was better to dry it slowly in the wind. They finally made it back to Ben's place and got the stove going for some coffee, and took out some of the smoked fish Ollie had brought along as a treat. "Ollie, I didn't know you could fly", said Ben, causing a spray of coffee from Ollie's lips, some laughing and choking. Because of Ben, Ollie realized fame around the lake. As flying goes it was a first for Saganaga Lake. Ollie wanted to keep his flight a secret but Ben thought praise was better.

Memories of a Family Living at the Rail Portage

There was a time that a colorful family of six lived at the mechanized rail portage between Saganaga and Northern Light lakes. The kids slept on springs in the rafters, parents and pets below. The shack was sixteen feet square. For a fee, they hauled boats to and fro, for anglers, mostly. The kids were a Huckleberry lot, tough, healthy, and happy. Their school was their life, and correspondence was their hero.

In the spring, with snow patches on the ground, I saw them running around in bare feet, playfully snapping dad's braces. They embraced life on the terms they were given. Dad hustled odd jobs around the lake, repairing docks for cabin owners on the lake and whatever other work he could find.

Long gone and since grown up, I run into family members in Thunder Bay from time to time. The Huckleberry kids are grown up, all married, in well secured jobs and raising families. I admire this family because they didn't gripe about circumstances. They overcame. Others had problems with their lifestyle, but it was happy and normal. In the spring, I saw feet so tough they could run barefoot with snow patches on the ground. I can't recall ever seeing the kids with a cold or sick.

I ran into one of the kids, Peter, who now has three kids of his own. He's a long haul transport driver. From him, I learned that all the kids had found productive lives. Two girls married well, one moved to the States. Of the four siblings, not one had problems adjusting to life in the city. Peter said that they all cherished memories of the past life on the portage between two lakes. He laughed about the time when the family moved to Thunder Bay, their dad contracted all of them—his sisters along with his brothers--to dig basements using shovels. He seemed proud that his sisters could dig so well. I'll always admire their humour and grit.

John Crossing the Rail Portage in the 1970's

The Age of Aquarius Arrives at Saganaga

Turi Benson was the best drug-buster at Canada Customs, he didn't need a bloodhound to find illegal goods. He earned respect from both sides of the border for his skills and intuition. In the 1970's the Age of Aquarius had arrived on Saganaga Lake. Customs officers were often accused of harassing young canoeists entering Canada. Turi insisted that he didn't type-cast certain people, he let geography be his guide. If the person came from a large urban center they were more likely to be in possession of contraband, so he looked at these people more closely. He told me he'd found LSD, Heroin, Peyote buttons, and everything else you can think of on people who were so clean cut you would have thought they were graduates of Westpoint Military College. He told me that drugs could be found in every walk of life, he had even found stashes hidden in the diapers of babies.

When working Government Island, Lands & Forests and Customs Officers always assisted each other because we were all we had. I remember one occasion when I arrived, at the Customs house, Officer Duffy was backed up against his desk. Officers in the 70's were unarmed. Two young men were shouting "We still have our knives, give us back our stuff and let us go! The border is just out there, no one will know the difference". The fact that I arrived to even the odds changed the situation on that day.

There was an unwritten signal between Turi and I. He would be working the dock and I knew he was on to something the moment I heard him start a dry, monotonous, tuneless whistle. I would go over to offer assistance and almost always he would be in the process of a search for drugs or contraband. Whenever drugs were found, the RCMP, having the enforcement jurisdiction, had to be called in. They would arrive in a float plane to process matters for court. On one occasion I had gone to assist Turi, since we were the only ones on the island. Sitting on a bench behind the barrier were two young men, pale and emaciated, two women and a child. All sat silently while a young RCMP officer removed a small packet of white powder Turi had found on his inspection. The officer told us that if we saw a tail follow the substance as he dropped it into a glass of water, it was likely heroin. It would look just like Haley's Comet. The young mother seemed nervous and held her baby tighter. The test was

Heroin Test

positive!

On another occasion a huge young man was being strip searched for drugs and paraphernalia after rolling papers were uncovered in a preliminary search. As I entered the office, there was an uproar and I saw a huge sasquatch leap over the barrier, bolt out the door and head for the back of the island, all while wearing only his underwear. Without thinking I was hot on his heels. Not long after I started thinking "what will I do if I catch him". I watched as he threw his stash under a pine root and I realized why he was running. Like a fullback he was weaving and dodging around stumps and trees all in his bare feet. There was really no place to go on the relatively small Government Island and soon his youthful advantage began to fade. Just as I was closing the distance between us, his foot caught a pine

root and he flipped to the ground.

He showed no aggression and I ordered to "Sit on a stump, catch your breath, and don't make matters any worse for yourself! Turi knows you were scared" Later, once the RCMP arrived they determined that the offender had to pay a fine for possession, and they teased me that I must have tripped him during the chase. I was unable to convince the two officers that a root did it.

We want the truth,
You tripped him, didn't you?
No, he did it himself

Some months seemed endless. What once seemed uncommon had become common with over 18 drug charges in a month.

Turi Benson, never gave up battling drugs because he believed the cause was important. Unfortunately Turi passed away shortly after he retired but his footsteps are being filled by his daughter who is now a Customs Officer herself.

Turi Benson, Canada Customs, examining some illegal weapons he had seized.

PETE

The Trout Bay Road southeast of Northern Light Lake was scenic but also dangerous. For some it was like running the gauntlet. Huge log-hauling trucks roaring down steep inclines would often hit hairpin turns and spew gigantic logs over the roadway.

It was fall, and I was trying to gather winter firewood. I managed to collect half a load, while ducking log-haul trucks coming and going. Then I ran into Pete. He had one log in his half ton. Pete was an affable man, with a penchant for personal history. We parked as far off the road as possible. "John", he said, "I've wanted to ask you a question for a long time. How did you get here to Northern Light Lake, and where did you come from? C'mon John", he said pouring me a coffee and offering me a homemade donut. His pale blue eyes and wry smile had a pleading look. This was not the best place to engage in conversation. We were parked between two steep hills. My head wigwagged between the two hills, as I was fearful of eminent disaster. I told Pete the truth. There was no wiggle room for anything else.

Checking my watch, my history had to be fast. I knew that more than thunder and lightning could come down the hills. "Lordy, why here, why now," I wondered. "Well Pete things started in the west. My best friend John Gabber and I landed a job in Banff, Alberta. We were hired as professional leaf-rakers at a posh golf course. It seems like yesterday. We saw two cougars lope out, not more than two feet ahead of us, long tails following. "Wow, no kidding," said Pete. "Scary!" "Not really we had our rakes." "Banff sounds exciting. Why did you leave?" asked Pete. "It was the fifties, we were both incredibly handsome back then. One day opportunity knocked, our big break was less than three miles away, at the Banff Springs Hotel. MARILYN was in town!" Pete's eyes narrowed, "Did you say Marilyn? THE Marilyn?"

"Yes!" "Holy cow, you met her?"

"Not quite".

"What do you mean?" After work, we pressed our strides, shined our shoes and slept." "Skip the details," Pete said. "What happened?"

"I hate to say it Pete, but it was jealousy."

"Are you sure you're not pulling my leg?"

"No Pete, I'm telling you straight. We woke early, with three miles to walk; there was no time to call the golf course boss." Pete said, "I get it. The boss was jealous?"

"No, that's not it. We didn't have the day off."

Pete looked perplexed. His eyebrows furled. "Please John, the suspense is killing me!"

"Well, in the pre-dawn light, Johnny Gabber and I began our irresistibility check. Every lock was precisely in place. It wasn't easy, because looking in the mirror, we both saw Marilyn." "So where does jealousy fit in?"

"At the Banff Springs gate we were stopped by a big Hollywood goon. He demanded a pass. He wouldn't listen when we insisted that we didn't need a pass. He wouldn't listen when we said that if Marilyn saw us she would invite us. His huge arm pointed to the road.

"Outta here!". "You could tell he was jealous the way he looked at us. We left with the satisfaction, knowing that if Marilyn found out, he would have big problems; and we told him so. But he refused to listen."

Pete said,

"You and your friend Gabber, are amazing! You actually tried to see Marilyn Monroe?"

"Yes Peter we did."

"But how did that get you here at Northern Light Lake?"

"Well, when we returned to the golf course, tired and worn out, we told the boss why the leaves weren't raked. We mentioned the two cougars and about Marilyn." He said, "Your services are no longer needed."

Pete said, "I guess your golf boss suffered from envy. But why settle here?" Pete asked incredulously. "Pete, it's really all quite simple. All you ever have to do is look up to the sky at night. If you did you would never ask. Northern Light Lake has big stars, far more brilliant than any in Hollywood. Out here you never need a pass. You can enjoy their company all night." "Mmm, never thought about it that way, John." We began to hear rumbles in the distance. The unmistakable shifting of gears that would soon bring clouds of dust. Pete nodded, "Guess we better go. You know John, those log trucks come fast, and don't leave much room."

"Thanks, Pete". I watched as he headed east, a lone log bouncing in the box of his truck. I was glad I had at least had half a load of firewood.

That night, I looked at the sky; thought about my old friend Johnny Gabber, and wondered if the goon ever got fired by Marilyn. I also wondered what Pete would say to his wife, about coming home with one log of firewood.

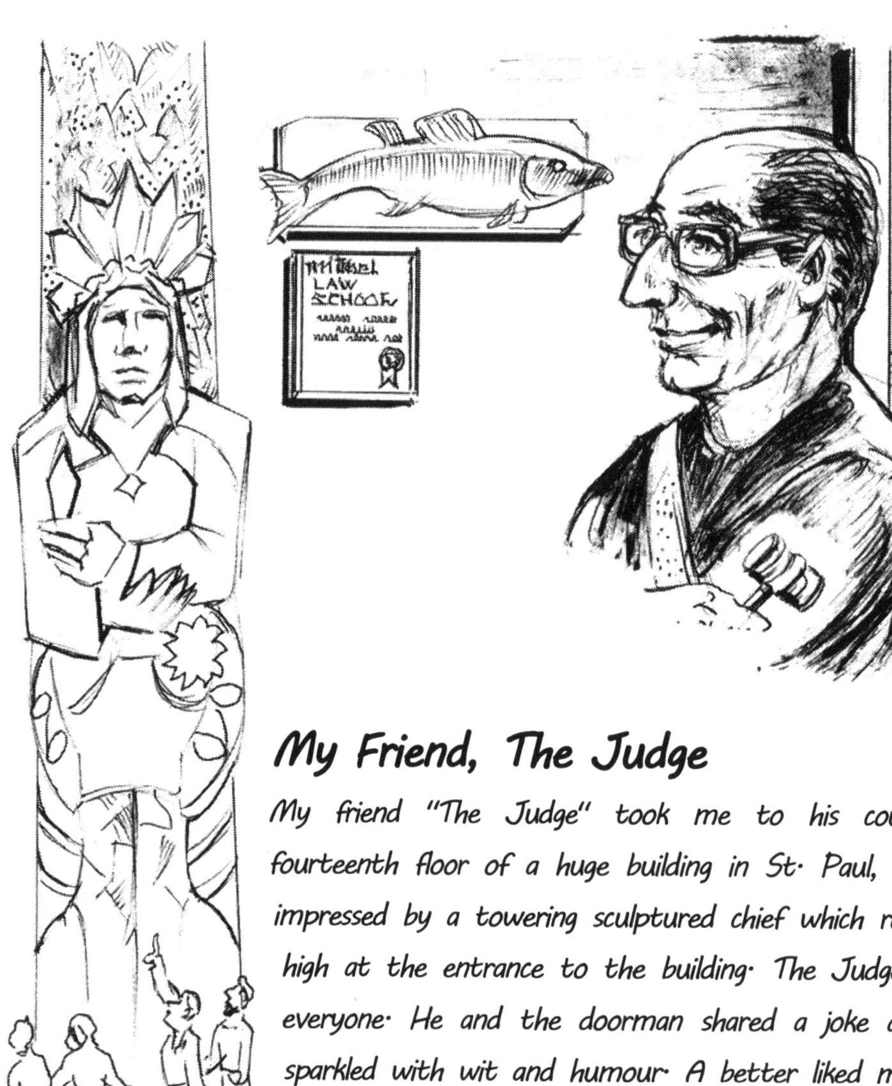

My Friend, The Judge

My friend "The Judge" took me to his courthouse on the fourteenth floor of a huge building in St. Paul, Minnesota. I was impressed by a towering sculptured chief which rose several stories high at the entrance to the building. The Judge was greeted by everyone. He and the doorman shared a joke and his grey eyes sparkled with wit and humour. A better liked man I never knew. He had time for everyone on a first name basis.

I was there on serious business, to conduct an interview. The Judge was vying for a position. During the Christmas holidays he had two weeks that he wanted to spend on my trapline at Kashabowie, Ontario. If he was nervous he didn't show it. I had tough questions for him to answer. The answers had to be straight no matter how tough, and he knew it.

"Have you ever skinned a Canadian beaver before?" I asked.

"No!" he strongly replied. "For me it would be unlawful. But I did catch a huge trout at Great Slave Lake," he added, pointing to his office wall. He continued trying to convince me. "I'm a good cook and know how to make tea in a billy tin. I know how to dry a beaver by dragging it in the snow."

"Can you ride on a sleigh and hang on?", I asked. "You're quite tall . . ."

"No problem," he said. "I served in World War II."

As though to pre-empt my next question he went on. "I own my own axe and can cut bait . . ."

Thinking quickly I shrewdly thought I had him boxed in. "What kind of bait?" I asked, as I studied his face for answers. "Poplar? What?"

"Poplar, small branches with buds for beaver."

I realized he had passed all criteria. To celebrate, he and his wife Alvirna took Eve and I to the Black Diamond Club to see Edgar Bergen and Charlie McCarthy. As we left St. Paul the Judge said he would report for trapline duty in six weeks. At this time I was live trapping pine marten which were to be reintroduced into the United States. The Judge filmed many of our furry friends about to be exported, along with our adventures on the trapline.

That Christmas at Athelstane Lake, we romped the trapline. Things were fine. Eve and Alvirna stayed at the Kashabowie Resort. The Judge was tough and hung on to the sleigh. A few miles from the trap shack we hit a wall of slush! My skidoo was at full throttle. The Judge was sorely slushed and wet. "Are you okay?" I asked. "I'm wet, not hurt."

I watched in wonder as he removed his big coat and dragged it through the snow. He quipped, "What dries a beaver's coat dries my coat too." Later, having tea in the tiny outpost shack, the Judge said, "Who would believe we have a dry cleaning business out here in the bush?"

Our trip was not without disaster which haunts me to this day. The Judges' 8mm camera perhaps froze up. Whatever happened it ruined of all film taken at Athelstane Lake.

George & Hildegarde

The Moonys hailed from Minneapolis Minnesota. They had a fine summer camp on Saganaga Lake. They weren't the kind of people to give you the gears, except for Irv Benson, a local friend and caretaker of their property. Moony ran a large manufacturing plant in the Twin Cities and actually made gears for outboard motors and other applications. Once summer arrived they couldn't wait for their trip up north, away from the hustle and bustle of city life. They would bring as many of the supplies as they could, due to the remoteness of their property. They would plan carefully and try not to forget anything. This trip as they headed North on the Gunflint Trail from Grand Marais, they planned to stop and let Charlie their dog stretch his legs. Both Charlie and Hildegard rode in the back seat, and Hildegard decided that she would stretch her legs at this stop as well. George, sitting in the driver's seat, didn't pay too much attention; he was daydreaming of the summer days to come on the lake. The moment he heard the car door slam, and saw the black blur in his rear view mirror he knew that Hildegard had let Charlie back in and they were back on their way. Somehow as he unwound his plans for lake activity he noticed that Hildegard wasn't answering him. He figured that she must sleeping. Good, George thought, she must be really tired· After 40 minutes or so he said "Wake up Hildegard"· He didn't get an answer· He adjusted his rear view mirror· No Hildegard· A new thought entered his mind, Ohhhhh, Hildegard, where are you?

He turned the car around and drove back another 35 minutes· He spotted something coming in his direction· She was walking on the side of the road· "Oh Hildegard, I'm so glad I found you", said George· All in all they made it to the lake before dark, family unit intact·

The Moonys Got Bombed at the Minnow Pond

Once I returned from lake patrol and found people laughing on the Customs dock. My interest was piqued so I ambled over to see what the commotion was about. I was immediately incensed to hear one man say that he heard the Moonys got bombed at the minnow pond. I blurted out "That's a foul thing to say about the Moonys, I happen to know that George and Hildegard do not drink". It seems I was wrong and this was not a matter of gossip. The Moonys had indeed gone to the minnow ponds and while there, they found an errant campfire, left to burn by careless campers. They were using homemade plastic bailers and whatever else they could find to try and put the fire out and while they were very engaged a big yellow plane came in. It was Ontario Lands and Forests. The Moonys got bombed by water and fire retardant. George said the darn pilot couldn't see them, or thought they caused it. Either way the fire was put out, George said, and the retardant was very sticky stuff. I guess the best way to get bombed is by friendly fire.

Emile

I first met Emile, a Royal Canadian Mounted Police, many years ago at Northern Light Lake. He was a friendly affable man. What I didn't know then was that he was a man with a past. Little did we know from first impressions, but eventually time would reveal the truth. I wondered why he appeared on the lake with sneakers and blue jeans; he didn't even have a horse! Everyone knows that Mounted Police wear scarlet tunics, with golden braided lanyards and tall brown boots and hats. Emile showed up without even his britches. I wondered, "Why? What was he hiding?" Soon I learned that his garb was for boating. He and his supervisor were the enforcement component for Canada Customs, responsible for clandestine goods illegally entered across the border from the USA to Canada.

On this day, the three of us would patrol together. There were many cabins to check and people to see on the two large lakes. To save time and cover both lakes meant that we might get back by dark. Wherever possible we decided to take shortcuts. Our decision was to carry the boat, motor, gas, and all equipment across Mosquito Portage. Emile and I did! The

supervisor decided to help by giving us directions. He didn't have any work gloves! The loads were heavy, but eventually we made it. Emile and I realized that we were the only two true voyageurs. The man in the tall black hat continued to assist us with his directions. As in the days of early fur trade, we were "les coureurs de bois". Supervisor was the well-dressed dignitary who might as well have sat in the middle of the load, as depicted by artists of earlier times. Emile and I didn't have to communicate our thoughts, we had twin instincts, a glance and a knowing look was all that was needed. A faint smile with a nodding head said it all. We worked like beavers all day. I continued to wonder about the mystery of this man Emile. Fortitude was boosted knowing that patrols like this only happened once or twice in the summer. We knew that there would be no pemmican for lunch.

In time, Emile's past and history were revealed. As we became friends, I decided to interrogate him. Finally, all of the pieces fell into place. Emile was an Acadian! No wonder he could persevere. He was a direct descendant, whose history went back as far as the 1700s. His ancestors were here for more than three hundred years, before this land was to become Canada. His ancestors were here during the Great Expulsion of the Acadians, when the growing population of French speaking Acadians became a threat to the British. Laughing, Emile quipped, "I'm the youngest of eighteen brothers and sisters, and I'm proud to say that all have done well in life. Imagine if we had lived back then, how the British would have raised their eyebrows. Not all Acadians left this country. Some stayed, contrary to the edict, right under the noses of the armies in control. The British with fixed bayonets, forced many to march south under miserable conditions. Many Acadians failed to complete the journey, however many others did. Those who survived created a new culture. Their French language took on a nuance, mixed with a southern drawl. Acadians were called Cajuns. You could say that spirited people die-hard. The facts are that most thrived. In the deep south they are known as hardy people."

History needs not to be concise. As the earliest French settlers left for life in their new world, who could have known what fate was in store. Their original journey from France was steeped with mystique; as much as a trip to Mars would be. Their spaceships tackled the oceans. How could they have know what fate waited in the long term? Nova Scotia, New Brunswick and much of the Maritimes became home. The Great Expulsion changed everything. From the north, they moved unwillingly to the land of swamps and gators. Adaptation included mosquitoes and likely malaria. They carried their fiddles and clogging shoes, and introduced their unique style of dancing with their wooden soled shoes. As I said, spirited people die-hard. Their jambalaya music, born on the bayou, to this day can be heard from where they were forced to resettle; Georgia, New Orleans…

Emile went on to say, " We are not all fishermen even in Bluenose country; carpenters, craftsmen, farmers… Some of the best tall ships in the world are built here."

Looking back to Northern Light Lake and the 1980s, over the years, time moves fast. We became friends. Our bond formed early on at Mosquito Portage. Many times, we carried heavy loads to and fro, while the man in the imaginary tall hat provided directions. We shared toil and hardship, overcame rocks, burdens of weight…and like the Dubois' of old, we did not gripe. Like allies, we overcame. Work is nothing as long as you have directions, much like assembling shelves: fig.3: connect to shelf B, place nut in line with C, do not over tighten… I was working on shelves at the time of this story, and thinking about Emile. He's back to his Acadian roots, with his partner Maggie, working on a summer home.

SISU and SAUNA: My Friend Harold

1967-1994, was the essence of my career; a time of pro-active wildlife enforcement. Given the same circumstances, I'd gladly do it again. Great memories remain. Old wardens and new wardens visit often, and renew a bond. Conservation and preservation of wildlife remains the common ground. There are others beyond enforcement who validate history; such as my friend Harold Alanen, a retired teacher and former principal. Harold is part and proud to be a descendant of the largest community of Finnish people in North America, at Thunder Bay, Ontario. M.D. applies... He has a passion for metal detecting, in every way he is a metal detective, with a dogged determination for early history; voyageurs and that of the paleo-native people, at a time when Lake Superior was known as Minong. His solitary pursuit takes him to many remote lakes.

I first met Harold as a young man in the late 60s. I recall distinctly that he proudly said, "We Finnish people have sisu and sauna." I understood the word sauna, sisu at best was a special determination. In 2010, I learned what sisu truly meant. It wasn't anything genetic, but rather a belief that one has to perservere no matter the odds.

Aware that Harold had recently gone to Dog Lake, and having viewed his collection of arrowheads, copper points, musket parts, including a device the voyageurs used to pluck live coals from their firepits to light their pipes, was more than fascinating! One evening, over the phone, I said, "Harold you're back! Any luck at Dog Lake?" "Yahhh, I'll be over to see you in twenty minutes." I met him at the door. Sisu and Sauna had a big grin. I can only say that I was awestruck. Harold produced the largest paleo-native knife-sword known. He explained, "At first I thought it was only a long piece of cedar bark covered on both ends by sand. The signal on my detector was strong, so I picked it up." Shortly after he left I reflected that sisu brings luck. I believe that Harold's "aha" moment deserves to be shared with the reader, and to the reader, I wish you SISU!

Early Fall Hunting Season at Wantello Lake

Below the falls, I tied the canoe securely. I crossed the portage next, the roar of the falls masking my approach perfectly. A man in buckskin tones was placing scarlet maple leaves into the cracks in the rock.

"Sir," I said, "do you think that's legal?"

Unworried, he slowly turned with a wry grin. "Ah. The warden, I presume?"

By the tripod beside him, I knew he wasn't hunting.

"Using props?" I asked.

"Yes, maple leaves," he said. "They will suggest the falls are Canadian.

"What's your name?" I asked.

"Les·" He said he was from near Minneapolis·

"I hope you don't mind if I say I don't like what you are wearing, especially the colors· Do you have anything red?"

Never was there a doubt in my mind that this man was bush wise, but he was not a big game hunter· Anything he shot was with his camera·

"The only thing I have red is this leaf," he said· Having no interest in hunting, he was unaware that the season had opened·

"By tomorrow this place will be crawling with hunters," I said· "With the colors you're wearing, you could be mistaken for a deer or a moose· Anxious hunters sometimes overreact·" I gave an example· "One day, a hunter said, 'No luck today, but I did get off a few sound shots·' He didn't really know at what though·" I also added the fact that two hunters a year ago on Saganaga Lake had success: they bagged a huge bull moose· How they loaded and portaged it out is beyond my comprehension, but one had evidently shot his partner in the thigh· I heard but never confirmed that he had his leg amputated back home in Minnesota·

I asked Les to do me a favor· I gave him my red vest and told him to return it to the MNR station·

Later, he came to my house to deliver it personally· My wife gave him a loaf of bread, freshly baked· Over the years, he would stop in with his son, Craig, on his photo journeys· His trophies were the photos that adorn many walls and earned him prestigious awards· Once I was given a photo of a red fox, which he had signed: Les Blacklock·

The Game and Fish act says: No person shall shoot over water· Les was an exception, he shot with his camera·

Women of Wilderness

Northwestern Ontario...

In the early sixties there was a railroad line. Locals called it the Sioux Lookout Line. It served a vast stretch of forest, from Thunder Bay, north to the town of Sioux Lookout. Scattered in between, and sparsely populated, the area was compromised of trappers and mink ranchers. Mid-way, at a place called Quorn, near Selwyn Lake, time would turn a trap line into a fisherman's camp, for anglers from the USA, and as far away as France. My mother Margaret and her partner Pat, started with a trap line that expanded into a five cabin resort, with a two storey lodge. Considering that they were both in their fifties, it was no small feat. My mother often said, "Our resort was built from scratch. From the abandoned remnants of railroad buildings and abandoned hamlets known as whistle stops; places like Valora, Quorn and Petry. The railway sold buildings for a song. Materials were precious in remote areas. I guess you could say that the first woman of wilderness I knew was my own mother. I suppose that the apple doesn't fall far from the tree. I began a career as a wildlife officer. A unique aspect of my mother's life was how she received her mail. Mother received her mail on a hooped stick. For me, it was much like an Olympic sport; the train did not stop, it just slowed down. In the baggage car stood a man, who aimed the hoop stick toward her outstretched arm. She retrieved her mail from a slot in the wood. All outgoing mail went east the next day. Now the roles were reversed. The baggage man held his arm outstretched to receive the hoop. This train took pride in the fact that it could never be on time, because it dropped

off supplies on the way.

One of the unique parts of living in the wilderness is the interactions you have with wildlife. One such occasion was when my mother came upon a moose stuck in a swamp near Wassau creek. Without intervention it was obvious the moose would never survive. After some creative thought my Mom went back and got help and the tractor. Together they rigged a sling and managed to pull the moose to safety. Mother waved goodbye to the moose as she wandered away. The cow moose hesitated, was the hesitation nature showing appreciation for the help?

As I said, the first woman of wilderness I knew was my mother Margaret. Little did I know how many more I would encounter, during my career at Saganaga Lake. So many names come easily to mind. Ida, Dinna, Tempest, Charlotte, Betsy, Dorothy and many others...

Some achieved fame because of wilderness. Tempest Powell was one of the women born and raised on Saganaga Lake. She shared with me stories that were passed on to her by Elders. They spoke of battles over territory between warring tribes as old as history. The narrows above Silver Falls was said to be such a place. Even today Silver Falls is a perfect place for an ambush as many erstwhile anglers found out. Pictographs in the area support the stories passed on in the tradition of aboriginal culture. Tempest recalled visiting a cave at Cache Bay as a young girl, thought to be, how that area of the lake got its name. Tempest was well known for her skills and knowledge in wood lore, she carried so much understanding of nature and survival and was always willing to share.

Tempest Powell

Consider Minnesota's famous root beer lady, Dorothy Moulter who has a museum named after her. Another great example would be Quetico Park's historian, Shirley Pruniak. She received acclaim in 2010, when she was awarded the Order of Ontario.

It comes to me as no surprise that many women do well in wilderness settings. Some raised families on the islands of Saganaga Lake. For me it would be a treason of reason, that only rugged mountain men do well in wild remoteness. Looking back millenniums ago, how else did we get here? Even Little Red Riding Hood lived in the woods. Wolves usually don't dwell in cities. I think we simply forgot about nature as we survived and advanced toward civilization. I have no doubt that the nature of man has little to do with understanding the value of our natural world, other than to contrive man's world. We accept life as it exists; the artificial reality of food stamps, coupons and bonus points. It's not my job to advise people that pre-packaged meat began with four legs underneath, or that when the cashier smiled, she exposed canine teeth. We live near nature but are hardly in rhythm with it. Few ever give it a thought that even the vehicles we drive, when you dig deep enough that all things come from nature. All I know is that the keystone to life will be another pipeline.

In 2010, I decided to revisit my corner of the natural world, Northern Light Lake. My object was to find one of two women I had heard about, that had left urban life for a life of wilderness. I decided to visit Wendy. She had left Thunder Bay and moved ninety miles south-west to Madeline Lake. I had left my home at Northern Light Lake eight years prior. The two and a half hour drive was familiar, and brought back great old memories of my years as a wildlife officer. On the road, I had reason to muse over change. Fresh new hydro poles lay along the roadway at intervals. I knew that soon the tentacles of civilization would soon be stretched deeper into the wilderness. When you think and drive, time passes fast. I chuckled to myself, that in all my thirty years in this corner of the world, I never had to pay a hydro bill. The next thing I knew I was pulling into Madeleine Lake at Wendy's place. The lake was still and placid in the spring sun. It was strangely quiet. I worried that she might not be home. Looking around, my eyes caught shadows near the beach.

I'm not sure when I last saw Wendy; but the girl I remember was a young woman now. "Hi John!" She remembered me. She was gathering brush, winters ravages, and piling it into a sandy fire pit. "Hold on a bit, I'll put the coffee on." Observing, I noted several things; fresh cut blocks of stove length wood. She laughed. "Imagine a Finn girl using a Swede saw. Her saw leaned against the remains of a fallen jack pine tree. A wry smile, with a quizzical look appeared. "John, long time no see!" She was full of banter, anticipating... "I know you want to know how my bucksaw winter went. Surely you know, you spent years out here", she laughed. "Everyone in Thunder Bay worried about me when I left, much more than I did."

Chiding, "Poor little waif, sold her house and went to the woods, forgetting that my dad and I had spent a lot of time here, when I was growing up." Pointing to a pile of hand-forged tools near a shed. I came here often as a kid. I knew full well, that being alone would be a learning experience. The biggest problem was fire wood, so I found dried trees on the hill, used an old snow scoop as a toboggan and brought the wood down. It was up the hill to fetch wood."

"Wendy, it sounds a bit like Jack and Jill."

"Exactly, a pail for water, and a snow scoop for wood."

"You mean you hand-sawed all of your wood?"

"Of course," Wendy replied. It's still a skill we women can do. Men need gas and power saws. Our power is patience."

Touché, she made a good point. My collection of handsaws only gathers dust; at best, as a collection of antiques, or something to paint pictures on. Amongst the green reeds of Madeleine, mallard ducks swam toward Wendy. She threw them breadcrumbs for lunch with a flourish; while two frolic-boxing squirrels sparred for crumbs. Above a blue jay urged them on. Words came, "John, out here what's to want? What is is enough. Look, even those ducks are mine." She began to describe her plans and innovations for next winter. She had created a box top lined with Styrofoam. It was useful on the lake, to keep the ice thin when drawing water. She described how she was surprised one day to find neatly lined shells, neatly placed under the cover. For her it was water; for an otter it was his dining area. At her cabin she poured coffee, and pointed to a back window, explaining, "There's where my new environmentally friendly refrigerator will be." Her plan was to remove the window, build

another Styrofoam box with doors on the inside, letting the elements supply the cooling power. "In the summer, I'll use my dad's fridge. He kept his food cool by placing it in an old well."

I thanked Wendy for my day at Madelaine and headed for Thunder Bay. The two and a half hour drive gave me opportunity to exercise the ability to think and drive, perhaps the greatest freedom we've ever had. Somewhere during the long climb up Sandstone Hill, nearing the top, I thought about Mount Olympus in ancient Crete, and discovered a zinger. Triggered by the name Icarus, I visualised Icarus. His waxwings wide- stretched, about to make history, so that man could one day fly. I imagined his wings melting in the hot sun, as he plummeted toward the ground. I felt the strong winds from the Adriatic Sea that blew him to his final resting place; next to Wendy's place at Madelaine Lake. I revelled in the fact that I had discovered something with proof. This was no myth. Before I knew it, I was back in Thunder Bay. Tired, I decided to make sure. I pulled out a map. Yes! There it was, right next to Madelaine Lake. Like twins, both lakes are separated by a small narrows. I was almost blown away to think that Icarus had not perished in the sea as previously thought. Instead, he had landed in northwestern Ontario. No wonder Wendy had moved there...

I never met the other lady who chose to live at Whitefish Lake. I'm sure that she is adding dimensions to her life, as many a wilderness women have before.

Sometimes the past catches up to the future; 1953-2001, means that fifty years had passed. When young I was in Vancouver, the western end of Canada. There I met two women of adventure. They had never hitchhiked before, and did not want to go it alone. Vancouver, the mountains, to Edmonton was our goal. Coming along with me would be two Irish girls, the McAuley sisters, and an old Scottish plaid suitcase that had a broken *hasp. The three of us found ourselves in mountain passes and long lonely stretches of highway many times. Rides were short and in between. The old suitcase was a curse. Each time a car might stop, usually one hundred feet ahead, a shrill chorus went up, "Hurry, hurry John"; and each time the hasp would let go, spewing lady things all over the highway. As I hurriedly gathered my wits, and as I scrambled to retrieve the contents, a laughing chorus went up echoing through the mountains. "Never mind John, the car is gone!" Half way to*

Edmonton innovation kicked in; black leotards held the suitcase shut. It has been said that wherever you journey a part of you has been left behind.

In 2001, I found out that after all those years the passing of time had caught up. I am forever grateful that I met my daughter Carole for the first time. She was a French Immersion teacher. She would bring the McAuley girls, back in to my life. To this day, Carole is helping me, so that a book called Life on the Invisible Line might be possible. This story is an example that the best of stories should have a happy ending. It all became possible; it was not simply "Bonne Chance". Carole brought us all together. Life has been a reunion since then.

I learned that time does not erase everything. The McCauley sisters have never lost their melodious voices. We often discuss the old suitcase. We argue and laugh as to who owned the old suitcase. I say it was theirs, they sing it was mine, their voices rising in complete harmony.

Life is truly an incredible journey!

The Day We Bent the Law, Slightly

One of Saganaga's favorite people in life was a legendary prospector, Ben Ambrose. A trapper and woodsman, he embodied the spirit that stories of life in the north woods are made of. There was conjecture about his age. Was he 83 or 86 when he died? Was the cause only fire? Ben lived alone on the Otter Track, a narrow place west of Saganaga Lake. He lived his life directly across from a magnificent rock face, where on the face the tracks of an otter by nature's hand and legend were etched. From his log house and tent kitchen his view was north to the Canadian/Quetico Provincial Park side. Somewhere in between this narrow stretch the invisible line between Minnesota and Ontario exists. He had the US Boundary Waters Canoe Area on one side, Quetico Park/Canada on the other. Both sides had a strict policy: no motors allowed in order to keep both sides pristine.

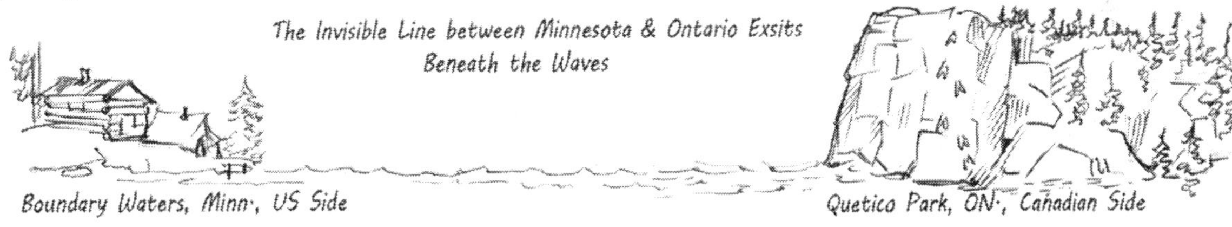

The Invisible Line between Minnesota & Ontario Exsits Beneath the Waves

From a canoe, Ben's ashes had been spread by his daughters Bonny and Holly. A great crowd attended the ceremony. Numbers of motorboats were seen tethered to shore, where portages to Ben Ambrose's place had to be made. As I recall, US enforcement officials were in the crowd. Ben's passing had bridged the laws; all came to pay respect. There are not enough pages to tell about Ben. He was revered in memory by all who attended.

Months after his death, old friends of Ben's, Joseph and Elaine Rollins arrived at Northern Light Lake from Minnesota. With them they brought a blank granite stone. Not yet clear I heard, "John, Will you carve something for Ben on this stone?" she asked.

"I can try."

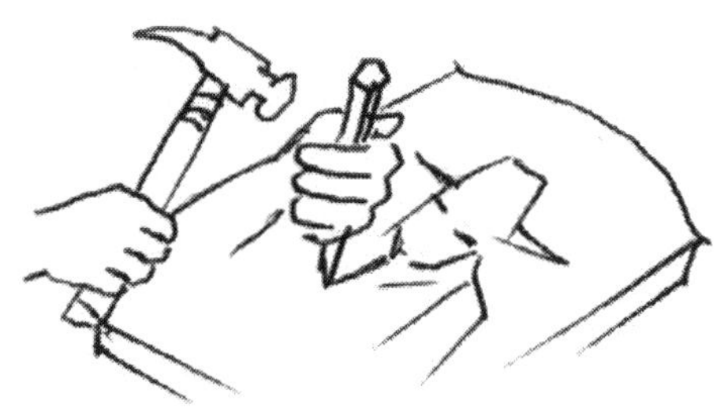

"We brought a special ink as well," Elaine said. "But we don't have power, and we don't have chisels for the stone," Joe added.

They wanted Ben to have a headstone. I knew the stone would have to be stylized like a linoleum block, contrasts emphasized by India ink. Hand chiselling, my hope was that nothing would crack.

Eventually the day arrived. "Co-conspirators", Joe and Elaine brought Rocky, a history teacher and well-known coach from the Twin Cities. He and his wife, Marion Elton, were a welcome addition. They also had an interest in Ben Ambrose and his headstone.

This day would use all the muscle it could get. We had to motor twenty-two miles by boat, then we portaged all goods; including the stone, a motorized Honda generator, boats, and canoes over the rail portage to make it to Quetico Park. We traveled eighteen miles west down Big Saganaga Lake, beached the boats, then by canoes we traveled west and over several more portages. We managed to achieve the task of getting to Ben's place on Otter Track Lake.

"The generator is quiet", we thought. "It shouldn't disturb nature's tranquility for too long."

"We'll need to set steel anchors into the sheer rock face to anchor the stone", I said. "Ready mix cement will do the rest. That is, if we don't drop the stone in the lake. It must be a thirty-foot drop straight down." We had reason for concern. We did all this work from canoes. The job had to be done carefully. Keeping the motor sounds to a minimum, we managed not to disturb animals or park rangers. Lifting the stone was not easy. Several shaky starts were harrowing. With each failed attempt, we managed the stone back into the canoe. The lifting was near impossible. The canoes, lashed together, would push out from the face of the cliff wall. The canoes had to be lashed together tighter and tighter to the cliff's face. Any mistake would render the mission impossible, and could send Ben's stone to the lake's bottom, lost forever.

Nature was stingy. A tiny plant, an inch or so in size in a ridge crack had to be reached and hold the stone. Its weight was formidably increased as we held fast with our arms extended. Shakily lifting, our base foothold was not solid no matter how we devised or tightened the ropes. Up again went the stone, straining, straining. Finally the stone took to the ridge and the small root growth and held it precariously, which gave us enough time to secure the stone to anchors in place.

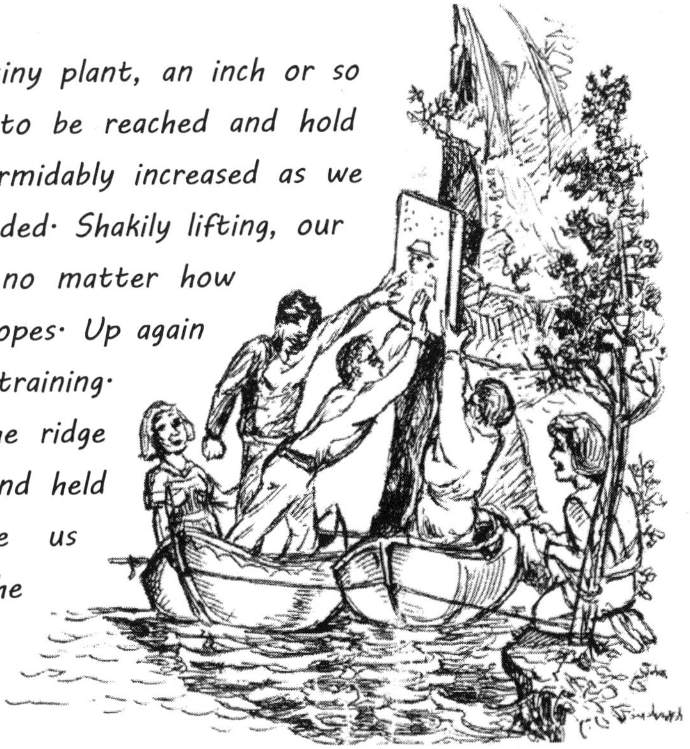

Giddy and relieved we all enjoyed success. All who

were there knew that nature punished that day. Sore backs and muscles, we knew that motors were not allowed in the park. No, it's no excuse, not even if we were on the extreme edge of the park. "This time you all get a warning", a voice in the wind seemed to say.

In the many years since, it is said that park rangers often paddle to Ben's stone, adding cement, tending whatever they can. They've never seemed concerned as to how the drilled stone got there. Obviously this case had run cold with the passage of time. Besides, the park remains serene and undisturbed. Quetico Provincial Park is nature's best.

In the end, Ben's memory was addressed to meet the occasion. He was a friend to us and many strangers. A prospector and trapper from the old school, Ben was a man who spent most of his life on the Otter Track.

There was no room for error or Ben's stone would be lost forever.

Fish Hawgs

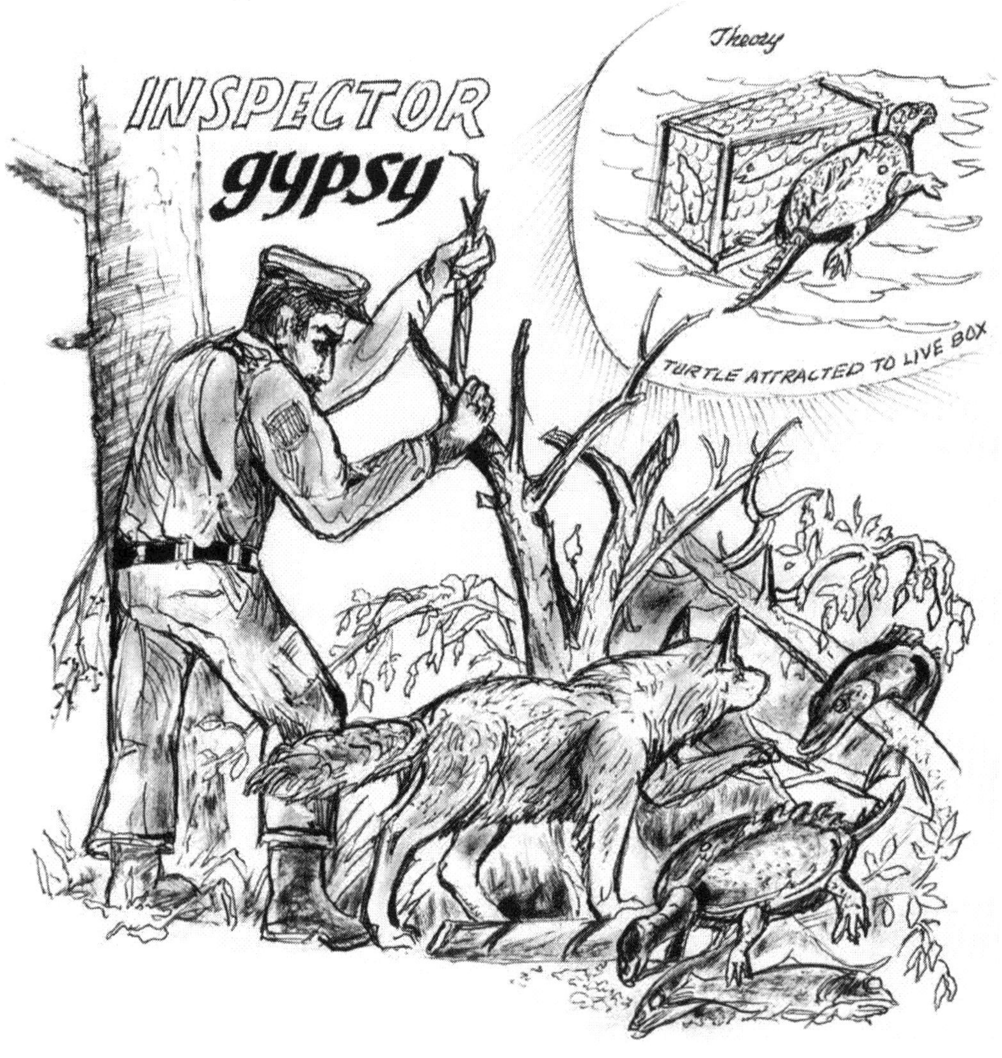

On Northern Light Lake, at the Old Ranger Station site, my dog Gypsy was with me.

Gypsy taught me that campers whom I had previously applauded for cleaning up their site were not as nice as I thought them to be. In this case, after three days had passed, I was to learn a surprising difference. I revisited the campsite again. This time Gypsy patrolled with me. She no longer attempted to eat any seized evidence as she had done in her puppy past· She self-graduated and began to support wildlife enforcement·

I stopped by the campsite in time to say goodbye to the campers· Their trip was over· They showed me that their fishing had been good; full limits in coolers and properly dressed skins on fillets meant easy identification and count of different species, proper for travel· I was impressed as they poured lots of water on their fire· Satisfied, I thanked them for a clean site· As I was about to leave, I went to my boat and called Gypsy· She ignored me· She was by a brush pile, which was odd, because normally she would be in the boat before me· She loved the wind in her face as we travelled the lake, especially on a hot day· I was a bit exasperated when having called her repeatedly I realized I was getting nowhere· Normally on command she'd obey· She was a perfect PR dog!

I decided to collar her· On my way passing the anglers, I heard them say, "Hurry up·" I thought they were busy loading their two boats hoping to make the border by night fall· As I approached Gypsy, she was pawing the brush pile· A bit of an odor suggested I should lend her assistance· We discovered four whole walleyes (that had likely succumbed in a chicken wire live box set by the shore in shallow water captivity)· With brush pulled away the wasted fish tumbled out· The worst was yet to come· We found a young snapping turtle that appeared to have been shot, a fair sized northern pike and filleted fish remains· Our friendly relationship turned into business· I *said that I wanted to see a rifle, and that until I did no one was going anywhere. With a knowing nodding look, one of the younger campers unrolled*

a sleeping bag, revealing a small 22 rifle considered to be quite rare; one that I recognized as an Ace. I informed the campers that there was no hunting season, convoluting problems with the reptilian act. The likelihood that this rare rifle would be returned was about as rare as the snapping turtle that had been shot. Charges of wasting fish were levied and the wasted fish were added into the count. This factored into having fish over the limit, resulting in multiple charges. Having insufficient funds for bail, they left the area not as happy as when they had come, because I also seized their canoe.

Sometimes full credit is inappropriate as to who did what in investigations, even amongst officers. To avoid misguided accounts, let it be known that Gypsy had solved this case. I only assisted as her deputy.

Millard Tew, aka "Pinch Me Too" & Joe Freare

As Millard would count, his partner, a rookie from Minnesota, would tally. One day as the counting reached 150 over limit, tension was visible and everyone began counting fish for different reasons. The more fish the greater the fines and court repercussions.

Our day started out at Government Island where officers from the US and Canada converged. Occasionally we paired with our counterparts and conducted Fish and Wildlife patrols together. Millard, aka "Pinch Me Too", paired up with a new young officer. The three of us chose the west side of Saganaga Lake; the other dual patrol officers covered heavy traffic areas.

It wasn't unusual during spring opener to find over a hundred boats and anglers dipping lines at Horsetail Rapids. We decided the west end might offer less traffic but more serious violations because of its remoteness, narrow waterway, and close proximity to the international boundary line.

It takes time to learn from experience. In the wilderness, rookies need to learn fast. To ease tension and boredom, sometimes officers play games. Banter between officers' works on both sides of the border.

"The next campsite will have violators," Millard predicted.

"Yeah," the young officer bemused, "Like the last five. Zip, zip. Two cans, bottle infractions and a warning. BORING." He continued, "I'm sure the other guys will be impressed tonight when we get back."

Time and miles later, we entered the narrow reaches, which meant we would run out of enough water suitable for our motor vessel. For us, west would end without a canoe. We would need to turn back, mission accomplished. Then to our left, on the US side, we spotted a large rocky outcrop with two tarps that provided a campsite. We saw two women, a child and diapers scattered about on a very messy campsite.

We pulled ashore on the Canadian side to watch. We didn't see any men around, but there were two gas cans on shore. We did not approach immediately. We decided that surveillance was in order.

Eventually a boat pulled up. Four men unloaded large coolers and brought on shore what looked like picnic items. Coolers? A picnic? Everyone on the site gathered under a plastic canopy strung above a large folding table.

We were not warmly greeted as we made shore and approached the group. Perhaps our varied uniforms caused wonder.

"What's up?" one in their party asked.

Millard Tew spoke. "Well, we would like to know . . ." He pointed to the messy conditions: cans, bottles, diapers, and pieces of chicken wire scattered on the ground. "You people should know cans and bottles are not allowed in the BWCAW."

"We plan to clean up before we go," someone said.

The officer shook his head. Then he asked, "How's fishing?"

Whatever cordiality existed soon faded as Millard began to count while his partner tallied: ninety-five, ninety-six, ninety-seven… I believe the counting stopped at one hundred and forty. The legal aggregate for the six adults in the group was thirty-six.

We brought matters to court in Grand Marais, Minnesota. I was summoned to witness and testify. Heavy fines and other penalties were levied. In the end, the judge said, "I'm glad to see both sides of the border working together."

As a footnote: Our poachers kept their secret about how they amassed so many fish. It was close to spawning season and the scraps of chicken wire suggested methods of old; yet there were no gill net marks on the fish. Purpose for the wire was never determined. I believe I know the method used as to how the fish were caught. However sharing this information would not be beneficial to wildlife. My fellow office Joe Freare tallied 140 fish over limit.

This was one of those times when I knew before I looked what I would most likely find. I was on Harmon Lake north of Graham, Ontario. The people at this site were extra polite, but a bit nervous. One of the anglers appeared like a pillar of salt suspended midway between up and down. He did much to accommodate me.

"Let me move this out of the way officer," he said as he lifted a cooler to clear it from the path. He explained that four others were out fishing and should be back soon. "By all means officer, go ahead and look around." He nodded around the site.

"Frankly I'd like to check the cooler you're holding," I said. His look of gracious confidence changed to the look of a kid with his hand in a cookie jar.

"Damn," the angler said. "We kept good count. These were for eating."

My partner, Officer Bill, was down by the lake as the rest of the crew returned. He found five fish too many dangling off stringers. A count of fillets in the cooler combined with the latest arrivals totaled forty fish over the limit.

Forty fish over the limit is not extraordinary. The biggest over-limit found at the US/Canadian border was the result of **Observation over Clairvoyance**. During a border check, outgoing anglers showed young conservation officer Forbes coolers that were seemingly in order. However Forbes noticed unusual condensation around the periphery of the camper on the truck. Tiny beads that seemed to match the beads of sweat on the foreheads of the anglers. The anglers had built hidden fish storage spaces into the shell of their camper. They were busted with 740 fillets over the limit. I couldn't help but wonder if all the fish were just for eating?

Border checks yielded bizarre innovations—from false bottomed tanks to knitting...

Serendipity Café

Greg Kemp, one of the Canada Customs Officers and I had dual roles today. He was interested in reports that there were clandestine aircraft landing in Canadian waters. I was interested in fish violations. We decided to patrol together for different reasons. Relief staff arriving at Government Island allowed the opportunity to get away from the station and have some adventure. We headed to Saganagons Lake about 4 miles north our location, then across the half mile portage at Silver Falls. Saganagons is located partially in Quetico Provincial Park and partially on crown land so different rules applied to different areas of the lake. Another several miles by canoe would take us to an area where there were several islands and the aircraft had been reported to have been landing and unloading. On the very first portage we had a chance to exchange disciplines. I pointed out a mass of wasted fish fillets sitting on the bottom, close to shore, while whole dead fish floated on top. Obviously these culprits were long gone. As we paddled our way down the lake progress was slow so we looked ahead for any signs of activity. Seagulls circling an

island directed us toward a target. As we approached the smoke from a campfire, a tent and 2 men made for an idyllic scene.

As we approached the men, identities were exchanged and valid fishing licenses displayed for us. The men we happy to tell us how great the fishing was, that they could barely get a lure into the water before they had a fish on the line. They were happy to show me the number of walleye fillets they had. The men were very surprised, and bemused to see the Customs Officer out in the wilderness and in a canoe. Greg explained that he was interested in the numbers that may have been on any aircraft in the area. The fisherman said that they had seen a plane landing a few days prior but didn't pay any attention to the numbers on it. They thought it was a red and white Cesna and that it had delivered supplies to a large group camped on another island nearby. As we were about to say goodbye I spotted a live holding box containing fish nearby. Unfortunately, the fish in the live box put the men over limit. They were very apologetic and co-operative, saying that they were so excited to be catching all the fish they were that they forgot to keep count. They were anxious what the penalties would be. I explained that the crime came with a $25.00 fine,

and $5·00 a fish for every fish over the limit· I explained that the penalties are set by the court·

Enforcement is unpredictable· In this case there was no residue of contempt· It was as though our presence was part of their adventure· They were in no hurry to see us go, and asked about why I seemed to have such a dislike for liveboxes· Staying to talk allowed me the opportunity to tell them why, that they always seem to be the cause of wasted fish or over limit· Turning their attention to Greg and his customs work they offered coffee· They told us they were still willing to help solve the mystery of the numbers on the plane, they said that if they spotted it they would send the numbers back to us, and asked for our address, post office number and zip code· They poured Greg coffee, and offered him both cream and sugar· They then turned their attention to me and asked how I liked my coffee· I said with both cream and sugar· A hint of mischief in his

smile, as he passed the cup he said that will be $25·00 for the coffee, $5·00 for the cream and another $5·00 for the sugar· Greg laughed and soon we all laughed in the moment· Our policy at the Seredipity Café, for Customs Officers coffee is free, for Game Wardens, there is a charge·

Some sportsmen really do bear no malice· The proof arrived by mail several weeks later· It was a postcard with the registration numbers of a plane on it addressed to Officer Kemp· This is a copy of postcard that he kept for many years· It always brings back fond memories of the Serendipity Café·

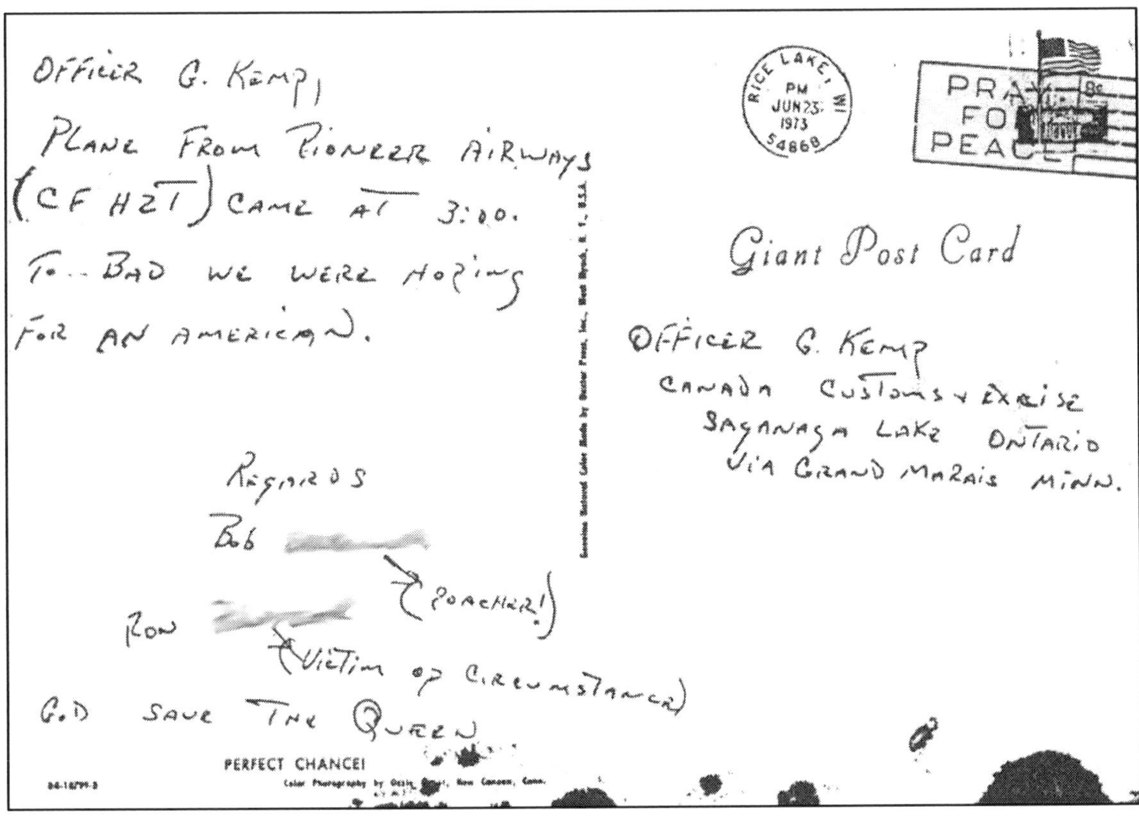

Officer G. Kemp,

Plane from Pioneer Airways (CF HZT) came at 3:00.

Too bad we were hoping for an American.

Regards

Bob

(Poacher!)

Ron

(Victim of circumstance)

God Save the Queen

PERFECT CHANCE!

RICE LAKE, WI PM JUN 23 1973 54868

PRAY FOR PEACE 8c

Giant Post Card

Officer G. Kemp
Canada Customs & Excise
Saganaga Lake Ontario
Via Grand Marais Minn.

Symbiotic Relationships?

The young fishing guide sat across from me.

"I think you're harassing me. You gave me three citations in a month," he said. His wallet on the table was yawed open like an empty canyon. Soon the wallet might echo if things didn't change.

He knew it.

I knew it.

"I think you got it in for me," he said. "Y'know, we don't make that much guiding."

I decided not to preach with a heavy hand. Assuming a relaxed position I said, "You've got things wrong. I actually look forward to our office visits. You and I have a symbiotic relationship. You bring your wallet, I collect bail bond, and in return each ticket issued helps me look good at main office. Why should I not appreciate what you insist on doing for me?" I asked. "I'm not nitpicking. I'm merely doing my job by not accommodating your ways. All I want from you is that when you're caught, I don't want you crying about it. Better we rejoice in every encounter now and in the future!"

The next time there wasn't a bust at the custom's dock, our guide had arrived clean. Nothing was hidden in his pack as before. His booty of live bait fish had been stashed on the US side close to the border, to be retrieved later after clearing customs. Some tricks utilized after clearing customs, included that his stash would be retrieved on the US side of the invisible boundary line. His new tactic didn't work.

We understood this technique of illegal recovery. From my office, he would next visit the Custom's office to confront other errors in judgment. It would not serve his profession well to be denied entry into Ontario. He now knew that his entry could be revoked.

Ontario fishing was good. Over the months our understanding seemed to work, no more problems. In time my friend moved away. It seems he wanted a new symbiotic relationship deeper south with the US wardens. Officer Warden Hiedibrink brought me disappointing news, or maybe it was Officer Tew? It seems that this young guide had found new problems in Chicago, selling trophy-sized walleye. His enterprising ways seemed to be on the wrong side of wildlife, whatever he tried on either side of the border.

The markets of temptation and illegal profit manifest themselves in many ways and are the reason why game wardens are needed on both sides of the border. Conservation is a noble occupation. It has every need to flourish!

Experience has provided us with the understanding that some people have no love for the outdoors. They are addicted to nature for the wrong reasons.

Symbiosis doesn't always work. How is a bird expected to know when a hippo has a gigantic toothache? Sometimes the bird gets chomped!

A Little Temptation With Survival?

For some people, the more they talk, the less they understand. The question for conservation officers is, "How do you deal with issues and still allow for some dignity?"

"I know what you're thinking Officer, and I know it don't look right," he said. "In fact, Officer, I know it ain't right. . . "

This man was bent on explaining, but his train was de-railing. Motioning to a brown paper bag he continued. "We found the hand lines, understand? But we didn't bring them. They was in the boat all hooked up an ready."

''Are all the lines baited?" I asked.

"T'be honest, they are," he replied. "I was teachin' 'em how to put on minnows," he said, nodding in the direction of three young boys. "Y' could say I was teachin' kids survival, passin' on knowledge." He kept going. "Y' see, I'm from Alaska. I useta live here. Now I'm just visiting, and I want you to know we didn't bring the lines. The lines were in the boat that we

borrowed."
"You say you once lived here sir?" I asked. "Did you understand or ever read Ontario's regulations regarding fishing?"

Seizing the moment, with eyes wide open in mock surprise, he asked, "Are you saying Officer that regulations have changed?" Looking at the boys he said, "Gosh, I shoulda looked! Yup. By golly, I made a mistake," he said. So that was how we were going to settle this.
"I wanna make things right," he said. The eldest boy began to giggle. The youngest asked, "Can we still fish?"
"Of course you can," he said. "As soon as Gramps does a little paper work, right Officer?"
"Right sir," I replied.
"The boys won't be charged?" he asked.
"No sir, not even a warning," I replied. "They're just learning."
"Right," he said. "They're just learning." He leaned closer to me. "Thanks," he said.
Gramps assumed responsibility and seem relieved, except when hand lines were seized. "But they're not mine," he said. "What'll I tell Bill?"
"I can tell Dad when we get back Grandpa," the middle one said.

We parted company on amicable terms, satisfied that issues had been handled satisfactorily. Every situation is different. In this case, with the young kids in tow, Gramps was trying to save face. It was understood from the very moment of our encounter that he was scrambling for a way out . . . The opportunity came with the word "regulations".

There are times on the job when you realize that some people are not lying, they just need more time to deal with issues. I'm sure he had great stories about Alaska. I knew better than to ask. It was busy on Saganaga Lake. Trout season was open; seagulls were milling around boats . . .

Frog Rapids: Walleye Spawning Season

"You scared me ...whew... I thought maybe you were the Game Warden," one man said.

"Yeah? Me, too. That's why I ducked," the other answered. "With my luck I'd get caught with a spear . . . Catch any?"

"A few," one said. "It gets better later at night. How 'bout you?"

"Nah. Ain't started yet. Waiting for my buddies to show up with the rigging..."

"Gotcha. Good luck."

Things that go bump in the night happen every season. Officer Tall Tom and another officer worked both sides of the rapids, each taking a side, both wearing long, green ponchos over their uniforms with warm hoods pulled tight.

A light drizzle was falling when Officer Tall Tom first heard the snapping twigs coming in his direction. At first he expected to see his partner; instead, he saw a stranger in a poncho lying on the ground holding an illegal fishing spear. This was not the time to raise issues of the law. The man had a spear. So he feigned friendship and made conversation.

"Man, maybe we'll bump into each other later," Officer Tall Tom said. "I'll show you a big one on the stringer. Catch ya later."

"Yeah, later," the other said. The man, relieved, slowly stumbled in the dark towards the rapids.

The sound of fast moving water allowed for radio contact. "Meet me away from the rapids near the landing. We got work to do," Officer Tall Tom said. The small hand-held radio worked well in rugged terrain.

"No lights, got it?" Officer Tall Tom said. "Over and out."

The officers met. "We have the spear. We need the fish," Tom said. "You stay out of sight. I'll approach him, while you pick a spot and move in slowly. He knows the area, and could run into you."

"Good plan."

Tom sauntered down. "Hi." The other guy looked side to side. "Nah, don't worry. It's good tonight. Probably the drizzle. Where's your buds?"

"Not sure should be here soon," he said. "Hey. look it there! Ain't it a doozey."

"Wow. Yes. Must be 10-12 pounds."

"Look at the fish. Must be a millions of 'em," he said. "Wanna give it a try?" He handed over the spear.

"No," Tom said. "But I will keep the spear."

The other two officers stepped into the scene.

"Boy, you guys are sneaky."

"No, sir," Tom said, "you are. You're out here at night not only taking spawning fish but also illegally spearing fish—and two weeks before the open season, which is also illegal. You can explain your reasons before the judge."

The man became silent, eyes and mouth so wide you'd think he swallowed a frog.

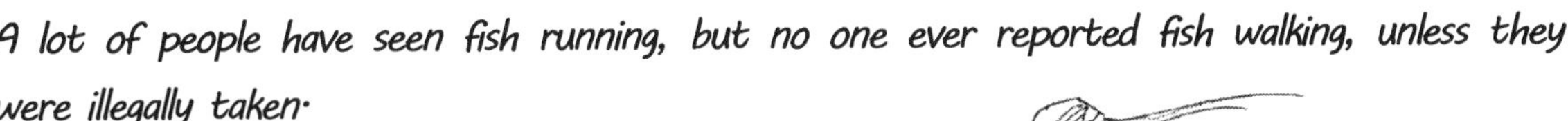

A lot of people have seen fish running, but no one ever reported fish walking, unless they were illegally taken.

"I Found It, Boys! The Motherload?"

Some officers give their all going beyond the call of duty. So often working alone, late at night, caught in storms, they understand the inherent risks in nature: hidden rocks under water have to be understood to avoid risk or injury. Nature has secrets. It's not hard to conjure images of voyageurs when officers occasionally rendezvous and work together. A certain boisterous exchange usually ensues. Adventures, exchanges and solutions are well explained. Of course, you could well expect great zeal given this day's task.

The objective today was to search for hidden coolers of fish, hidden beneath moss, stock-piled by bushwhackers during the week. The plan was

these illegal over-limits would then be claimed by others: friends, family members; who would claim fish as theirs. They would drive long hours from the city in numbers to match the legal catch numbers they were transporting. Such genius deserves attention.

Our objective was to find the fish and coolers quickly. We had information that the transporters would arrive this evening. Once found, surveillance from nature's hidden reaches would be in place to greet those who came to claim coolers. Their magical catches would then have an opportunity to be explained in court. The courts might ask, "How can you catch fish from afar whilst being in the city?"

Good Time Charlie Blues and words from the song, "Sometimes you win, sometimes you lose" was not anywhere evident as officers fanned out to search a mossy area. Serious as matters were, this was something akin to a treasure hunt. In all the misses, who would be first to find treasure? Suddenly and not too loudly a recognized voice was heard.

"This is it, boys. I got it!" one officer said. "The motherload!" This officer had given his all, and without hesitation he dove under a mossy depression, hands and arms deep. He knew that nature, once disturbed and no matter how cleverly disguised, often reveals a secret. A small twig out of place and

instinct put together·

Immediately officers converged with anticipation· By now expressions changed from wonderment to nearly uncontrollable mirth as bags of soiled diapers were retrieved·

Ted was the kind of officer who liked being Pampered, but we didn't think he would Pamper himself·

"Yup," one officer said· "It's the motherload all right·" The others laughed· But then the officers began to poke around with sticks, and eventually, under moss, large coolers with ice and fish were found· The travel-weary transporters arrived late afternoon· Unable to establish how they had caught these fish, and with reluctance, they revealed who caught them· Many identity papers matched names of workers in the area· All involved received personal hand-written invitations to appear in court· Justice prevailed· Heavy fines were levied, and the treasure, golden walleye, went to charity·

The case of the motherload is solved but not forgotten· This story bespeaks how wardens and conservation officers give of themselves, facing the unknown with due diligence, sometimes beyond the pale of normal routine· They earn a place in the sun for what they endure for the protection of fish and wildlife in Ontario and the States of North America·

The Day Poachers CAUGHT US

One of my fondest recollections of enforcement occurred in the early 80s. Funding was available which meant that my seasonal contract as a deputy could be extended. I could resume duty as early as mid-February. Officers gathered at my home at Northern Light Lake. We had a theory to put to work. Instead of one or two officers on patrol, we would dispel the notion that officers were few and overextended. A group of officers might be viewed as simply another gaggle of fishermen. Our hope was that the wary would be less suspicious.

With extra gas and many miles and lakes to cover, we avoided slush from Northern Light Lake to Saganaga. After another hour heading north, we were at Saganagons Lake. Upon arrival, we were astonished to see, like quills on a porcupine, illegally set fishing lines covering the lake as far as the eye could see. The many snowmobile tracks indicated that a large group were somewhere on the lake. As we checked the lines in play, snowmobiles appeared from behind an island bearing down in our direction. We knew that we had been caught

out in the open. To run and hide would only arouse suspicion. We assumed a role of fishermen pretending to use the lines on the ice. We turned our backs as though engrossed in our own activity. As the first machine arrived, with his helmet visor up," Moon Walker" ran in shouting. "What are you guys doing? Those lines are ours!" I'm sure that every officer present observed that our unusual ruse had worked. We were caught by poachers and yet we prevailed. Now we had a bonus, music to our ears. A clear loud spoken admission, "Our lines!", left little wiggle room for denial, here or in any courtroom. As others arrived shouting expletives, we didn't mind being called lousy sportsmen. If this investigation wasn't true, by now it could be called hilarious.

People who live on the edge of the law expect to see a lone officer or two, proving that our earlier hypothesis and planning was also true. We believed that officers brought in from other areas would lessen the identity of the officers who worked the area. It might also confuse the issue that we didn't have enough officers to cover huge areas of the wilderness. This winter would be different. We would cover each area in turn, covering many miles of twisting trails and absorbing the bumps which go with snowmobiling. My area near the border was the first to use the gang buster approach.

The lights came on as we showed our badges. "SWAT, Special Walleye Attack Team!" They looked dazed. Soon charges were pending, and being that they had already made claims, there was no turning back. All assumed their responsibility and bore the effects of being caught, after they had caught us first. I suppose our situation was similar to what a married man once told me. He said, "I brought her flowers, chased her for years, bought her candy, and chased her some more, and eventually she caught me."

The day at Saganagons resulted in a variety of violations, including too many lines, unattended lines, and importing live bait fish.

One of the group members looked at me hard and asked, "Is that you, John?"

"Yes it is", one of the officers replied.

"I thought you got laid off in the fall. What gives?"

"I was hired again."

"Oh…", the member responded.

As the sun sank low turning the snow pink, a dispirited group of fishermen realized that their fishing trip was over. Their illegal equipment seized they had no spare equipment, and adding to their woes they did not have necessary permits to enter Canada. We all noticed that their faces were uncommonly red. It's hard to say whether the sun or the wind had caused it…

By nightfall empty handed anglers headed south and we headed north. At Northern Light Lake, Eve had the wood fire burning and soon the SWAT team was enjoying Indonesian style moose.

On our next patrol we'd all meet in the Red Fox area. Ted would lead the way to Upper, Middle, and Lower Shebandowan Lakes. He knew his area the best. Once again enforcement had success.

Eventually Ted, the last of our group retired in September '07. With him went the end of an era; a time when conservation officers lived in remote areas. He remains in the very area where he once patrolled. Today young officers knock at his door to share knowledge that cannot be found in books or anywhere else. Every seasoned officer knows that to understand an area one has to be there.

To make a short story longer, as of 2011, retired and new officers often visit. We reflect on old adventures, encounters, and stories of past Fish and Wildlife violations. Inevitably conversations seem to settle on two words: "Found Committing". Magic words that light up the room for *seasoned officers and new officers alike· Those words are tinged with nostalgia, a longing for the good old proactive days· Old sayings like, "Nipping things in the bud" still apply and seem to be imbued in the psyche of all who aspire to be game wardens·*

There seems to be a message in all of this, especially when new officers nod approval and long for the good old days· Could it be that enforcement has gone from proactive to reactive over the years???

I cannot speak for wildlife, as animals or fish don't understand concepts of time, attrition, or fiscal priorities· If I could speak for animals, I think they would say that they prefer protection rather than becoming grim statistics with after the fact investigation·

This Late Call Was Different

It was late night and the knock came from the back door. Usually people came to the front door at Saganaga station. Hopefully it wasn't someone reporting a runaway campfire. Whoever was knocking at the back didn't come to see the red kitchen, chairs, table, and cupboards that rangers had previously painted from leftover equipment paint. Imagine, furniture and cupboards painted fire engine red! This was my summer home on Government Island, Saganaga Lake.

I was surprised to see the silhouette of a guide I recognized at the door. Usually guides are cordial but keep a professional distance from enforcement people. "I came to see you about a problem I got, and I want your help, and I want to keep it low key." Because we were not always on the same side of the fence, I realized what he had to say did not come easily.

"How can I help?" I asked.

He replied, "Tomorrow I want you to check me, my boat, and all my coolers—every time you see me."

Obviously, I had to ask, "Why?"

Tugging his beard, he related nonstop: "I got me this client tomorrow. He's big, a millionaire. He's big on transportation, huge eighteen-wheelers coast to coast. I'm told he likes to fish nonstop. Don't know when to quit. And don't like no from no one. A lady I know went out with him a few years ago fishing. She warned me about him. I don't want problems. It's my boat we're using. Don't need it seized if there's trouble. I'm still paying for it and I ain't no millionaire. That's why I want coolers checked every time you see me. See you tomorrow! We'll be fishing Curran Bay. Check my fish under the seat too. Got it? 'Spect a hundred boats at Horsetail Rapids tomorrow." "Yes, it won't surprise me." "Good weather for seasonal opener of walleye. Well, goodnight. See you tomorrow!"

The next day: "Gentlemen, just a little peeky-boo, if you don't' mind?" Five times seemed enough. Each time I checked the cooler and fish under the seat. And while I found things within limits, I also believed that any temptation was likely removed. The day turned out to be uneventful.

That evening I attended a local meeting at Chippewa Lodge. Owners and resort owners discussed the business of the day and then adjourned the meeting. The people in the large gathering socialized a little before leaving.

"John," a voice said coming from my side. "You checked my cooler so often today. Once more and I was going to give it to you! Then what would you do?"

"Sir, I would take it and ride around, and each time we met I'd ask if you would like to look into the cooler."

The man slapped his hat against his side, laughing. "Darn, I like that answer!"

Over the years, I never found the man in violation. I don't know the reason for his past lady's ire. I tried to broach the subject but never gained clarity as to anything relative to illegal fishing having occurred before. I did come to understand that they had been friends a year or so before, but neither was as enchanted as before.

Some things in life are never meant to be understood.

Bush Pigs Are Coming! Hurry, Run for your Lines!

Some anglers see two as twenty· These anglers, when approached by officers, have the mistaken notion that if they win the foot race they circumvent the law and punishment, forgetting that their very actions provide strong probability that an offence has taken place· With fish rigging in places immediate to drilled holes, all things including the foot race are noted· Convictions are made by the weight of strong circumstantial evidence·

At Shebandowan Lake, Conservation Officer Red Fox (who was also involved in the famous motherload fish scam) and Axel, a young rookie, were out patrolling Shebandowan Lake on snowmobiles· Red's seniority allowed him to render Rookie to have gopher status· Axel, a new officer on the job became hybridized; gopher this and go for that, and was also part mascot· He had to earn his rite of passage· Task master Red would relish in his role· He was in tune and knew his area best, therefore he was king of his turf· Knowledge is power on big lakes· Shebandowan Lake consists of three long adjoining lakes with portaging links and dangerous narrows· You must understand the weak spots in the ice before travelling· Snowmobiling requires more than just a map·

Axel was about to learn a lesson not found in books or lessons at Ranger school· Ice fishermen on shore were panting and resting after their foot race· They had cut excessive lines·

"There ain't no hooks on them lines Officer, so how can we be fishing?" one asked·

"Rookie, fetch me a long slim spruce pole," Red said. Soon a pole was on site. "Now cut all the branches off except for those near the top. They'll look like an umbrella, and the branches will bend and spring back once they go through the ice hole." Once the pole was inverted Red said, "Slowly spin it around all the way down to the bottom. Now bring it up slowly with no spinning all the way up." The slender spruce pole invariably would do its magic. The boughs twirled and snagged several of the cut off fishing lines.

"Well, what do we have here?" Red asked. More than a bit of line was wrapped around the limbs. The anglers seemed bewildered. "There's still more line dangling down. Pull it up easy," Red said. "My oh my, not only do we have line, but also a beauty of a jig with a live minnow."

"Okay, you got us," one angler said. "Now what do we have to do Officer?"

Later, when recounting the day's events to other officers, one officer was heard to say that some anglers deserve to be kicked in the ice hole.

Trying to Escape Justice
Anglers forget, cut lines don't disappear, monofilament floats and can be snagged

Like Father, Like Son?

Like father, like son is not in our books.

A lone vehicle parked with a canoe rack caught the attention of Officer Bill and I. We saw a man and a young boy in a canoe angling below a rapid. Without a canoe, we observed them from shore.

The fish were biting fast. All the while they pulled in fish; the man seemed to be unusually dehydrated. Can after can went from his lips to rest in the water. Partially submerged cans were held down by his paddle so that the cans could rest on the bottom. The man continued this action, obviously aesthetically attuned to his environment. He didn't want empty beer cans floating around. Officer Bill and I took precise notes, and the time of each of his actions was recorded.

The day was wearing on. We knew that in time we would all meet on the portage. Eventually, a coffee can cement anchor was pulled up into the canoe while the last can was held down. This ship was about to sail. We scrambled through the bush with our copious notes. It was time to have an official meeting. We waited and watched as they lumbered up the path with their canoe, gear, walleyes on a stringer, and a 12-pack before we made our presence known.

"Where the hell where did you guys come from?" the man asked. He was obviously surprised and angry. "What do you want from us? What? You got nothin' better to do? Jeeze."

"Sir, we are doing something right now as we speak," I said.

"Yeah, yeah," he said. "What are you, fish cops or bush pigs?"

"Sir," I said, "we want to do a little counting."

"A little counting," he repeated. "Right. What you gonna bust us for? Three fish over the limit? Big deal."

"It's your 12-pack we're interested in." I reached for the carton.

He looked confused.

"Your 12-pack is missing five cans," I said. "We know for certain they're on the bottom of the rapids." I opened my notebook. "One was held under by your paddle at exactly 11:53 AM. The second..."

"All right, enough," he

said· "Okay, so my kid was playing·"

It was hard to believe he was blaming his son· The look on the boy's face told it all·

A final tally disclosed that the 12-pack held four full cans· We observed five being sunk; three were unaccounted for·

The 12-pack case was seized for more than one good reason and later presented in court· No unflattering comments were made before the judge by the accused· In fact, the man was clear that he was guilty of both offenses· Fines were levied and life moved on· The greatest offense the man did on that particular day however, was to his son· Without an apology to him, that offense could last a lifetime· The Game and Fish Act does not provide for everything encountered· It covers nature, the animal and fish world· It does not cover the attitudes or nature of man·

Oh No, Not Waldo!

As I seized Waldo, it was a highly charged moment. The danger was they might cry!

"Officer, are you saying we can't keep Waldo even if we buy a license?"

"No, Sir, you can't." I explained to the young men that Waldo was no longer a fish. He (or she) was now evidence. At over eleven pounds, Waldo was big evidence.

Waldo was taken against his will, without a license. They didn't have a license for Minnesota or Ontario. My job was to prevent violations when possible, and to stop violations when I could. The courts demand evidence.

"Technically Waldo is out of my hands," I explained. "He is a victim of circumstance, and he will be available to the courts on the date indicated on your ticket."

One of the young men kept repeating, "But I'm from Arkansas·"

Exasperated I replied, "You're not in Arkansas, you're in Ontario·"

The young men listened· "You can appear in court, or pay a fine, and write a letter to the courts," I continued· "You can obtain a lawyer to represent you· Depending on innocence or guilt, the disposition of seized evidence is for courts to decide·"

"What happens to Waldo if we're found guilty?" one of the men asked·

"Poor old Waldo will wind up in a halfway house, a mission, or given to charity," I replied·

"Gee, we planned to have him stuffed!"

"No, fellows," I said, breaking even more bad news· "Exactly the opposite will happen· People will be stuffing themselves on Waldo," I explained· "We operate somewhat on a Robin Hood policy· All game or fish taken illegally is preserved appropriately· This includes deer, moose, birds and fish· After court, if found guilty, then the fish or game goes to charity· If found innocent, fish or game is returned· All equipment used illegally, including aircraft, boats, ATVs, anything directly related to a violation can be retrieved at high costs or may be sold at auction· It is for the courts to decide· Every detail must be noted on anything seized; scratches, scrapes, serial numbers····"

They listened attentively so I continued· "An officer notes each item's condition· Finding persons without a fishing license is fairly routine and happens all too often·"

I chose this story of Waldo to show that beyond fines, other losses are also incurred· Some fishing gear can be expensive· This incident included a trophy fish on the border lakes· I always knew that Americans referred to yellow pickerel as walleye. In fact, I've been converted and many Canadians have adapted the term walleye.

The young men I encountered had flair. One was from Arkansas; the other from California. They'd introduced me to a new term "Waldo". I took it figuratively and physically. I liked the name so much that I painted it on the back of a blue denim jacket I wore when fishing. I caught some great fish in my day, but never the likes of Waldo!

After the fact, solutions often come a-plenty. The young men thought to mitigate problems by offering to purchase a license later. To me, this was like trying to undo speeding or running a red light. Once done, you can't take it back!

I could not blame Waldo for leading them to temptation . . . Waldo was a beauty!

My job was enforcement. I'm not saying Waldo had no part in this; however, he was innocent!

Moosterious Encounters

Ending a Deadlock

When two moose lock antlers it will mean certain death for both. On one occasion Bob & Russ shot the antlers to set both moose free.

Return Call

The last leaves of fall barely hit the ground. The clacking sounds of diesel engines were shut down for maintenance. The drill crew welcomed the silence. Racked core samples showed promise in the Shebandowan area, 1965. Hearing sounds from hills and forests, a young drill-crew member took a section of steel pipe, and, clowning for the crew, went into a clear cut and began to hoot and grunt through the pipe, enjoying his stage and audience.

He was a hit. The waving from his friends encouraged him, and he faced them doing a clown dance. They began waving and screaming. He turned. The dry ground leaves seemed to be shaking. A black blur was pounding toward him. A huge bull moose was interested. He knew he couldn't reach the drill shack. Running, he let his feet do the thinking. A huge pine lay prone, and he joined it on the other side and waited. The bull raked the ground and paused, grunting and for what seemed like forever, turned, and trotted toward the tree line. The young drill crew member said he found it hard to leave the old pine even when the crew yelled "It's okay". Suddenly, the drone of engines seemed all right. He reported the next few days it was hard to keep his head on straight. As he worked, his head kept turning around.

Old stories seem true. It's bears in spring you should be wary of. With cubs or hungry after a long sleep they can be grumpy. I also understood that Indians who camped, pitched their tents in the worst tangled up roots they could find, for they knew that in the fall, moose were the most cantankerous of all. A moose's small brain, not much bigger than a golf ball, is well imbedded in a cavity of bone, beneath protecting antlers. Moose, by railroad engineers' accounts, are a sad sight to see when they run, heads down, headlong into a train.

My job involved more than 100 aftermath encounters between moose and man on the highway stretch between Shabaqua and Upsala, Ontario. There was hardly a clear victor. More than severe injuries were the result, to moose, man, or vehicles involved.

My experience with hunting moose provides that calling moose does not necessarily require great skill in the calling process. Moose are unpredictable at times, for different reasons. They do their own hunting during rutting times. Experience shows that moose have an uncanny honing ability to locate the spot where the call came from, a mystery of skill of mythical proportions that should be understood as true. Sometimes they come fast, trees cracking, sometimes slow, raking the ground with their antlers. They mean business, and it's not just saber rattling.

Many years of hunting and calling moose taught me that it is wise to move 40-50 feet away from the exact site where the calls were emitted. On approach, a moose can be behind you staring. On such occasions, the hair on the back of your neck will stand at attention. As late as November 18th a young moose surprised me. On that day, the notion that once they run, they're gone, it's over, must be discounted. Thrashing the brush with my axe handle, as I was grunting and calling, the moose came back. Unpredictable means unpredictable! Back then, I only wish I had a movie camera. In 1983, a moose went home in my boat. In 1984, a moose answered my call. In 1985, I responded to a call and moved to Nakina, Ontario. My hunting and trapping days had ended. I became a Conservation Officer full time.

The Contest/Calling Moose on Mowe Lake

The Contest: There were three groups of eight people: office staff chose different cut haul roads. I called for my group. Gollat, the moose biologist, had hatched a competition to see which group would call in a moose. Secretaries, clerical staff and people from various branches had a break from office. A staff photographer, Karen Wylie, was in my group. We sat on a steep hill near an old haul road that dipped into a valley and climbed another ridge and disappeared.

After an hour of calling I began to feel foolish. All of a sudden there came an unmistakable grunt, and another. Everyone looked around. A black silhouette appeared about half a mile away coming from the thick timbers in the valley below, swaying and rocking side to side. A huge bull in no hurry was heading straight in our direction. The hill was sparse where we sat, so we had a clear view. We sat in silence. The bull was very dramatic and moved in slow motion. His big antlers raked brush from the roadside, pulling up red vines stretched across the road.

The steep hill made him disappear for a time, but his grunts told us of his methodical rocking, and his stiff side to side movements told us he was still down below. The tension in the group was high and only got worse as we observed a huge rack strung with dangling vines on the bull as he slowly came grunting up the hill. As his head appeared, followed by a great body, things got scary. The bull resembled a Hollywood witch doctor, vines all over his face

There was no plan, and very little protection. Karen said later, "I tried to take pictures, but I shook too badly during the stare down, I wondered if my heart would stop. He was barely 30ft away." I don't know what instincts took charge, but as if on cue we all nine of us stood up. To the moose, it may have seemed as if the earth exploded. Whatever the reason, he turned and burst down the hill so fast his shadow couldn't keep up.

Karen did manage a blurred close-up and another shot in the distance as he wandered down the road in a cloud of trailing dust.

The office buzzed for a week. Our group was happy. We won the contest, and bragging rights belonged to the Wildlife Branch.

Every moose that comes to call is different. Some come like a freight train. This moose liked drama. Of all the moose I've observed over the years, only the Mowe Lake moose displayed the slow side to side rocking motion, his antics well displayed. If his only intent was to scare us, he definitely succeeded—and he more than met any of our wildest expectations.

Lucky are we who live and work in nature.

As our Mowe Lake Moose crested the hill he presented a formidable sight. He looked more like a bride than a groom but was too close for comfort.

Three and Three Is Equal; Four Is Illegal

Acting on a tip from a lumber camp located in a dense bush area in the remote north of Graham, Ontario, while assisting Officer S·Elliot, we roamed the vast maze of ever-expanding logging road systems and lucked out· We heard the sound of a skidder· An empty haul truck indicated that it had recently been unloaded· This particular area was not flagged for hauling logs· Earlier we had received word by radio that four moose had gone down· The hunters had three licenses and would give one away to anyone who would help haul the moose out of the dense brush kill sites· The plot overheard at a nearby logging camp seemed correct; the hunters had travelled far, were tired and had one too many moose· We located a tent site and met a lone man at the hunt campsite· He claimed he was not hunting, he was simply the camp cook·

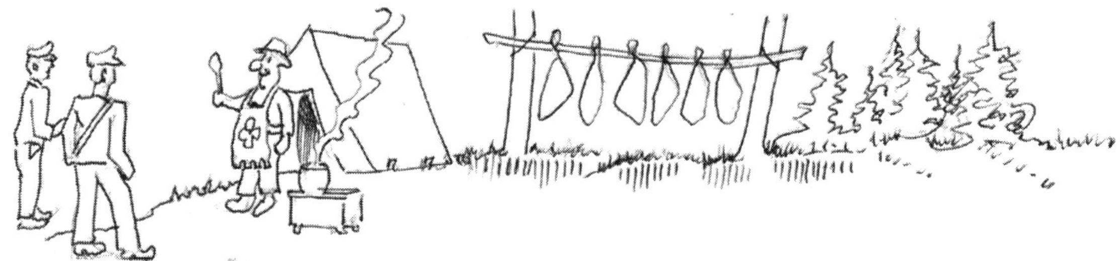

We asked, "Did you see a skidder in the area?"

"Yeah, he's in the brush retrieving equipment", he replied·

We asked, "Where are the rest of your guys?"

"Not exactly sure· I think two on a ridge and the other is in a swamp somewhere", he answered·

Trekking along a twisted trail of skidder tracks and twisted saplings, we encountered two hunters on the trail· They claimed to have been hunting on a ridge and were heading back to camp·

"Any luck?" I asked·

"Not yet, we need a break from the black flies·"

"Where's your buddy?"

"He's somewhere in a big swamp· We all separated·"

"Do you have means of contacting him?"

"No·"

Steve and I walked on for what seemed like endless miles· In a grassy area above the swamp we found moose meat wrapped in linen hanging from a ridge pole· We counted eight hind quarters, which aroused our attention and confirmed that we were on the right track· Trudging on, somewhere in the tangled green swamp near a thick balsam grove, we shouted out several times· Steve heard a response, much like an echo·

"Over here! Over here!" Faint signs in spongy moss led us to a solitary figure· Perhaps he thought we were his buddies? He seemed surprised, nervous, and certainly excited·

"I shot three moose, all in this location·"

Steve read him his Miranda caution· "Wow! You shot ALL THREE? You must be a great shot!"

I asked, "Are you sure it was three?"

"Yeah, I guess", he replied without much enthusiasm.

"We'd like to see the gut piles," I said. A long silence followed.

"Okay guys, I guess I'm in deep trouble. Things got very confusing", he tried to explain. "They came through the trees like great shadows. A moose went down and I kept shooting. I later discovered that more than three had gone down. You'll find four gut piles. I alone made the mistake. I'm wrong. I know that one and one and two doesn't equal three. When this goes to court will it make the papers? If it does, I'm more than sunk. Like I mean, will the papers keep out my occupation? This could ruin me! I recently received a prestigious award, and one of my buddies is studying to be a lawyer."

"We're investigating moose. We don't have time for a discussion on biodiversity. If all you say is true, it will sort itself out."

We took photos of the evidence, and made necessary seizures. Steve and I then went to the lumber camp. A mechanic said that he had observed two men standing in a doorway. He wasn't sure but he thought he heard the name Cook talking to a bushworker, and that they weren't discussing beans. He was offering a free moose to anyone who had a skidder and would help retrieve moose from a very tough place. I immediately called Berny at Fish and Wildlife. Steve and I returned to the hunt camp.

The hunter repeated, "I alone made the mistake."

"Not so", we advised. "Your biggest mistake was not reporting the four moose in the first place. Your second mistake was implicating your friend the cook who didn't have a license, a well as a bushworker. This will be settled in court." The consequences of their actions were substantial. Heavy fines were imposed, including the loss of equipment and moose.

The papers read, "Four Men Charged and Found Guilty in MOOSCAPADE"

Mon Doux - Moose Case North of Graham Ontario

Foreword: I chose the words "Mon Doux" / "Oh my", as a fictitious name for this story. Thunder Bay: The Land of the Sleeping Giant. Population: 113,000

Aside from shipping, Thunder Bay also employs many in the forestry and logging industry. The city is reputed to have the largest Finnish community outside of Finland. Migrant workers as far away as Quebec are found working in bush camps in the outlying forests. Logging companies often apply for no hunting permits in work areas due to worker's safety and equipment concerns. Conservation officers know that occasionally some workers take advantage and use such places as their private hunting preserves. (They shoot moose illegally)

Officer B. Stewart and I discovered, unfortunately a little too late, a moose hide draped over a tree trunk, minus its legs and head. Little clues were found at the scene inside the No Hunt zone. As luck would have it, on our way out we met a perturbed hunter, a park employee. The day before, he had been hunting partridge in the proper hunting area. Concerned, he handed us a small piece of wood. Scratched into the surface was a license plate number. He shared information in fragments. "A blue 4x4 truck, gas tank and hand fuel pump in back . . .man driving . . . woman passenger . . . seemed in a hurry . . . came from the No Hunt zone . . . big blue tarp covered the back." The fuel tank in the back was a helpful clue. We headed to a logging camp that was in the general vicinity. En route, a man and woman were accosted. They were heading for Thunder Bay. Soon we were all at the logging camp office. There the man said, "We was on our days off. Got our moose yesterday. We got our cow took it to town already for butchering."

In response to our questions he said, "No, we did not go into the No Hunt zone. See my license. See my tag." He told us the cow moose came from a road system that was near a small lake which is open to hunting. Mr. Mon Doux said, "Come to our house tomorrow. We swear on the graves of our ancestors, we don't do anything wrong."

Tired from bush roads, we took turns driving to town, moose-hide, notes, and statements with us. Disparities were not enough! We needed more evidence.

That night after contacting several meat processors, a butcher who knew his moose anatomy, advised that a bull moose had been dropped off by a man and a woman. He wasn't certain about the make or color of the truck, but he seemed to recall a blue tarp.

Early the next day Mr Mon Doux said, "Ah, you come early. Come we have coffee, we show you nice meat in freezer." Officer Stewart and I knew that the hide we had found in the No Hunt zone would be difficult to match to the processed meat. We queried anyway. Nervous, but friendly enough he responded to our questions. Using a ruse, so as not to divulge too much information, we substituted the term swamp for lake. Excitedly he replied, "It's not our moose hide you say you found at a small lake. I call dat a swamp!" Laughing he explained the difference, "Our cow moose she come from lake, most of lake is open for hunting." Having created confusion we asked Mon Doux, "Could you draw us a picture?"

He stroked pen past the hide location. He's taking us to another place? We couldn't believe it. We did not want him to see the look in our eyes.

"Yes!" With his head down and concentrating, he ended with an X that raised our eyebrows. His marking was within one quarter of a mile from where we had found the hide. We both knew that we had to re-explore the area. His map revealed more than we knew, only that what he knew was not the same, as things were not in sync. Hurriedly we returned to the area. His map was hand drawn but accurate. Assisted by crows we found decimated remains. Again, no legs, no head, no hide. There were clues, skidder tracks and drag marks, with no activity toward the lake. On the shoreline, there was no boat nor signs of lake activity. Unusual, but not proof positive. We had our hide found in close proximity, but little else. We were running on resolve, close was not enough. Once more we had to revisit. Time enroute allows for chit-chat. Suddenly I told Bob, "I finally figured it out!" "What?" "No not the case but what my mother used to say." "What's that?" "Catch as catch can. That's what we're doing." Bob conceded, "Maybe you're right, but we're not there yet J. B., we'll have to tread softly and pose the right questions. Things are suspiciously iffy." During field investigations we mull over the fact that we are running behind. The violators having a head start. A lot of curious circumstances existed. For instance, the evidence of skidder activity and trampled branches indicated something other than logs had been dragged out from the tangles of brush. Supporting factors included that the crude trail had no stumps to support logging activity, and yet the entrails were in the No Hunt zone. A mystery unresolved...

Revisiting their house again, Mon Doux greeted us. "See, I told you correct, we do nothing wrong." He was in his yard seeming confident. As for Bob and I, it was our luck that the dog wagged his tail, and not the other way around. His movements lead us to investigate behind a shed. It was there under a tarp that the magnificent head of a bull moose, with a great rack was discovered. A dispirited Mon Doux could not explain how his cow turned out to be a bull. He knew it, and we knew it. We had our questionable hide and Mon Doux had a questionable moose. Gone was the rhetoric. Confronted with our facts, the dam burst. Mrs. Mon Doux , running with her head down, crying, and yelling , "See how you make da liar out of me!" Soon, he too joined his wife in tears, fully aware that his trophy meat was all for nothing. Perhaps even his job was in jeopardy. He knew that the No Hunting zone was posted for his protection, by company request for the safety of all workers and their equipment. It was never meant to be a private hunting area.

Sometimes you win, sometimes you lose. Often it's help from others; the wooden chip with the scratched license plate number and public concern, when even the wrong hide can lead to the right moose. Whatever it was, perseverance has a pay off. The courts see to that!

As for Bob and I, it was our luck that our hide had been so close to Mon Doux's kill site. Oh well, close was enough. His license allowed for a cow, he shot the bull. Mon doux!

You Won the First Round Not the Next . . .

Curious remarks came from a man who claimed to be a sheriff.

Nothing at the site supported the Sheriff's theory or story

"The moose went down and was bleeding heavily," he began. "It made it up and into the no hunting zone, nearly a mile away. Then I shot him again. The first shot was in the open hunt zone. The second shot was, uh," he said, "necessary."

While explaining two shots in total, one at point A and the other at point B, he could not account for two spent casings in the no-hunt zone, nor the vagueness of any supporting evidence at the reported first location: no signs of blood or casings, no tire marks or disturbances of nature. Only the no-hunt zone bore the earmarks of hunting activity: blood, casings, tire marks... Two shots were confined to only one area. The kill site alone bore all the evidence, including easily discernible boot marks and tire tracks, only from the wrong direction. He'd made contradictions in his own admission.

The court did not find his defense credible.

Hours later, when I was at the main office doing paperwork, our secretary mentioned a curious call. Someone wanted to know if once a court case was resolved, could horns be retrieved? She told him no, as it was not in her hands to decide, and that the courts make decisions of seizures. Besides, she knew nothing of the circumstances. She asked the person on the phone to elaborate, but the phone went silent with a clunk.

As the day wore on towards closing, and the visiting public was slowing down, a voice caught our attention by the front door of the building. I stepped out of my office to see the sheriff-hunter wagging his finger. In a not so quiet voice he said, "I want you to know that you won the first round, not the next." He didn't wait for a response. He turned and went out the door.

My boss wanted to know what had happened. I said, "I guess he wanted you to know he wasn't happy."

"Make sure you make a note of it on your final report," he said. Then he continued, "As to sheriffs, you should be aware that in some places such positions are made by election, not recommendation. Often there are no criteria such as law and enforcement training. Positions are made by popular vote. Even business men run for sheriff and compete for the prestige or clout." "Don't equate anything to images of the Old West," he said.

"Badges can be had through many sources. Some are fake. Some are for boosting egos." He nodded in the direction of the front door. "That's what I think you're dealing with," he said. "A bloated ego."

"What makes you think he's fake?" I asked.

"Any real sheriff would know moose have antlers, not horns," he said. "Also, in a dilemma, a real sheriff would know to keep his mouth shut."

Strangers come and strangers go. No one ever saw our sheriff again. He did carry a badge. That's all we really know. This happened over twenty years ago. Maybe he went to Dodge City, or maybe the Alamo? Maybe, like all good sheriffs, he simply faded into the sunset, as all good cowboys do.

Even If You Found Something . . . Officer, Warden, Huh.

"Have y' ever wondered if a man might be sitting on those hills?"

Something in the way he asked, his demeanor and age made me wonder if this was expressed curiosity or a veiled threat?

This humour aroused no laughter. It was goading, not banter. Intense glaring, gesturing, waving and pointing at the hills as though to make his point. This man had made his point...

He was a tall man. Tired of being harassed he said. He'd come a long way to moose hunt in Ontario he added. His partner, a shorter man, merely gazed ahead. They were both testing the waters.

While I found things in order I advised, "I'll get back to you regarding your question of a man sitting on the hills," and that I needed to consult with higher authority for answers appropriate to the question.

"Nah, we was just kidding," the tall man said. "Just joking, y' know what I mean?"

Somehow we parted on a more somber note. "See you later," he said as I walked away.

Following the dark tree lined hills back home to Northern Light Resort, I covered my front light to make visuals better in the dark. I placed a phone call to Officer Red Fox at Shebandowan Lake, knowing that the head office in Thunder Bay was closed.

Ted answered, "What's up, JB?"

He listened. Who, what, where, when and why questions followed, as I filled him in on the day's events. The radio phone cracked. "Yeah, I got it," he said. "Those same guys got charged last year, one was charged with loaded firearms. How about I pop up and give you a hand tomorrow? Those two are a bit strange . . . yeah, they're different all right. Ok, see you in the morning."

The next day, we looked in vain for their campsite. Large as it was, it was abandoned, likely in the pre-dawn hours. We checked every bay including areas and landings where vehicles from provinces or states would park. No one to my knowledge ever saw them again. Perhaps they got lost in the hills… From the 70s to the 80s I looked to the hills at Northern Lights . . . mostly to get home in the dark. I never had finite answers as to why anyone who would sit on the hills in the dark . . . other than to carry a good supply of repellent when mosquitoes and black flies came out.

My mother used to say, when you ask a stupid question you might get a stupid answer. I'd like to think these two may have had the same early advice and had decided to vacate.

Most officers know the difference between jokes and dark humour, and most expect it to happen. I recall a social event where a friend introduced me to a hunting buddy.

"He's a game warden," my friend said.

"We hunt together every fall." My friend and his buddy nodded in unison, recalling adventures together. "He uses an old 303 savage beater to shoot moose," my friend said.

"Yeah, but at least I get my moose," said the hunting buddy. More banter was exchanged.

"Bo-diddly here says he's always prepared," my friend said. "I'll never forget his new 30-06 going 'Click, click', and the grin on the old moose's face as he ambled into the bush."

Bo-diddly said, "I'm more prepared this year. I'll have two guns; one for old moose and the other for the Game Warden." "Aye, aye", came with an exaggerated wink.

Conservation officers know that what goes on in the bush is as mysterious as what goes on in the minds of some individuals. Some people say what they mean; some mean what they say.

The hunters who broke camp seemed to indicate that they were not comfortable hunting in this location. Whatever our brief conversation implied had nothing to do with safety issues. They wanted wilderness to themselves. Early in my career, unarmed as a deputy, I learned when to fold and when to play my hand and show respect even when it wasn't deserved. When a man lied, I never called him a liar. I told people that certain disparities exist. They could plead their case before a court, whatever the test.

Charging people is one thing; winning them over provides a greater satisfaction.

Enforcement is not easy. It is unfortunately necessary. You do your job even under threat, and then after a long career you measure success by the fact that you survived.

To Serve and Reflect

Fall hunting season reflects the best and worst in sportsmanship. Hunters come from far and wide, looking for the monarch of the north, the moose. Crown land is generally for everyone, however hunting licences designate specific moose management areas where a moose must be harvested from. Some hunters push the limits in what they do, including blocking roads like mad miners guarding a claim. Guns and liquor can lead to ugly disputes amongst hunting groups.

One such incident involved shots being fired across the road in front of approaching vehicles, as two groups vied for vantage and territory, to which neither had legitimate claim. Fueled by alcohol, ordinary people can take on unusual personas, and make bizarre dispositions: "It cost us plenty to get here and we don't need competition". The dispute escalated into a mêlée of pushing, shoving, and uncomplimentary remarks about origin and parentage. With 15 people all arguing my priority was to diffuse the situation and let settlement come later at the MNR office.

Hunter A:
I fired twice – the bull went down – did not get up. I was ½ way there but he beat me with his ATV. He was about to tag my moose. I hit him in the hump and spine – Big Bull!

Hunter B:
He was wounded. I raced over and shot him dead. I killed the moose – it's my moose. He put his tag on my moose. He was wounded. I gave him the coup des gras, he couldn't walk.

Separated from the group, both proponents settled down. The moose was seized on site. Hunter B agreed he did not act on humane principle; he thought speed was his advantage. First come first served. Both parties were advised the issue could be settled in court but reason finally prevailed. The first shooter by mutual agreement won the prize. The cheerleaders (both sides) did not attend the settlement.

A new Conservation Officer nearly ended his career when a loaded rifle went off inside a vehicle he stopped. The bullet missed his head by inches, passing through the upper door frame. Would defense lawyers claim that it was just an unfortunate misfire even though it was illegal to have a loaded firearm in a vehicle?

I once arrived at a Lac des Milles Lac dock at sunset. The officer on

scene before me was being herded toward the end of the dock by drunken mob rule. The timely arrival of a second officer changed the outcome. Conservation Officers, like no others, work the wilderness alone, facing groups and firearms equal to any army. Despite what they face on a daily basis, in nearly 30 years, there has been no use of deadly force by any officers in these trying conditions.

Now that I am retired I still long for the day when the law will be enhanced to make hunting while intoxicated as clearly a defined offense as impaired driving is. The danger it creates surely deserves equal treatment. Penalties like demerit points could be applied to anyone carrying a loaded firearm in a vehicle or vessel with removal of hunting privileges for repeat offenders. In recent years the green uniform of the Conservation Officer is often paired with the blue uniform of the Ontario Provincial Police, with positive results.

Nature Can Confuse Visitors

Each year hunters with scopes and open sights head for the woods. They sit near ponds and creeks, straining necks, eyes, and letting imaginations run wild. In swamps, sounds and wind can make a stump breathe. There are times when the stump blow-downs and craggy shapes can seem to move as water sways them. Massive as they are moose can appear where nothing existed moments before.

Over the years many hunters have related surprises which they had encountered; perhaps a long month of hunting anticipation causes some errors in judgment. Investigations have shown how errors have occurred; common and repetitious. Hunters erringly shoot a cow they thought was a bull hiding in the thick. "The moose appeared in a clearing. I scoped a look and was sure I saw antlers" a hunter would say. The hunter did see antlers, phantom antlers; twigs or branches above the moose's head appeared to be antlers. I recall when the U-shape of an open sight may have contributed to improper identification.

When bullets fly there is no room for error. Improperly colored clothing can be confusing. Accidents do happen on highways, when swimming, or in the woods. Whatever the cause of the accident, victims and families suffer in the aftermath.

One tragic reminder is a hunter who attended a friend's funeral. He had accidently shot his friend. Filled with grief and remorse he had to be restrained from the coffin. Witnesses attending the wake reported that he had tried to crawl into the coffin.

A trigger squeezed can never be undone. In the woods it pays to be wary.

Early on I'd heard that native guides would never carry antlers on their backs. True or not it certainly made sense to me.

Hunting is thought to be a game sport; sometimes on TV it seems to be more like a sports game. Imagine that virtual hunting can be accomplished via a computer linked to a game farm! From a corporate tower a mogul hunter can select a trophy of his choice from his chair. His "bang-bang" of choice gets him a trophy much like a mail-ordered tiger, and has it delivered. If this is truly the case, a trophy pays homage to the tiger and his ego, and hangs on his wall. What I do see on hunting and game shows indicates that computer harvesting seems likely. On a lesser note, I marvel at the sight of televised he-men with soot covered faces having shot squirrels, breathing hard with hoarse whispers, congratulating themselves before I change the channel.

Strangely, in all of my years, I never saw a tiger or water buffalo.

Pardon my pun, anything for a buck! Captive game hunting hardly equates to hunting in the wilderness. For me some shows are surreal. So much for TV... In real life, wildlife officers encounter virtual nightmares in the field; like boozing hunters. I call certain camps "Willies' Camps", because approaching them is enough to give an officer the willies or a sober man the DDTs.

Approaching such camps at night can be hazardous; a normally friendly hunter can turn aggressive at the drop of a hat. Impaired judgement can cause ever changing mood swings. While I mention such things I am not disillusioned: most sportsmen believe in fair play and follow regulations when hunting.

Hunters should not be surprised to find conservation officers paired with policemen. Rest assured it's all for a good reason.

Strangers in the Night Exchanging Glances

Allow me to set the scene. It was a cold wintery night. The late night went into the a.m. hours. There were officers on the hill wearing parkas. Some were in five-star sleeping bags to conserve body heat. They had radios and night binoculars. They were focused on a huge bull moose who appeared to be browsing near the tree line cut edge of Highway 11. Many a moose feed along this lonely stretch. Travelers and truckers are wary in this area. Moose and transporters collide with bad results to either side of the equation. Unfortunately for moose, the area also attracts night hunters. Poachers. The types that often boast that they can shoot the eyeballs out of a mosquito before it hits the ground. To the north and east, officers Russ and Bob were in patrol vehicles. They awaited the night from the main route on small tertiary roads used to maintain the pipeline that runs parallel to the highway. Their focus was on radio contact with officers on the hill. Traffic had slowed; the last transport went west more than an hour ago.

Officers in their sleeping bags are now out slapping their shoulders to fend off the cold and whatever snow had clung to them as they rose from the ground. Radios alive announced, "Something's happening." An older vehicle with dual lights? The dim lights were straight on. The high beam went left and right off center of the highway. It was moving slowly.

Literally, it must be said, all hell broke loose. The vehicle stopped then flashes and rapid fire ensued. At times it can seem like an eternity to the poachers as well as us. Well-placed shots from the vehicles nearly blew our friend the moose's head off. I can only have a guess to what the poachers thought. I doubt that any self-congratulating took place, more than likely, for a brief surreal moment, they entered the twilight zone. Why did this moose not fall?

For the poachers, it must have been traumatic to see a large bull moose holding his ground, eyes staring back, while most of his head was on the ground before him. In a flash, the car roared off into the night and passed Bob. It was headed northwest at high speed, kicking up light snow, and further to confuse the chase they turned the lights on and off. Bob later said this wasn't a matter of high pursuit; it was more like fast tracking. When in the distance lights went out, left or right, I'd slow down. The old fish sanctuary road, unplowed, showed fresh vehicle tracks. You couldn't go very fast without four-wheel drive capability.

A few miles in they were spinning around, attempting to regain the highway. I reached them and asked, "What's up, guys?"

"Nothing, sir. Just driving around," one said.

I asked, "Do you have any firearms?"

"Nah. Nothing. You can go ahead and look." No shells or casings on the floor, no rifles anywhere. By this time there were more officers at the scene. "It's a lot easier if you follow in our tracks out to the highway," the officers said. "We'll go real slow. You guys stay well back."

These men seemed very relieved, knowing well if they led, they could spin sideways. The road was narrow, a brush-swatting mirror road. Beneath snowfall, there were holes and good boulders. Officers were leading the procession and were craning their necks out vehicle windows, scanning the road left and right very carefully. We wondered, "Where are the rifles?"

The officers were driving up a thick Jackpine ridge that was windswept with snow nearly gone. Officer Bob yelled, "Stop! Stop!" In the snow he noticed where a truck had previously stopped and backed up, adjacent to a huge fallen tree. Bob walked weaving his way through a maze of limbs. At the end of the tree, there in the deep snow, Bob did not come up empty. He weaved his way back with an armful of rifles.

Once the officers proved what the men had done, the matter eventually went before court. The poachers gained ill-gotten fame. They lost valuable equipment, paid hefty fines, and lost their right to engage in legal hunting activity. The judge made it a super long period because it takes some people longer than others to learn their lesson, and he wanted to make sure the poachers learned to respect others, the land, and nature because they deserved protecting.

The poachers were found guilty of offenses. The judge said, "Your fine today will be $$$ and I can make it more!"

Can You Believe It!

Oh how often officers have heard the words, "Would you believe it?" Having reached Hwy 11 near Upsala, Ontario, we found a scene that occurs all too often, and each time it is different. We listened to the aftermath and observed the result of colliding with a moose in the dark. The lead vehicle tried in vain to avoid the moose, but unable to avoid impact the vehicle careened and hit the rock cut. The boat being towed, snapped its tethers and shot forward through the vehicle, the hull nesting inches from the driver's neck. In this circumstance, the father who had been following in another vehicle explained, "It all happened so fast!" This phrase is a comment we had heard too often that summer.

"Officers," he said. "I'm worried that my son might not make it. He's in shock, pale and unable to speak."

"We have an ambulance on the way", we assured him.

The son, chalky white and somewhat dazed, sat rigid behind the wheel.

The ambulance came and took him to the station. The worried father went on, "Can you believe it? We were three miles from the motel we booked. Almost there!"

"Yes, we do understand," I said. It was best to keep things simple. "Can you believe it?", could never be answered in full. At best we nodded in empathy, as we had done in every instance when we'd attended moose/vehicle collisions. We needed no explanation, because collisions of this nature occurred so frequently.

Often tired after long days on patrol, with court in the morning ninety miles away, we knew the moose had to be removed and the highway cleared as more traffic would be on the way. A tow truck would come to tow the wreckage away. The night had not ended. In the morning light, we would again pass this site. Heading east, with scant sleep, and the sun in our eyes we thought, "Yes, we'll remember."

We will continue to be amazed that people actually remove small moose hazard warning signs to embellish their bar at home or as souvenirs. We know as conservation officers—more than what the public realizes—how many signs have been shot and removed. Today travellers passing by Shabaqua, Upsala, and English River will see much larger signs regarding moose hazards. We hope that size will add emphasis to the danger, and that people will feel the need to slow down and to be extra wary especially when driving at night.

We know that the ghost of a moose struck in the night or at anytime can haunt victims long after the big bang. Severe injuries, even death, and expensive repairs have spoiled many a dream vacation . . . We understand that such events can also change a person's former enthusiasm and lifestyle. I can't speak for the moose or from its point of view, but if the moose happens to survive any impact with a huge transport, it's hard to visualize the moose roaming freely again. There are no moose ambulances or hospitals. If his leg was severed and was lying beyond him some twenty-five feet on the hard median of the highway, the moose probably senses that after being softened up, whatever its ambitions had been, his future will be as hamburger. Sometimes things were so bad, I wondered if we needed new signs to caution drivers that they were now entering a proven roadkill area.

This unintended game of chicken in the middle of the night never benefits man or beast. Those who depend on vehicle whistles to avoid collision should consider that whistles are likely loudest once they've passed, but are not as effective as they approach. Whistles are not foolproof. Seeing is believing. Moose, as big as they are, have the uncanny ability to appear and disappear before your eyes. This has caused many a motorist surprise, as he or she could not slow down in time before impact.

Imagine for a moment, driving at night on a two way highway, everyone driving within the speed limit, but on a particular stretch, suddenly the top of your vehicle is crushed or ripped off, because a furry underpass was struck without enough clearance. You see stars, some in the sky, others in your head. If you're lucky, the moose that crashed through your windshield didn't enter hooves first, but mostly flattened the vehicle's top.

Experience teaches that when man, animal and vehicle encounter, no one comes away unscathed.

Today we find larger moose hazard signs in place. Thanks to supervisor Dave who believed as I did, that sometimes bigger is better.

Bear Tales

Sometimes "Whoaohah Sasha" Didn't Work!

Sasha was a Kodiak bear who stayed as a guest at the Chik-Wauk Lodge. The owners of the Lodge, Ralph and Bea decided it would be nice to show Sasha around the lake. To convince Sasha to stay in the large freighter canoe they put some honey in the bow. Leaving their secluded bay, Ralph and Sasha headed out past the point at Snapping Turtle Rock. Witnesses from a passing boat said that Sasha looked quite demure as she rode along. She was well behaved like a proper lady; the honey in the bow was a stroke of genius. She sat still and dignified, no more walking back and forth, she seemed in bliss with the wind in her face, created by the movement of the canoe. On the blind side of the point, anglers also enjoyed the moment with rods in hand. The view of the lake was a welcome and healing sight away from city life.

Attracted to sound of another boat approaching, the fisherman looked up and recognized an enormous canoe. Soon a great brown blur sailed over the bow creating a thunderous clap and near tidal wave on the still water. Ralph realized that even a Texas "Whoahh!" could not stop Sasha. She was a free spirit. If she decided to bail, she bailed out! Ralph explained later that he never recalled so many anglers cranking their motors in unison to get away, as he did that day. Sasha did not jump ship to be menacing to anyone. She viewed her job as a work-holiday. She felt an overwhelming urge to swim and she was only acting in accordance with her instincts. One never knows what the fisherman thought. They likely recognized a Kodiak Bear and wondered if Saganaga Lake was a part of Alaska? Sasha learned all too well that anglers are very unpredictable as they scurried away. Sasha must of thought that some folk have the personality of a cut worm.

The Legend of the North Lake Bear

Customs Officer Doug Grandfield bolted upright. In silence he shook me awake. A dark shape was mere inches from my feet. The pup tent was small and made it difficult to swing

the long barrel 303 around so we waited in petrified silence, not moving, barely breathing. The shadow was a big one, caught in the lst light of susnset at the North Lake Portage. The rain had stopped but the reign of terror was inches away through a light nylon tent. I'd known more than few bear a few feet or yards away, grunting and whoofing. A few chomping clicks of its teeth told us this bear owned the portage and was interested in collecting his toll fee. He had exacted a variety of gifts from canoeists, leading to many complaints received miles away at Government Island. He ripped a few tents and dragged off useless things like life jackets. Part of this dual role canoe patrol between Canada Customs and the MNR was to do enforcement checks and cover both mandates. We were looking for illegal entry into Canada, illegal fishing, and the nuisance bear problem at North Lake portage. After travelling here we were tired from setting up in the rain, and now near nightfall, the nuisance bear had caught us napping. I hate to think that he was intrigued by our smelly feet. Our boots had been wet most of the day. He hung around grunting for too long. Doug later reflected that the hair was standing up on the back of his neck. City born and raised he had never canoed in the deep wilderness before.

Eventually the great shadow ambled off. We sat still and after a little while I motioned for Doug to lay back down. He knew the need to create enough space to turn the rifle around so he followed my instruction. Once the rifle was in position it became his job to unzip the tent. Tension was high, quietly and deftly the flap opened. Some 25 feet in front a huge black bear, back to us stood high and was reaching for packs tethered high over pine branches. He was intent on what he wanted. Never had a gun shot sounded as loud as the one did from that tent. It was like an explosion. It was a good hit but the bear's adrenaline was high and he tore off into the bush, crashing and thrashing. It was little comfort that darkness fell as things went silent.

There would be no sleep this night unless we followed and found out what happened to the bear. Doug managed the 5 cell maglight and I the rifle, side to side and straight ahead. Every shadow moved and threatened. First 100 feet then 50 more, through evergreens, slow progress. Birch bark flapping nearly had us running. Was he wounded, just waiting? We'd head back, take turns standing guard all night or pack up and head out on the lake to find another campsite on an island if necessary and resume our search in tomorrow's light. The wind was picking up, rustling and swaying willows as we circled back to our campsite. Suddenly a large dark shape was observed prone, it seemed to be breathing. I knew it was not but the wind and the woods moving gave it life. It had all happened long ago, near dark on a trapline, another bear, another story.

We prodded the big male bear with a long branch. He was gone. My guess was that he likely weighed about 400 lbs. As big and powerful as he was, the North Lake bear would no longer menace anyone.

Interesting to note, East Flower Lake, not too distant from North Lake, produced the largest black bear ever taken in Minnesota. That bear weighed in at 735 lbs.

Doug Grandfield, now retired, also teaches bible classes at a church in Thunder Bay. I've been told that when asked to share a story of the scariest time in his life he tells the story of the North Lake Bear to a wide-eyed attentive bunch of kids. The North Lake Bear lives on in legend.

Are Asian Markets Benefitting from Residual Bear Parts?

In the 80s, Rent-a-Wreck vehicles brought novice hunters to the northwest. Bear hunt outfitters completed the package with competent guides. All one had to do was shoot; the guides would do the rest. Organized group hunting was a lucrative business. Outfitters promised no fuss, no mess for hunters. The skinning, butchering, salting of hides came with the package. At times baiting was also included.

Once, three stands were set up in place for arriving hunters. These hunters were not local. They came from faraway places, eastern provinces and states. Locals were soon buzzing about this an unusual trend. The hunters and out-of-town outfitters arrived in large numbers. They didn't mingle much. Local small bear outfitters felt their areas were being displaced and encroached upon.

Allocated areas were not yet established for bear management purposes. The land was vast and private hunters were not restricted to any particular area. The licenses they held were legal, and hunters were well versed to keep conservation to a minimum, no matter how scattered their geography or origin. Bear hunting is different than other hunting. Often the bear are baited for days or weeks in advance, and then tree stands are set up in the area. A small marker on a trail will indicate a tree stand nearby. Conditioned to come to the spot for food the bear is easy prey.

Curious anomalies can occur at any time, and some are bound to raise suspicion. Exporters from as far away as the Pacific Northwest, Vancouver, British Columbia, sent letters to local bear hunters, soliciting gall bladders from legally taken bears, along with instructions on how to prepare and dry bear gall bladders for a lucrative Asian market, offering up to $3,500 a pound if properly dried.

As one Mounted Policeman would later say, "If you think aphrodisiacs in the market of Asia aren't big, consider the population differential between it and other parts of the world and its market potential." Much is known about elephant tusks and ivory, crocodile hides, and the illegal trade of animals, birds, and exotic species. Where does the North American black bear rank in the scheme of value in markets? Truly, the black bear fetches less than a live falcon or a rhino horn in Yemini, but in terms of valued parts in Asia, it had no rival.

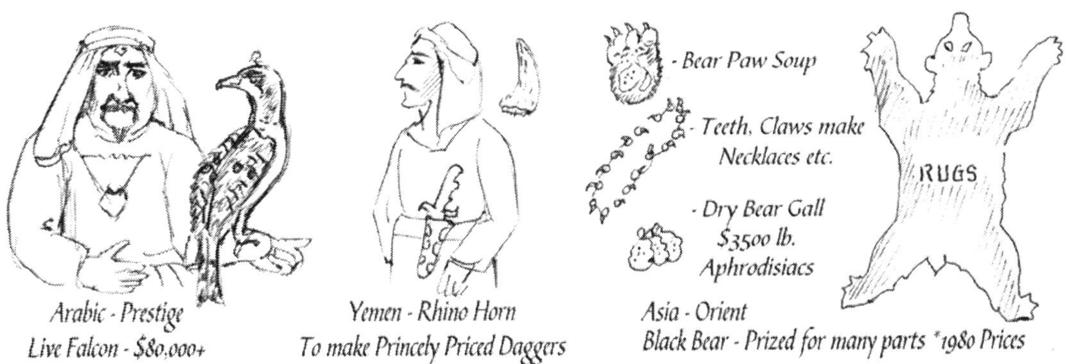

Consider the following incidents from the 1980s. Conservation officers throughout North America began to report black bears which for the most part were found intact, dead near dumps with telltale slashes that indicated only gall bladders were taken. Even now I wonder who got the body parts from bears taken during organized hunts in the 80s, when all things were looked after by guides and all the novice hunter had to do was shoot?

As of 2007, the laws regarding bear hunting have been changed and revamped many times. Now, for example, shooting of bears with cubs and hunting in dumps is illegal. Most hunters generally comply with ever-changing often controversial laws. I like to think that some confusion over laws may favor the black bear. I'll never forget one Magistrate's comments in court to me and a defendant in a case over shooting a bear in a dump.

"Officer, shooting a bear in a dump?" he asked. "Would you agree that such an act would be similar to shooting a man sitting on a stool while he was eating his lunch in a restaurant?"

"Yes, Your Honor. I would."

Officer:
Shooting a bear in a dump,
Isn't that like shooting at a
man eating a sandwich on a
stool in a restaurant?

Nuisance Who?

In the latter days of my career, I had the privilege of practicing catch and release. Black bears had to be removed from new developments in the city of Thunder Bay. Ancient trails and spaces were now man's domain. We caught bears in the developments, spray-painted their bottoms red and released them, many miles north. Unfortunately catch and release works better for fish than it does with bears. Distance was critical. If the bear returned, it could be shot. Man is least tolerant in matters of space. A bear's best friend is distance, ideally in a place near a creek or a river with a conifer-poplar mix forest. Of course, we wondered if a city bear could survive the territorial claims of other bears. We thought that at least it had a chance.

One such assignment involved a family of bears. The large female followed my concoction of bacon grease, oil of anise and honey into the live trap. She slammed the door with her own kind of thunderclap. Two cubs soon poked their way out of a small tree and were captured in an old fish net. They bawled and Mom was not amused as they were placed in galvanized garbage cans secured with heavy barbeque iron grates roped to the handles on each side. Mom grunted, hollered and tested the quality of the hinges on her trap as we headed north on the Spruce River Road to find them a new home. I chose a place with mixed evergreen trees and sandy loam soil so she could den before winter. The problem was, it was now me and 3 bears. Who do you unload first? Obviously the 2 cubs, since the other way would be far too perilous. I released the cubs and waited until the cubs moved far enough way that they would attract the Mom in that direction. I left my truck door open and carefully opened the trap. I made the sprint back to my truck without falling and slammed the truck door. In the rear view mirror I recognized a new dilemma. It was my turn to be entombed in the truck. The 2 impish cubs decided to play in the box of the truck while the mother bear circled. They were in no hurry to leave. I tried moving the truck forward and back, and honking the horn to dislodge them to no avail. It seemed much longer but after about 10 minutes the cubs went overboard and scampered away into the Jackpine. I cursed that I forgot to bring my camera.

Sometimes I had to shoot bears. It was a duty I disliked, so I devised a plan to avoid it as much as possible. Typically, a controversial demand resulted from complaints. Some circumstances, such as deep wilderness campsites, with no paved roads or other means to wheel in culvert-sized traps prevented use of live-trapping devices. About half of the complainants were against killing bears. Knowing this, I devised a democratic approach.

Tucking pants into my boots, I'd leap out of my truck announcing, "You people have a bear problem? I'm here as your hit man." A bit of silence usually followed, and then a question. "You mean you're going to kill the bear?"

"Yup!" I'd pause to be sure I had their attention. "But only if you say so. This situation does not allow the use of a live bear trap. So you decide if I kill the bear, or if you can come up with a better idea I'll listen. I'll wait while you decide." I made it clear that it was not in my interest to shoot the bear. My interest was to ensure safety, including the bear's safety. Democracy often led to dialogue. Ideas would begin to flow, and most of the time the ideas were good.

"I suppose we could move," someone would say, "and maybe even leave a note for other campers that we moved because of bear problems. . ."

Usually there was accord. If not, consequences and responsibilities were shared evenly. One way to catch a bear fast – brush and rustle trees to the trap in 3 directions. Concoct a mix of Honey, bacon grease, blueberries; include oil of anise.

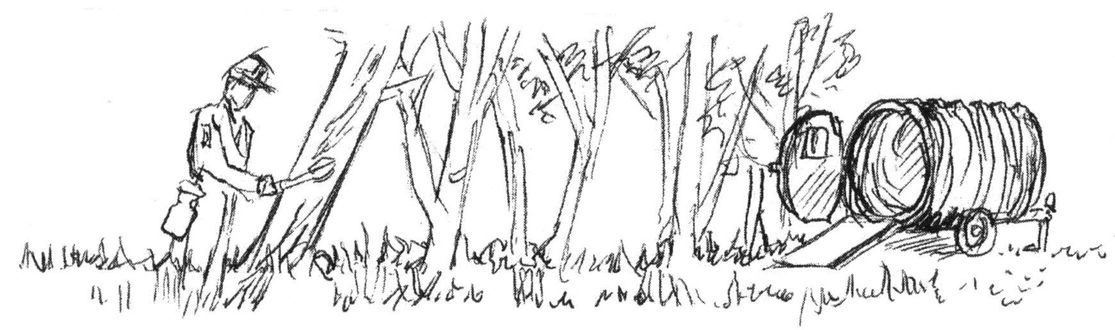

Violations

NIGEL: 3RD VICTIM, SAME MODUS OPERENDI – We could have a SERIAL KILLER on our hands!

I Once Met a Snake Named Garter

I once met a snake named Garter. A rocky island on Northern Light Lake was his home. He was tied in the hot sun. Beer cans and a cold fire pit told much of Garter's history. He was too tired to speak, but I could see what he wanted to say, "These fishermen were camped at my home celebrating their catch, when one saw me, and using monofilament looped it around my waist. For good measure, he placed a hook in my belly. Then they tied me to a tree. You could say I was their merry-go-round. They stayed up late drinking and laughing. One threw a tin can at me. In the early morning sun, after a long cold night, they loaded their boat. One guy must have liked me. Just as they roared off, he yelled smiling, "S'long, old snake."

Over the years, whenever possible, it became a routine to visit the island. I had hopes of meeting these sportsmen. No luck. While I never did see Garter again, on occasions I saw small snakes in the rocks that bore a striking resemblance. I hope they are his kids. Descendants of the first tree snake I ever saw in Ontario. Their bodies formed a shape that seemed to spell the word thanks.

If conservation work was the topic of a game show, categorizing and using Good-Bad-Ugly, I would ask that panel of judges to allow the use of the word despicable. Ignorance may have been bliss for the individuals involved, but for this unfortunate harmless garter snake, no joy at all. I hope the people involved grew wiser with age, and if any are in nursing homes, I can only hope they are not employees.

Mr. Guide Man: "Boys, There Are Other Ways to Skin a Fish Cop"

There is a lake 18 miles long near the US/Canada boundary. One portage north of Saganaga, a border lake, the lake of interest is called Saganagons. It runs parallel to Sagnaga. One third of this lake was bound by the rules of Quetico Provincial Park. Here was a walleye mecca. I don't know Saganagons aboriginal translation. I do know that more than one non-resident viewed the lake as paradise found. One phenom in particular was known as "The Guide". He worked for a worldwide company in the USA. He knew how to turn a long holiday in the wilds of Canada into a lucrative venture. After two seasons we were on a first name basis, Glen Guide and JB. As time went on JB could be reversed and stretched to BJeez, not you again!

The reader must understand that this is not the fabled story of an overzealous inspector chasing Jean Valjean, over a stolen loaf of bread. Ontario resources were being exploited for profit. No officer goes through a career without ruffling a few feathers, especially when you helped curtail lucrative well-organized illegal enterprise. The con man paid the locals peanuts while he made the money. Problem was, he had no work permit to operate in Canada. He was a tourist operator of his own making on a remote lake in Ontario.

The reader will notice that this story is longer than most. Perhaps because it took longer to resolve the situation encountered.

Enforcement is not a slam dunk. It can be a long and ambiguous process. In the wilderness you stumble into situations not knowing where they began or how things will ultimately end.

The name Guide has a mystic appeal. The farther north you ply your skills the greater the acclaim.

On Saganaga Lake, in the 70's, I met Glen, who everyone referred to as the Guide. The first season he spoke very little. By the second season he was more than flamboyant. "Heh JB. Heard you caught some of my crew. Guess you got no other places to patrol? Picky picky." I learned early that it was better to smile than show disdain at taunting humour. Glen Guide seemed to revel in his image, providing entertainment for his friends and cohorts. Who-ever they were they seemed well schooled as to what to say to Canada Customs.

Saganagons, known for its tranquility, was fast becoming a circus. As summer progressed more planes landed more often with arriving guests. I once spoke to a woman who said she was a volunteer cook for the group. Most people questioned stated that they were co-employees. Inevitably, with overcrowding, violations increased, and seemed to be the price of doing business.

Wilderness with all the Amenities

By fall more tents were set up in the periphery of the park. The drone of aircraft could be heard in the late fall. By the second season things had grown to the *ultra-ridiculous. The park portion of Saganagons had stringent rules. Again and again his friends were cited, no live bait fish in the park, littering charges, etc... His friends said, "We didn't know Officer, Guide didn't tell us."*

Back on Government Island on Saganaga Lake Customs saw cracks in the veneer of Glen the guide. Stories came from two cities, Minneapolis and St Paul, that city anglers gladly opened their imaginations and wallets. In the cities, Glen the guide was sunset mythical, like a mountain man, a smooth operator. On cold winter nights he knew how to outhustle pool players, without a cue ball. It was said that after work he came out of the frost into local pool halls.

There he offered summer gold; golden walleye up north in Canada. All inclusive meant, cooks, bunks, flying in and out and bring your own fishing gear. Listening to tales I thought that even Minnesota Fats would be impressed at such a spiel. One complainant asked, "Why would a man in the wilderness carry a wallet bulging with cash?" The stories seemed credible, however no one was willing to testify or sign statements. It seemed Glen Guide's aura and appeal was becoming tarnished. With time he had garnered more than a few disgruntled souls.

One day G. Gravelle with Canada Customs said, "I think it's time we went on a canoe trip. Can we go after my shift? I need to see things for myself and hear it from the horse's mouth." All officers know that truth and proof are two different things.

We crossed the portage at Silver Falls and elected to wait by one of three glory holes which drew fishermen like magnets into the park. Inevitably Glen Guide showed up with a guest. I don't know if he'd had a few nips, but this time he was more than vociferous. "Yo man, I see early wardens trying to catch Old Glen again! Hah! I see you brought a trainee. Hah,hah! You're wasting your time JB." Waving a wad of papers, licences and daily park permits, he gloated,"Looky looky! I even have a brand new Quetico Park official Guide Permit! Like you told me the park has its own rules. I took your advice, talked to the park ranger and he said like you said that to be a guide in Quetico a permit is required. After months of game playing things began to unravel for Glen Guide. Suddenly Gravelle, Canada Customs, interjected. "Sir, I'm not a trainee for Fish and Wildlife. I work for the Federal Government; Canada Customs. I need to see your Canadian work visa." "What? What work visa?" Fumbling with his wallet was an error. He exposed his fabled wallet of cash. His exuberance crashed. I never watched a demeanor fade so fast, like gas escaping from a hot air balloon. Sullen Guide came back, "Since when does Customs patrol out here? Dirty pool JB!"

"Since you," I replied.

"You told me to get a guide permit! You tricked me!" "No", I replied, "I provided you with information only. It was you who decided what you were in obtaining an official guide permit."

Customs said, "Sir, stop all activity immediately. You entered this country as a bonafide tourist. My findings are that you are not."

Soon Glen Guide's passenger piped in, "Officers, I don't know what's going on· I'm here to fish· Frankly I'm lost out here, he's the guide·"

Customs Gravelle said, "Sir, I observed the tents and the entire set up for myself· This is no one man operation· You are free to take matters up with Canada Customs· As of now, you are restricted any entry to Canada, with family members only·" With the stop and desist ordered, the drone of aircraft continued for a few days· As all things went packing, Saganagons Lake returned to its natural state of remote silence·

The story didn't quite end with the guide man or his Midas touch gone· Weeks later Natural Resources received a petition style letter· In order to impress Government, it had many signatures· Fortunately with time it also had a boomerang effect on the senders· They had made mistakes· To add clout, the authors had included their companies world recognized letter head and logo, without permission· Complaints are taken seriously when they are received· Those adjudicating can only deal with abstract matters· They were not at the scene· All any officer can do is hope that common sense prevails· I was puzzled over so many signatures· One chance night luck was on side· While leafing through old field notes of past violations , I discovered addresses matching in close proximity to Guide Man's address back in the cities· Others were fellow co-workers· Many ways to skin a fish cop, or a customs officer did not work· Simply because the renowned company wasn't happy to have their name affiliated in matters of dispute involving violations in Canada. We did hear that the unsanctioned use of the company letterhead did have its repercussions.

Does anyone know how to spell "harassment"?

I recall the words of a senior officer who'd said years before, "John Boy, when you embark in a career in enforcement, if you look for problems, you will find them. I also came to understand that those who do not see the problem first hand may conclude that problems do not exist.

During the late 80's as Government Island closed and the waves of time washed away the incidents of the 60's, 70's, 80's and into the 90's, I do know that somewhere musty records languish in the dark or lay rain soaked in a leaky warehouse. Yet even now and then, we hear of problems on the border. It's not always about drugs or guns. This story is about the exploitation of natural resources.

There is a place called Blarney. Every country has one. This Blarney happened to be in Minnesota. It's a secretive place, where exclusive peoples gather. Mostly males and occasionally females, who all have egos. Some are wounded. They talk of past exploitations, a world without boundaries, freedom without taxes, paradise found and lost, a place without rules, endless resources for profit and free enterprise taken to the outer-limits. They gather to ensure that someone knows how to spell harassment. They gather with pens on Grunge Street! A harmonious group, who don't like fish cops.

At Saganagons there is a rock just beneath the water's surface. In good light you can stand on it. The photo result appears as though you can walk on water.

Time surpasses all things. By the mid 70's great change affected Saganagons Lake. The Quetico boundary expanded to include all of the lake in its entirety. Aircraft and motorboats could no longer ply these waters. Access became by paddle only, which meant difficulty. Six miles to Silver Falls portage, then a rough rocky half mile of portage, after which a stiff paddle through two rapids, and then more paddling to reach three glory holes. The last hole was dubbed Thumper by Judge R.E. Hachey. I remember each hole well, and think of each place far too often. Such places get lost after thirty-six years. I travel the trip in my mind recalling every detail, and like the Lost Dutchman and his goldmine in the deserts and mountains of Arizona, I too know in my heart my knowledge has become a heavy burden, for I know of gold not measured in ounces. On Saganagons gold is measured in pounds (4 to 8 lbs average). I paddle on into a bay and look to a fallen balsam tree. The top juts out over the water. I anchor my canoe near the tip of the tree. Here lays the Thumper hole. It's very deep, 40 feet. Here you plumb the depths with a lure, count to 15 slowly, down deep you feel a great thump. Up, up, up comes the best fishing I have ever known. Dark backs with bellies so vividly yellow, make these walleyes seem unreal. Unlike the Lost Dutchman my story secrets will not be lost to an unknown fate. Saganagons has had a lot of rest in the last 36 years. I think of the treasure trove wondering could it ever be better than it was? Oh how I wonder the thought of making the tough arduous trip to Saganagons. Someone please pinch me, because more and more I dream of making the journey. In the event I cannot, I chose to share my long ago secrets by passing on those glory holes to you. I do not go only for the gold, I also go to search for truth. I urge anyone to go without me. Remember my directions, seek out the fallen balsam tree. There are golden walleye on Saganagons. Remember to respect the Aboriginal name, even if you do not know its meaning. As for me this lake will always be my lake of dreams. Should you go and come up empty, my offer still stands, feel free to pinch me.

Truly a Retired Fish Cop

Exotic Species – The Source of Reptile Dysfunction

The law says ignorance is no excuse. I say sometimes it can be a mitigating factor. Using the heavy stick of enforcement without education only leads to hostility, not preservation of fish and wildlife, which is the ultimate goal. Compliance comes with a meeting of the minds, if not in the moment, sometimes good results come later. **Basically the Law says…NO PERSON shall IMPORT LIVE BAIT FISH and/or Piranha**

In all my years as a deputy Conservation Officer I never did see a Piranha. What I did

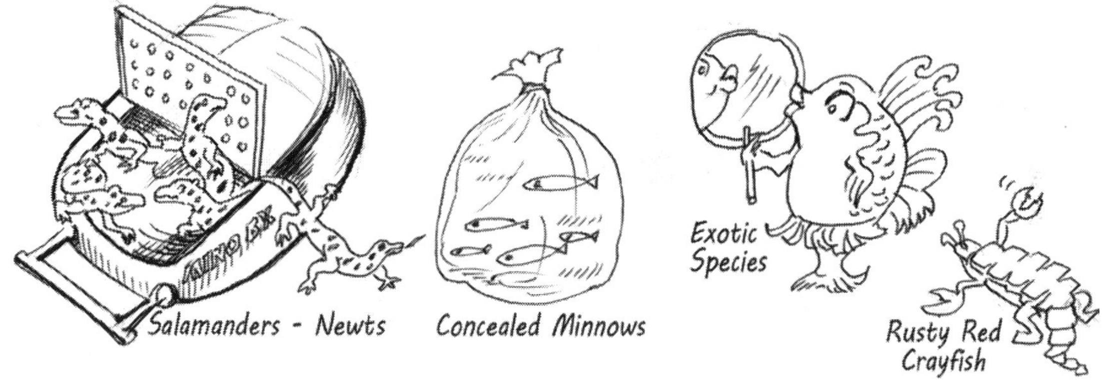

see were a lot of Houdini minnows. A minnow frozen on ice appears lifeless. Fisherman would claim that they were dead as though they had attended their funeral. Great miracles occurred when the dead minnows were dropped back in water, hence the name, Houdini minnows. Some wallets became much lighter as a result.

Enforcement in this area became a game of wits. The Game and Fish Act seemed to indicate that the offence was species specific. There was no way for a blanket approach that just said No Person shall import into Ontario Live Bait or Non-Indigenous species. I was told to work with what the law said so I developed a new technique. When I approached a boat where a person was fishing I would leap-frog from my boat into their boat and grab their fishing rod. I tried to prevent them dumping their bait fish overboard but as long as I had a minnow on the fishing rod I had all the evidence I needed for a charge.

Accusations began to fly. Some of the American outfitters accused me of doing this enforcement just so the American anglers would have to buy their minnows on the Canadian side. At least this presented the opportunity for dialogue and education of the resort owner. Whether he agreed or not at least he understood what the Ontario law was and would tell people one of two things: a) don't take live bait into Canada, or b) don't get caught taking live minnows into Canada. I continued to lay charges and avoidance tactics were developed. Some guides would try to fake receipts or change the dates on them. I devised a plan.

My plan was to create a unique linoleum stamp for each of the resorts in the area that sold bait fish. I carved the stamps knowing that it would be extremely difficult to forge or imitate them. I asked that the stamp be applied to each receipt with a clear date and signature on it, done in pen. My plan worked, but there were still offences occurring. Over time live bait infractions continued to drop.

Dr. David Etnier, Professor of Zoology, University of Tennessee and cabin owner on Saganaga Lake had warned me many years ago that certain species could decimate fish populations in a lake. Unfortunately he was correct as we have now seen with zebra mussels and certain crustaceans that are now being found in Quetico Park lakes. Fisherman need to know that the simple act of importing live bait can lead to reptile dysfunction.

The Man in the Canoe with a 12 Volt Battery

One day on Saganaga Lake, a young mountain man arrived at the docks. He was cleared through Canadian Customs. Alone, he would camp on the lake's islands. He seemed to be a clean man, without drugs or weapons. He was just a quiet mountain man with a huge 12 volt battery in his green canoe. My interest piqued by his heavy battery, I watched as he paddled westward through a small line of islands straddling the invisible line of the US/Canada border. I pondered. As heavy as the battery was, it could be ballast to hold the bow down in windy situations, but so could a rock.

I decided to patrol west towards Quetico Park in the area of Seagull Island, home for herons and nesting gulls. I began to hear loud cracking sounds. As I neared the island I observed a well-concealed tent, off shore with no one around. As I looked around, I saw an unloaded shotgun propped against a tree along with a big battery hooked to an animal calling device. While standing and listening, I detected movement at the far end of a clearing. A shadowy figure seemed hesitant. Suddenly, a man ran toward the tent. Somehow, I instinctively knew that I'd have to beat him there. I dove into the tent hands first. My fingers slipped under the air mattress. I felt a revolver. With all things in hand, I told him that his actions were illegal. I seized his guns and paraphernalia. With charges pending, the seemingly gentle man contritely explained that he came into the wilderness to escape and live off the land. He showed me a tree with a target, and told me that the gulls and herons were not his intended target. I advised him that his very presence was potentially harmful. On nesting sites, when young herons are disturbed, they often fall to their death or perish being caught between limbs and branches.

He made his way back to the United States. Returning to Customs a day or two later he paid additional penalties for failure to divulge illegal entry of firearms. Customs is well aware that some people stash illegal items on small islands in the US. After clearing Customs, they retrieve their drugs, booze, and firearms at a later date. In this instance, it would also have been wise to stash the big battery.

While I never did see this adventurer again, I don't know what would have happened if he had won the foot race to the tent. Some things you never know; some things you do.

A week or so later, Customs told me that our man had returned. This time I was told that he didn't want to stay; he had to get back to the city, and was wondering if he could ride along on a patrol.

The Customs officer quipped with a laugh, "No, not with me." She chided, "It's you he wanted to patrol with." I think the mountain man wanted to be a game warden...

Mergansers Lost at Koss Lake

Fowl Hunters came out of the fog

In the 1980s, Russell and I, after many portages, arrived at Koss Lake. Remote, it seemed unusually quiet, not a soul in sight. Being that it was a great walleye lake, we thought we'd see more activity. We pitched our tent and bedded down early. In the morning we woke early. Great fog patches played games in the early light. A few places on the lake had clear spaces. We waited for the sun to burn away the fog patches. Eating breakfast we watched merganser ducks; a mother with her brood swimming back and forth. Their world was undisturbed and they were seemingly unaware of our presence. They were simply being ducks. Suddenly, due to the fog, a boat seemed to come from nowhere. Transfixed we watched as two fowl hunters, one with a shot gun up front, the other driving the boat, shot the ducks wantonly. After the feathers scattered, they plucked the ducks from the water laughing. They drove off and threw the ducks into the shoreline brush. Unaware of our presence they decided to try fishing. They began trolling and casting adjacent to a point of land approximately a quarter of a mile from where we were camped. Our challenge was to catch a powerboat with a canoe! We donned plain clothes for the occasion and decided on a fixed direction of approach near to where they were, however not direct. Feigning that we were angling, we trolled inching our way in their direction· Sometimes turning and going opposite, a lulling action so as not to arouse their suspicion· We were in no hurry· Our object was to get as close as possible, and it worked·

Close we asked, "How you guys doing?"

"A few nibbles and a pike", the boat driver said· "How 'bout you guys?"

"Nothing yet·"

Russ asked, "Do you mind if we take a picture of your pike?"

Bow man responded, "Naa, no problem· He's not very big·"

Now, with our hands clutching their boat, they seemed startled· Announcing that we were conservation officers was like throwing ice down their necks· Both men cringed at the words·

"Let's all go look at where you threw those ducks in the bush·" Badges displayed, "We all know that mergansers are not meant for eating· But first we'd like to see licenses and duck stamps·"

It was not too surprising that they had none of the above·

They did attempt good sportsmanship after their firearm was seized· They accompanied our request· In time, the thick shore brush yielded five ducks· There may have been two more··· A slight smile entered Russell's face when I uttered, "Five in the hand, is better than two in the bush!"

Having read the men their cautions, charges were tallied· Hunting from a powerboat, wasting ducks, no license, no duck stamps···

The boat driver asked, "Is this serious?"

"Very serious!"

The boat driver anxiously thought he had an out· "I never shot anything, I only drove the boat·"

"True, but you were part of the violation·"

Soon bow rider piped in· His persona was somewhere between dejected and a ray of hope. He said, "What about you guys? You weren't in uniform. Is that right? Is that legal?"

"Yes we can when necessary. Today, was necessary", Russell replied. "But don't worry fellows, we will have our uniforms on when we meet in the courtroom."

"Courtroom! You mean we just can't pay a fine and settle out of court?"

"Not in this case, the judge will want to meet you."

We set the date and issued each a summons.

It was lucky we were there that morning waiting for Koss Lake fog to lift, and when it did, we found the unexpected. But they did too!

Of all enforcement groups, conservation officers and game wardens in the field are likely to encounter the most committing offenders, and when found, it's like being caught in the act, minus the use of radar. Observing a violation in progress means cause and effect are indisputable.

Thorough knowledge of an area provides an instinctual pulse of where and when occurrences are likely to occur. Being at the right place at the right time might be luck;

that is possible, but it's also true that understanding the pulse of nature's activity, such as when and where fish are spawning, also aids the instincts of wildlife officers towards apprehending offenders.

Poachers know when game or fish are most vulnerable; so do the wardens in the fields and areas of their responsibility.

It happened that on their day in court, the judge decided that stiff penalties and a permanent loss of firearms was in order. He was not sympathetic to the fact that the shotgun was a family heirloom. He also imposed a five year no hunting order, commenting, "I can make it more." Over the years, the courts have given penalties that show a keener awareness and need to preserve wildlife.

There was no response from either defendant to explain the cause of their senseless actions. Perhaps both realized that silence is truly golden, and like the ducks their pleas would also be wasted!

This was not a matter of hunger and need. It was more like vandalism.

I watched as they hid whiskey at Mike Deschampes trap shack

Pork and Beaners

History indicates that Voyageurs traveled the waters of Saganaga Lake. Some of their copper pots and kettles, nestled under the water a half mile from Mike Deschampe's trap cabin, were discovered below Horsetail Rapids, to the left of his cabin. Voyageurs of the North West Fur Company had a post nearby, perhaps a place for rest and repair of their canoes. A square grove of poplar is believed to have been their site.

Once, Mike found a musket in a tree. I imagine a Voyageur leaned it in the crotch, forgot it, and the tree growth cupped and held it.

Jock Richardson, searching for a motor that came loose from a boat and sank in front of his resort, was more than pleased when retrieving the motor, he also retrieved an ancient musket.

Voyageurs were called **Pork Eaters** *because of a concoction of pork fat, powdery dry pemmican, and berries mixed into gruel, which was often all they had to sustain themselves each day, months on end. It's uncanny how history clings to the notion of pork. My day saw its own Pork and Beaners.*

During the 1980s, tourist operators and locals on both sides of the border observed a trend: many people were arriving in boats and canoes, but there was little spending. From

Canadian Customs' viewpoint, little customs duty was being collected; yet many people were camped out up to one or two weeks. It was puzzling. Where did they get their food? Alcohol?

Simple. A US tourist operator said people avoided can and bottle laws on the US side by stashing goods on the Canadian side. They'd sneak past Customs and stash food. In the morning report-in, they'd obtain only a day pass to fish on the Ontario side. Everything they had came from their home state; gas, oil, booze, food. They didn't spend a nickel in Minnesota nor in Canada.

A young Custom's Officer with whom I worked was interested in what the operator had to say. This officer was not green. He knew it takes time for people on the lake to orient rocks, shallow areas, boundary areas, US islands, and Canadian islands. He also knew that all goods had to be declared on both sides of the border.

We set up surveillance on a tent full of goods without sleeping bags. After hours of waiting, we realized this group was wise. So we left a note:

"To whom it may concern
Persons at this site may have gotten lost.
No one has seen activity on site for days.
Please claim goods at a Government Island."

Shortly afterwards, a man came to our island office claiming he was a friend of the group, but not in the party.

"Sorry," I said. "Goods must be claimed first by the owners."

A day later, he came again. This time he identified the goods and ownership. He claimed he didn't realize the island was in Canada.

"You mean you thought you were state side, with pots, bottles and cans?" I asked.

"Okay, okay," he said. "You got me." He claimed he didn't want to break laws on the US side and forgot about reporting goods on the Canadian side. Customs levied appropriate penalties.

Another time a boat veered off the normal route to Customs. I observed occupants stash goods at a trap shack. They then proceeded back to the main route behind the islands and entered Customs for clearance.

The timing was right.

While they were inside, I scooped the goods from the shack, including a case of booze. I arrived just as they were making their oral declarations.

"That's all we have to declare officer," one of them said.

"I believe you forgot this at the trap shack, gentlemen," I said, as I held up the booze. Jaws dropped. I never saw looks and expressions so short-circuited. A lot of whiskey and booze went down the drain, and wallets opened as wide as the Grand Canyon that day.

Word soon got around on both sides of the lake. Eventually the Pork and Beaners faded into history, much like the Pork Eaters of old.

It is said, that the ghosts of Voyageurs-past, near the poplar grove and trap shack don't like the clandestine activity. On rainy nights, some say, you can hear their muskets, followed by a flash.

By the end of summer, the young officer had a great tan. I think it would be fair to call him Brown. He left Customs shortly afterwards to join the Ontario Provincial Police.

Mike Deschampes

Undercover at Crooked Pine

Predawn, T·C· and I were on our way to Geraldton District· We had been seconded to conduct an undercover mission· We would be briefed by Geraldton brass· As the sun rose over the trees, we pulled into the Ministry of Natural Resources in Geraldton, Ontario· I was elated to have been chosen for the task· T·C· simply said, "Many are plucked but few are really chosen·" Geraldton Officers seemed to be awaiting our arrival· "Thank God you boys arrived!" We were ushered to the briefing room· "You boys should know you came highly recommended by your boss· We needed somebody who could blend in with the riff-raff at the resort· Our officers would be too recognizable", the biologist said· "You guys look perfect· Your boss was right· He said that of all nine officers at Thunder Bay you two were the least likely to arouse suspicions because even in uniforms you don't look like officers·" It was hard to maintain modesty, but we were flattered·

Our mission was to gain the confidence of the manager at Crooked Pine Resort· We had four days to complete the mission· "Gentlemen, I need not tell you to plan your mission carefully·" T·C· interrupted, "You mean go in low down and dirty? No problem, we are good at that· We know every dirty trick in the book· I even have Kentucky license plates· Biologist, Stan Offal volunteered details; he gave a heart rendering account· He handed us a map· "You'll need this map·" Pointing he continued, "See here, adjacent to Crooked Pine is another lake called No-No· A narrow spit of land separates the two lakes· Low and sandy it's covered by cedar trees, perfect concealment for illegal activity· I do implore you both to reconnoitre this area· Rumour has it that Crooked Pine Resort has boats and motors stashed there· It is imperative that you obtain all evidence, including a receipt of all transactions· Gentlemen, the lives of thousands of baby walleyes rest on your shoulders!" "Wow that is a heavy load! Sir, why is this lake called No-No?" Stan Offal was near tears· "No-No means no boats, motors nor fishing· A sanctuary should have meaning; a place where walleye mothers can raise their little ones, then send them off in schools, without fear of predation·" We saluted these men, knowing there was no greater goal imaginable than serving walleye· T·C· consoled Geraldton's concerns, "Not to worry, we will get the goods·

We left early in the morning ready to play our roles at the resort· T·C· would be a Canadian heavy metal junk dealer, and I would be his American bud from the Minnesota Iron Range country· We were dressed for the occasion· I was amazed how my fellow officer introduced us so skilfully to the manager of Crooked Pine Lodge, all the while dropping subtle time bombs for the manager to absorb· Simple things like T·C· would use the term aye and I would use the term ongh·

"Can't you tell he's American, aye? Check out his duds·" "Welcome to Crooked Pine", the manager smiled· "Our aim is to provide service and welcome to Canada", he said as he shook my hand·

That evening at Crooked Pines, in the confines of our cozy cabin, blinds down we reviewed our objective; to catch the operator of Crooked Pine with incriminating evidence· To break any wariness we had to befriend him and gain his confidence· T·C· muttered, "Dirty job, somebody has to do it·"

Our role-playing had to be flawless and our script had to be followed· Any nuance, inflection of speech had to be correct· We practiced· We reasoned that T·C· was a scrap dealer and I was his Yankee-Doodle buddy· We had met at an iron ore convention on the great shores of Minnesota· "Remember at Silver Bay"· "Good one T·C· Iron ore and scrap metal go together, very convincing·" I had noticed that the resort had brand new roofs on every cabin· Flattery could break the ice· "How T·C·?" asked· "Well ongh, we could fake a dialogue with the wily manager·" "Explain J·B·!" "Next time we meet the manager, I could say ongh, you folks sure do have a beautiful country, and your new ruffs sure do look fine·" T·C· said, "Now you're thinking J·B· We will engage in banter·" "Roof, ruff, roof, ruff· Okay we'll use it· A few playful barking sounds are endearing· I'll say roof, you'll say ruff· Let's add a big bomb or two to our recipe; like you have a dream job in Minnesota· The mining companies hire you to scout out vacation packages for its thousands of employees·"

The next day as T.C. was cooking breakfast he suddenly crouched down. He was whispering and choking. "Hurry we're out of here!" At first I thought, "There's no smoke, what's the hurry?"

Soon heading north, dust was flying. T.C. explained, "While cooking breakfast I looked out the window and not four feet away I saw a man I knew from Thunder Bay. We locked horns in the courtroom recently." I asked, "Was he a judge?" "No!" "Was he an adversary?" "Yes". T.C. answered, "Stop asking questions and listen." "I pray you T.C, give me a straight answer. Keep your eyes on the road so you don't have to look me in the eye." Swerving, he barely missed a moose. "The man I saw was a poacher. Had he spotted me our cover would be gone. Our whole mission compromised." I asked, "Where are we going on this bumpy road to nowhere?" "We are on the road to Oden. We need to hangout for the rest of the day at this railroad hamlet and hope that by nightfall the poacher has left.

Oden provided its own answers. Population zero, a single small white church by the tracks hidden in overgrowth, with no other buildings. Curiously, the door to the church opened, displaying freshly ironed linens. "T.C. this place is being used, where are the parishioners?" "Don't ask me," replied T.C. "My guess is that Native people and trappers worship here. Hah, I thought you could use a bit of religion J.B." "Why me? What about yourself?" It was then that I realized my fellow officer was a man of faith. We prayed all day for many reasons; black flies, mosquitoes, no lunch and not enough repellent. We prayed for a miracle at Oden; that our man at Crooked Pine would be gone. We returned to the resort late that night. Our objective had not been compromised· A great obstacle was gone! Again, we hit the sack· "I know what you're thinking J·B·, don't wonder, miracles do happen·" As my lights turned out, I dreamed of the night that T·C· and I had witnessed a miracle at Oden·

In the early morning of the third day, a curious knock came to our door· A groggy T·C· said,"Yo! C'mon in!" In the hallway shadows stood Manager man· "Someone said they didn't see you around yesterday· We worry about our customers· Frankly, I've enjoyed our intelligent conversations· "Hot dang, oofta, us too!" I said· Looking at Manager I wondered if T·C·'s bombs were beginning to pay off? Would we wind up with a moment of truth? I recalled how skilfully T·C· had opened his wallet, exposing a great wad of cash, while ordering $60·00 worth of red-eyed suckers, explaining to Manager that fishing had not been good· After a long lingering silence, Manager spoke, "How would you like trophy size fish? I can arrange it for a fee, uh, but no receipts· You seem like good guys, and I see you as preferred guests·" T·C· asked, "What's the deal?" "I can supply you with a boat, motor and trophy fish; guaranteed·" T·C· acted exuberant, "Let's go fishing! I don't need a receipt·" I breathed a sigh of resignation, "Ongh, okay T·C· you go ahead without me· I can't go·" Whaddaya mean can't go?" "Well it's my bosses in Minnesota· They demand receipts to cover expenses· Employees are allowed expenses up to half their age in expenses·" T·C· replied, "Wow! Some vacation!" By now, Manager could hardly contain himself· "Bud, are you heading straight back to the States, non-stop? Maybe I can make an exception·" T·C· yelled, "Yahoo! Let's go fishing!", as he peeled off cash for Manager·

Soon we were dragging a boat into No-No Lake· We took photos as evidence· We returned to the resort and obtained a receipt· We returned as we came, pre-dawn to Geraldton, dropped off the evidence, then moved on toward Thunder Bay· Our mission had been accomplished·

Somewhere in the vast forests of the Geraldton District, a lonely juniper tree was planted, to honour two great officers from Thunder Bay· The location was kept secret due to the nature of the case· The case was code named The Miracle of Oden; and remains hidden in the secret files of undercover operations in the Geraldton District·

Bubba

Well after midnight, we discovered that the high rising Sandstone Hill had a sudden dip followed by another rise in the road. Tom and I decided it was a great set up for a road check. Late hunters would be surprised after the first hill to find us checking if their guns were uncased or loaded after sunset. They would have been in violation of the Game and Fish Act. Who was surprised doesn't really matter. Three vehicles in tandem came over the hill and lurched to a stop. Our blinding light rotated across red faces. Nine men were in violation, as all guns were uncased. The men told us they knew the regulation. The guns were seized from each individual. Aloud, I read off the serial numbers as I passed the guns to Tom, who then placed them in his truck. The offenders were unaware that I had activated

my small tape recorder.

Tom and I had a lot of paperwork to complete. We split the work between us. Tom issued five tickets and I issued four. Unseen and sitting in Tom's truck, I transferred the serial numbers into my field notebook. As no firearms were found loaded, we sensed there was no attempt to night hunt nor to hunt from a vehicle, therefore we would eventually return the firearms. The men were cooperative, accepting responsibility for the lesser charge, uncased guns.

To end the process we all drove to their rental cabins a few miles down the road. A moose hung from a cross pole, dressed, and properly tagged. One of the men who was jocular and friendly called me Bubba, and asked if we'd like coffee but we declined.

Eventually Tom told them they could have their rifles back. They were happy and relieved as each came to the truck to retrieve his own gun. Using my notebook I called out each man's name and the serial number and make of the rifle. The men were puzzled that I could remember so much at a glance in such a short time. Suddenly the man who had called me Bubba turned to the others beside himself with excitement. "Nine rifles! Jeez, man," he said. "Did you see that? Bubba rattled off every serial number! When did he have time? The other officer put the guns in his truck." "Man," he said turning to me, "you should be working at Cape Canaveral, not this job. How'd you do that? I never saw anything like it!"

I revelled in his notion that I had a photographic memory and the uncanny ability to recall precise numbers. They had watched from their vehicles, observing well and making sure their guns were in the truck with Tom. What they didn't hear were the recordings which I was replaying and transferring to my notebook along with their licence plate numbers.

It turns out that in the Deep South Bubba is the name for sheriffs and lawmen. It was not meant as anything derogatory; it was meant to be humourous. My fun was never to reveal my great source of infallible memory. Officer Tom kept my secret. As the night wore on, other officers contacted us via radio and indicated that they found activities slow. "How about you guys?" Inevitably we called back. Tom responded with a twinkle in his eye. "Yeah, we only got nine charges." The radio went silent. Tom said, "Guess we walked tall tonight JB, uhh Bubba?"

Forensics

In the last dying days of the leg-hold trap, a lynx paw was found in a trap which belonged to a local trapper whom we called Uncle Frank. Anyone in the know about trap lines would view this matter with suspicion. The behaviour of this lynx was dumbfounding. A lynx's snowshoe pad is the least vulnerable; a well-furred paw is least susceptible to freezing or wringing off. Suspicion was that the lynx was stolen and faked to appear that it had escaped.

For Russ this case was a Head-Scratcher. How did a LYNX leave a Paw in a Small #110 Conibear Humane Trap?

At the landing, clues around a small vehicle indicated that it had been recently parked and had left the area. Uncle Frank improvised and used a broom to measure the tracks in the snow. The broom was notched and later remeasured with tape. Perhaps he was not happy knowing that the lynx had been stolen from his trap?

It turned out a logging truck operator had observed a small green truck heading north. A village store owner knew of a truck matching the description which belonged to a local trapper.

At his house, he had a lynx hide and a license. The hide had four missing paws, which is unusual as missing paws diminish the value of a hide. One might fetch five or six hundred dollars rather than eight hundred with the paws intact.

The man explained that he had never skinned lynx before; therefore, it was a blunder.

"Where are the paws?" I asked.

"Likely buried in the dump," he said.

As luck was with us, the frozen carcass was found in the yard with four paws missing. We told him his lynx was being investigated and would be sent to Toronto for forensic evaluation. The man was adamant. "Man, you guys are treating this like murder," he said. "This is harassment as far as I'm concerned."

Later, forensics advised us they had a match. The cuts on the left forepaw came from the carcass that belonged to the snowshoe pad left in the trap. The blood was that of a cat. The matters and report went to court.

Word Came: We have a match

The man earned himself the dubious reputation of poacher and thief; heavy fines and the loss of his trap line were imposed.

Years later, while attending an enforcement conference in Toronto, I heard the guest speaker telling officers that one of his favorite duties was to conduct forensic analysis.

"Have you ever done this on a lynx?" I asked. It turned out that this man had conducted the analysis on our lynx.

"For me it came as a new challenge," he said, "a break in normal routine." He welcomed my full story and was pleased to learn that the results of his expertise had resolved the case so many miles and years ago.

Today's conservation officers often travel patrol areas with kits. They extract vitreous humour, which is a fluid taken from the eyeballs of moose or other game shot illegally before opening season. This helps in determining the time of death, which is critical to a case. Game wardens are capable of seeing in the dark and photo-evidence of extraordinary detail and features can be made to accompany other evidence presented to the courts.

It has been said that nature holds secrets. Conservation officers also have a few . . .

Twisting Wrists for a Bail Bond

Iron Range Lake, 1970s-80s

No one is impervious to making mistakes. After a winter on the trapline, I was in good shape. I could set the springs on a 330 Conibear with bare hands. One year when collecting bail bond, cash on the spot for violations was in order. I found three young men with an over limit of fish. The man charged assumed his responsibility and was cooperative in attitude. His brother-in-law, on the other hand, was not. He was mouthy and good at getting under my skin. He kept goading, and, even though he was not charged, he was adamant.

"I have the money for bond, but this isn't a right for you to get it," he said. "Let's see what your made of? Let's arm wrestle! Either way you'll get your bond."

His big friend, Finnish Frank the trapper, nodded in approval.

"Yup. Go 'head. I watch!" he said.

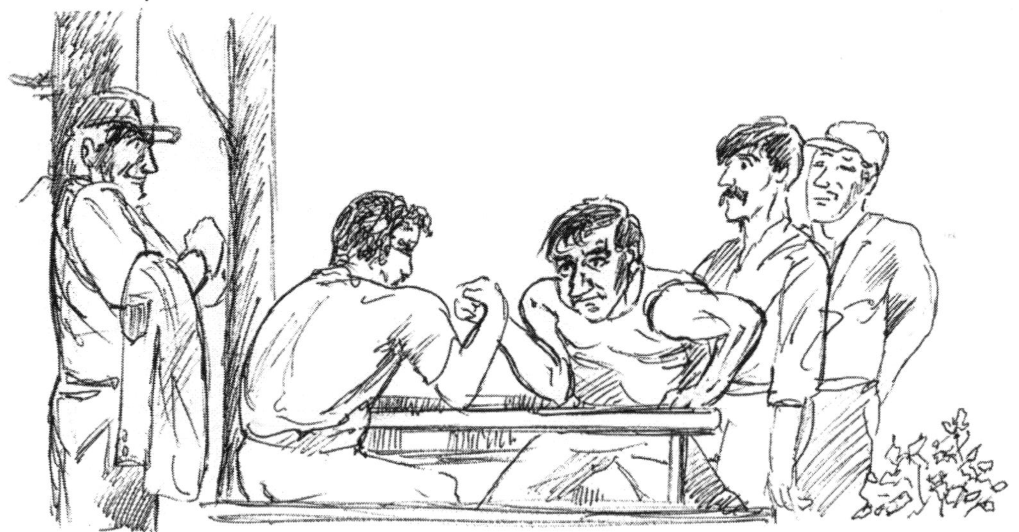

My antagonist was husky and had a glint in his eye. I decided my best strategy was to exert a lot of pressure to the top of his hand. Pin pointing the pressure to the outer edge was immediate as we gripped. I don't know if he observed more effort was on his hand that caused his arm to fade, but I was relieved that his arm went down.

Curiously, he showed a friendly respect, even if somewhat embarrassed over his loss with friends watching. I decided a little salt on his wounded pride was in order as he had handed over the bail bond.

"How old are you?" I asked.

"Twenty-five." he replied.

I said, "I'm 44, and I still beat your butt!"

Whatever apprehension in the moment turned to laughter. Like school kids, we stood the test. I sensed mutual respect but was aware there was risk. A loss could have meant more than just a fool's gamble. I made sure to remove my hat and jacket, advising this was not anything more than a personal thing. We both adhered to our made-up rules. Besides, it was lunch break. In essence, I was off duty.

My boss, Berny at Fish and Wildlife, had a different viewpoint.

"Don't ever do it again," he said.

He laughed but saw little humour in such engaging activity, and while I viewed it as a mistake that worked out, it never happened again. I learned that goading is a rant that, ignored, usually settles down. The pressure point of control comes in the lull of any storm. When frustration is spent, most people aren't happy being caught. Patience is the key that usually resolves most problems. Usually a calm cool approach reminds people that whatever charges are at hand could be added to more. This calms the waters, much like an antidote applied to a snakebite. So much is dependent on timing and the mood of any and every situation.

I always viewed the best enforcement resulted when even people with the worst attitude could shake my hand after court. It implies that notion that things can change for the better. Such occurrences do happen more than we think, and when it doesn't, the job is still worthwhile! Without rules, where would wildlife be?

Pigeon River is what we sometimes call a sitting duck border crossing. It is a testing place for would be actors, and large as life over-limits of both fishing and human behaviour. One wildlife supervisor decided it was time for an enforcement blitz at the border and arrived just in time to witness an altercation between an offender and officer. When a citizen from outside the province was charged with an offence, considerable funds were required to assure court appearance, since subpoenas could easily be ignored and were unenforceable in other jurisdictions. On this occasion the accused took exception to being required to post bail. The man stated "You got the fish, it's all you're gonna get". "Besides, we don't have money for a bail bond", his lady chided in.

The young officer responded, "Without bail bond, SIR, substantial seizures will have to be made to compensate", as he indicated the boat, motor and trailer, since they were used in the commission of the offence. "No Way", said the man, "I'm heading home, the trailer hitch is locked, the key is lost, there is nothing you can do about it! Anyone stops me, I'll get a lawyer and charge them with··uhh··kidnapping!" As he waiting for his words to sink in, our usually introspective supervisor reached his hand into the vehicle and retrieved the ignition keys for the vehicle· He said, "The bridge is there, go home if you like· When you return with the bail bond you can have your keys back"· As our supervisor walked away from the pair with keys in hand I thought I saw him wink·

The pair sat in silence obviously fuming but in no hurry to walk· After a while the truck window rolled down, a high pitched screech accompanied the action· "We found money, we found some money!"

As they day ended and officers gathered getting ready to head back to our home territories, we teased our supervisor· We called him hardnose, knowing full well he was strong on public relations· A few puffs on his pipe, he said "Good job guys· Some of you might be wondering why I came out today·" "Yeah" in chorus, "Yeah, sure, tell us···" "Well I came out to set an example, prove a lesson"

The Lesson: You're damned if you do, and damned if you don't· I came today to prove that P·R· alone doesn't always work!

Without Answers, Look for Clues (Inspector Clueso)

It was more than a campfire left burning. All three men were telling lies by the fire. The elder man claimed both younger adults because they were not yet seventeen could therefore fish on his license. He claimed both were his sons, but I thought not. There was no ID. They left their wallets miles away. I found no resemblance between the three. Even accents in speech seemed to differ. Scrambling for truth seemed important beyond seriousness. Years on the lake had taught me that one person's ploy can lead to trends. Furthermore, the notion of IDs left behind would not pass Canadian customs clearance requirements either. To me, a better story would have been more credible by simply saying, "We cleared customs and then lost our wallets and ID." You hardly start with a plan when doing enforcement. You improvise in nearly every situation.

As I followed the elder down the rocky incline to the boat, I discovered his wallet and ID were in his tackle box. He assumed responsibility for leaving an open fire on his campsite while they had gone out fishing. He would be issued a POA ticket for leaving an open fire unattended and fined according to schedule. A break came when the so-called brothers separated, one low with his father, one up high on a hill. Suddenly my eye caught a packsack off to the side. Inked on the flap a name appeared that did not match any of those given. I did not betray what was seen. As I processed paper work below and aware that I was standing center stage in view of everyone, my gestures included nodding and glances up the hill where the other brother watched intently. The group, with every query remained adamant, "He's our dad, we are brothers." The packsack gave me inspiration, sometimes you have to gamble. Knowing dramatics could make me look foolish I gambled. I ran up the hill as fast as I could. My sullen acquaintances below must have been bewildered. My friend on the hill was wide-eyed when I shouted, "Which one of you two is Shmengy?"

"Ssshhhoooottt man," said one of the men. "I guess I am."

"Don't guess . . ."

"Yeah, all right, I'm Shmengy."

"How old are you?"

"Twenty."

"All right," I said. "Things match up." You're not even related!

He glanced around at his companions below and shrugged. "Nah, I guess not."

"Thanks for the truth," I said.

"What else could I say? They gave me up. Why else would you come to me?"

" No Sir, your friends did not do a thing. Your packsack told me the truth."

"Ssshhhoooottt!"

The rewards of spontaneous utterance can sometimes have value in the courtroom. This day it helped in the field. Soon everyone had a story to tell: the truth! Now that things were out in the open, they explained how they had been to the area over the years. On other trips they had appropriate licenses, but never before had they been checked for licenses. (It seemed like such a waste, they thought.) The adult below was not a true dad, but he acted like a father. He was actually a distant cousin. They commented, "Seems to us that's pretty close. We knew sons could fish on a dad's license, right?"

"Right," I said, "but he's not your dad".

"Anyway, we figured this time we'd do it differently."

I advised all that their goal to be different succeeded. But the lying did them no good. Both young men in their twenties received tickets for fishing without a license. The cousin (dad) had a fire charge. No one met the criteria for a $2.00 group license. They failed all criteria in a cheap way. To qualify for the $2.00 license you had to be seventeen or under. Dialogue and communication lead to understanding that day, and that's the way we parted. They would never again have to say they had never been checked before—they all had tickets to prove it! Angling without a valid license.

I like to think back that the impasse was broken. When the lion waited for his prey to become separated from the herd, only until then did the lion attack, and hope for success. The risk could have failed and caused the lion to look like a Shmengy fool.

Enforcement has risks. Sometimes ruses work, even more so when a little guilt exists. Organized lying is hard to break, because lies offer no real evidence. It was never mysticism nor cynicism that caused me to doubt the word of this trio. The problem was that if they got away with it, trends could develop on the lake.

Other problems I encountered were that some parents sent money for licenses, but the kids never received licenses. It was not uncommon for large canoe groups to number thirty or even forty youngsters with fishing rods angling.

That's the name of the game. Some people play with enforcement. From a wildlife officer's viewpoint, the lakes may be true blue, but dealing with people, at times things get a little murky.

Quetico Vandal Hunters

A boring but true story . . . Dan Ross, US Warden: A bit of Moses from the sky.

More than once Dan's plane and loud-hailer skimmed Government Island. His greetings were loud and well known and would echo and boom through the landscape. "Wake-up you lazy Canucks! Put the coffee on!" It was always a fun get together.

Soon Dan was gone, back to the US.

As the day wore on, the custom's dock had hordes of tourists waiting to be processed. However, more ominous than that, disturbing reports were being received about trouble in the area of Quetico Park. Mike O'Brian, Cache Bay ranger, reported being threatened. Upon seeing rifles, he refused four men entry to Quetico

Park. The bandits continued along the border. Other allegations included canoeists reporting that shots had been fired over their heads.

The "boring" part of this story took place in my boathouse. At the time deputy conservation officers were not allowed to carry firearms. Facing the possibility of armed offenders I wanted to be prepared. I took matters into my own hands and I hand drilled a broken air pistol to make it look real. Officer Turi and I would investigate matters in the evening.

We approached Swamp Bay and accosted two men camped on the Canadian side. Baum and Ladd were hostile, especially after we found a dead loon, a merganser and several illegal fish. Turi also found drugs. One of the men defiantly expressed that we would never have gotten onto their campsite had they known that they would be arrested. They were advised that all goods would be seized due to their illegal entry. Matters became even testier. They began yelling to the point that I prayed I would not have to unholster my "revolver". One of the culprits goadingly suggested that I'd like to shoot him. I believe that I responded that it would not be necessary if they behaved.

Soon a recognized patrol boat arrived. It was Dan Ross, an ex-sheriff and now a US game warden. When he saw the dead loon, he was particularly incensed.

"That's our state bird!", he hollered. He asked us, "Are you sure it was shot in Canada? Couldn't it be possible that it floated in from the US side?"

Baum and Ladd looked nervous. There was no doubt in my mind that if Ross could have, he would have liked to have stretched his jurisdiction. Sadly we told him that the loon had been found at the tent site. Dan Ross decided that he could best render assistance by trying to find the other two men involved, somewhere on the US side. He and his deputy left through a maze of islands.

We did not know that this long night would be so adventurous. Near dark, our two prisoners, along with a heavy load of goods went back to Government Island. Enroute we encountered two men along the border line beside an island. Our arrested boys shouted and waved warnings.

"Stay put! Don't cross the line!" They didn't. All things we noted would be produced in court.

"Your actions will interest the Judge", bringing solemn looks.

We contacted Thunder Bay by radiophone. Two officers, Russ and RCMP Burke, would be at Northern Light Lake to escort the arrested duo to Thunder Bay lockup. This meant a long starry night boat ride. It was dark. Reving up the motor and getting the boat onto a good plane, even Baum and Ladd appeared impressed. After crossing the rail portage near a small bay at Northern Light Lake with 22 miles yet to go, one of the seized fishing rods fell overboard. The men laughed.

"How can you account for that?"

Near 4:00 am, we saw vehicle lights at the landing. Soon we met the two escorting officers who would escort the prisoners to Thunder Bay.

Turi's hunch paid off

Turi and I slept in a cabin. At daybreak, we headed back to Saganaga. Turi said he thought he had a hunch.

"The rods had bobbers attached."

I couldn't believe my eyes, when he spotted the bobber in the vast waters and pulled it up. All evidence was now intact.

Baum and Ladd were convicted. They each received 30 days in jail. All their goods were permanently seized. Their well known lawyer also had to be paid.

They both received hefty fines. After serving their jail time they were escorted back to the US. We felt that justice had prevailed.

I learned that what you read in the media is not always accurate. We received no mention as to our involvement. In memory of Turi Benson I'd like to set the record straight... Included are the actual notes from our investigation. They say the truth will win out, I merely want to help it. In truth there is justice.

P.S. The only existing notes regarding the investigation are the notes of Turi Benson and John Bouchard...

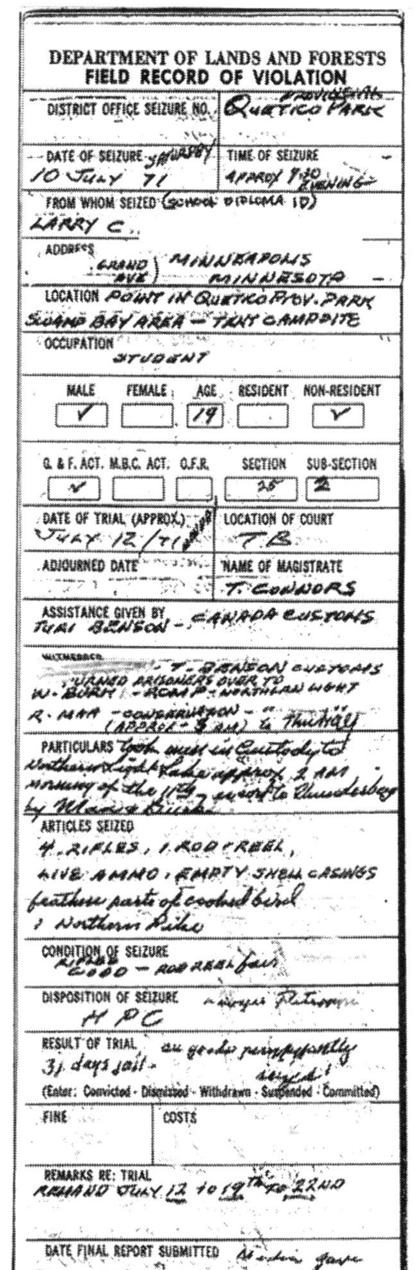

DEPARTMENT OF LANDS AND FORESTS
FIELD RECORD OF VIOLATION

DISTRICT OFFICE SEIZURE NO. PROVINCIAL QUETICO PARK

DATE OF SEIZURE SATURDAY 10 JULY 71 | TIME OF SEIZURE APPROX 9:30 EVENING

FROM WHOM SEIZED (SCHOOL DIPLOMA ID) LARRY C.

ADDRESS GRAND AVE MINNEAPOLIS MINNESOTA

LOCATION POINT IN QUETICO PROV. PARK SWAMP BAY AREA — TENT CAMPSITE

OCCUPATION STUDENT

MALE	FEMALE	AGE	RESIDENT	NON-RESIDENT
✓		19		✓

G. & F. ACT.	M.B.C. ACT.	O.F.R.	SECTION	SUB-SECTION
✓			25	2

DATE OF TRIAL (APPROX.) JULY 12/71 | LOCATION OF COURT T.B.

ADJOURNED DATE | NAME OF MAGISTRATE T. CONNORS

ASSISTANCE GIVEN BY TURI BENSON — CANADA CUSTOMS

WITNESSES — T. BENSON CUSTOMS TURNED PRISONERS OVER TO W. BURK — RCMP — NORTHERN LIGHT R. MAR — CONSERVATION — (APPROX — 3 AM) to [illegible]

PARTICULARS took men in Custody to Northern Light Lake approx 2 AM morning of the 11th — escort to Thunderbay by [illegible]

ARTICLES SEIZED
4 — RIFLES, 1 ROD & REEL,
LIVE AMMO, EMPTY SHELL CASINGS
feathers parts of cooked bird
1 Northern Pike

CONDITION OF SEIZURE RIFLES GOOD — ROD REEL fair

DISPOSITION OF SEIZURE [illegible]
H P C

RESULT OF TRIAL 31 days jail — [illegible]
(Enter: Convicted - Dismissed - Withdrawn - Suspended - Committed)

FINE | COSTS

REMARKS RE: TRIAL REMAND JULY 12 to 19TH to 22ND

DATE FINAL REPORT SUBMITTED [illegible] TRUE LARRY ?

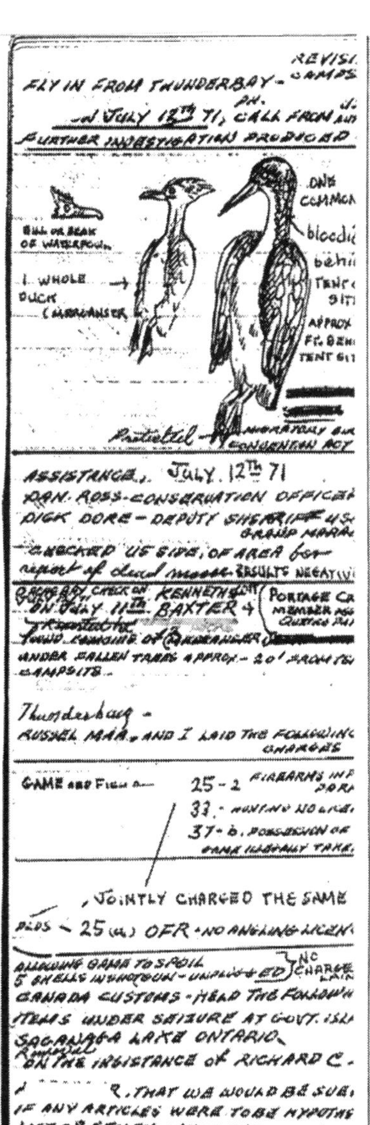

FLY IN FROM THUNDERBAY — REVISI[…] CAMPS[…]
… JULY 12TH 71, CALL FROM …
FURTHER INVESTIGATION PRODUCED …

ASSISTANCE., JULY. 12TH 71
DAN. ROSS — CONSERVATION OFFICER
DICK DORE — DEPUTY SHERIFF U.S. GRAND MARAIS
— CHECKED US SIDE, OF AREA for report of dead moose. RESULTS NEGATIVE

CHECK ON KENNETH … BAXTER + … ON JULY 11TH … PORTAGE C… MEMBER … QUETICO PA…
… FOUND REMAINS OF (MERGANSER) … UNDER FALLEN TREES APPROX. — 20' FROM TENT CAMPSITE.

Thunderbay —
RUSSEL MAR, AND I LAID THE FOLLOWING CHARGES

GAME AND FISH A— 25 - 2 FIREARMS IN P… PARK
33. — HUNTING NO LICE…
37 - b. POSSESSION OF GAME ILLEGALLY TAKE…

, JOINTLY CHARGED THE SAME

PLUS — 25 (a) OFR — NO ANGLING LICEN…

ALLOWING GAME TO SPOIL
5 SHELLS IN SHOTGUN — UNPLUGGED } NO CHARGE …
CANADA CUSTOMS — HELD THE FOLLOWING ITEMS UNDER SEIZURE AT GOVT. ISL… SAGANAGA LAKE ONTARIO. ON THE INSISTANCE OF RICHARD C. … THAT WE WOULD BE SUE… IF ANY ARTICLES WERE TO BE HYPOTHE… LOST OR STOLEN. IN THE INTERIM OF THE ABSENCE.

3 RODS 4 REELS, 1 CLOTHES BOX, 4 SLEEPING BAGS, 1 TENT, 1 TARP, MISC. COOKING GEAR, 1 PR BINNOCULARS, MISC CLOTHING ETC, 1 GUNCLEANING KIT, 1 L… BAG OF RICE.

1 CUBE OF BROWNISH SUBSTANCE, AND A QUANTITY OF PILLS, 2 PIPES, TURNED OVER TO W. BURK RCMP BY T. BENSON.

Turi Liked
my John
Wayne
Swagger

Quetico Park
High Noon

A Good Trade Off: I Had His Rifle, He Had My Tie

What happened at Northern Light on a small island in the evening lasted well into the night. The next day, a morning check showed they had left very early. Working alone on late nights is not easy and for some people this can be very stressful.

I had his rifle and he held my tie in his hand; a good trade off. It was also his shouting that gave me pause. He was the leader of his younger companions therefore seemed compelled to show his companions that he didn't give up easily, even he seemed surprised that my tie was in his hand. In the impasse I assumed a posture of resolve. I was not alone, I said, but part of an army. What couldn't be settled now would be settled far more seriously later. Of all things borne from experience, the mouth in any situation has to be dealt with. Listening also paid dividends, so I reminded him that penalties could increase if he continued to carry on, and I added that his rifle could be subject to permanent loss by court order. Early on in the debacle he yelled, "No one takes my rifle!" By doing so he indicated where his Achilles' heel was.

Sometimes patience takes more time stretch to reach compliance. A thick skin helps *in all dithering. In all situations I always maintain the offending item in hand. A better exchange for a tie was the rifle. Soon the tie came back in exchange for a ticket, with options to enter a plea or to attend court.*

Most often encounters are reasonably concluded. Some are less predictable. It's all part of wildlife enforcement. The ride home gave me time to ask myself a lot of questions. "Could the situation have been handled better? Did those words really come out of me? Did they turn the tide?" I learned that the way a person responds in one situation might not be the same as in another situation. Every situation and circumstance in law enforcement is unpredictably different; therefore each requires instant innovation.

Working alone, I learned that I couldn't afford to turn my back on anything. There are times to act before you think. Basic instincts become finely tuned. Adrenaline rushes must be kept in control. As in a poker game I never show my hand and never allowed a bluff to be revealed by any emotion.

I never called a man a liar. With some people lying is a habit, perhaps only in an attempt to save face or in a vain attempt to preserve a sense of dignity. My pointing to evidence usually worked best. Demeanor is best at eye level. If you elevate your head at each answer to a question, a subject looking up each rise of your nostrils will only realize you do not believe anything he is saying. Attitude, composure, and demeanor are assets that are conducive to good enforcement and positive results. Authoritative glares or grunts, even if they work, leave a long lasting negative impression. For me, good enforcement lasts longer than the moment of encounter. It seeks a lasting compliance. Enforcement is not a power trip! The nose up approach each time after every question leaves a lasting impression. It reminds me of, "Say what? Try me again?" It's hard to convey anything looking up nostrils. It's like standing close, calling someone HHHarry with a mouthful of garlic, especially if the person's name is Rastus.

Your Side, My Side

There are times when officer discretion cannot be used, especially when illegal acts are enforced on both sides of the border. For example: If angling with more than one line, both countries apply the law. Officer discretion can allow a warning. If a person strays over the line but has an angling license for province OR state, he may receive a warning . If a person has no license whatsoever: Charge. Non-compliance after being warned: Charge.

US Officer Hiedibrink and I often patrolled together, working both sides of the international boundary line, especially as the US enforced the "No cans or bottles" law in the BWCA (Border Waters Canoe Area). This type of enforcement was not the kind that stirs the imagination, but the results benefited both sides of the border. Today campsites are pristine and natural.

This day's patrol was not unusual. Habitat violations occurred as well as fishing violations. However, this day was a bit unusual, because it lead me to be a witness in a US courtroom. A prominent person from Grand Marais put up a vigorous defense on a relatively minor offense, a

misdemeanor· He denied and used jurisdiction as a defense· Judge Wolfe was interested in a sketch presented as part of testimony·

"I'm going to allow this to be entered into evidence·" He continued, "The resemblance to the defendant is clear, reasonable, and also objective · · · the placement of the equipment on the left or right hand side, even if taken from stick figures from a field officer's notebook made at the time, are likely correct·" He studied the sketch from my notebook· "The resemblance made relatively soon after, supports high probability that an offense took place· The fact that the two lines were both minnow baited, does not support any notion that the gear was alternated; one having a hook with a minnow and the other having a jig with a minnow, is suspicious·" The judge paused a moment and then said, "Officer Hiedibrink has presented maps and credible knowledge of the lake· Maps are available that provide reasonable guidance as to jurisdiction· · ·" He concluded, "A line has to be drawn somewhere· Two lines are a violation on either side of the international boundary· My decision therefore is to find the defendant guilty·" And fined, he did!

The judge seemed pleased that US officers worked together with Canadian officers· While both countries prevail, the justice systems are based on British systems of justice, the adversarial twelve person jury or Judge· I recall one feature which I admired in this judge's courtroom: witnesses, officers, and defendants are always in full view of the gallery and Judge at all times· No one is observed from the back at anytime·

I'm privileged as a result of having worked as an Ontario deputy conservation officer along the US/Canada border· Twenty years of such work allowed unique advantages and contacts: doctors of zoology, curator of Chicago Field Museum, renowned wildlife photographers, trappers, woodsmen, US officers, and sheriffs·

I'd like to see more parks with Judge's names, as is the case of parks in Minnesota· If I could name a few, they would be Judge Hachey State Park, including Judge Wolfe and Judge Bujold· Unfortunately such notions are beyond my reach or jurisdiction· Maybe somewhere a retired judge has my exhibit A on his mantelpiece·

Incorrigibles

On a good day, from Saganaga Lake to the courthouse in Thunder Bay it was a journey of about two hours by boat, and another one and a half hours by truck. Officers were required to be there by 9 am., when they had a case on the docket so an early start was required. As I entered the courtroom this particular morning the accused man turned, winked at me and gave me the thumbs up sign. I immediately thought "Oh, no, I'm late!" Not so. Another officer was in the process of giving his testimony and my turn would come soon.

I recalled my original meeting at Hoof Creek with this gentleman. He moaned that he was on compensation due to a shoulder injury. I advised him that his 4 line illegal angling activity was hardly doctor ordered therapy. Obviously one ticket issued wasn't enough. I soon learned that later the same week he was caught again. He decided to test other waters and another officer's heart and penmanship miles away at Shebandowan, with the same result. The officer known as Red Fox also obliged him. Red's advice was "tell your story to the judge". I think the Justice was surprised to see the same accused before him once more, same charge, same day. The Justice showed no mercy and doubled the fine. This was not a case of double jeopardy, it was repeated offences! I recall one judge, when imposing penalty *would say to a defendant, "Your fine will be __", hesitate, look over his glasses, and add "I can make it more."*

Back then a single fine was the penalty. Whether a person was fishing with two or five lines, they received the same fine. Today's penalties multiply with the infraction. There will be one fine for the violation of fishing with too many lines then an additional fine for each illegal line. Today repeat offenders can lose hunting or fishing privileges for years.

Some violators are addicted to a game of trying to outwit the system. I often wonder if a court appearance is seen as their moment in the sun. Some can ill afford the fine, they are not wealthy in life and the fine creates a financial burden. Perhaps their mindset belongs to the era when limits and rules were less critical, when game, fish and buffalo roamed as far as the eye could see.

The Court Jester?

Some Days Amaze

Nothing is ever routine. The charge was fishing without a license. The outburst came as I was writing a ticket. "You should know I represent a large law firm, and I will represent this matter in court. You know we had a park permit. I want your badge number! Make sure you dot every i and cross every T!" He seemed to want to amalgamate one into two. A park permit is not a fishing license. Each has its own purpose. I tried to ignore what the Romans said so many centuries before, perhaps because it all seemed to harsh. This was not the time to share my theory with this man, he was in a finger waving, feisty mood. I gave him his ticket, no one said goodbye. "You will hear from me!" were his words as he paddled away.

The occupational reality is that there are times when public relations and enforcement do not coincide. The shock was to come later. Several weeks had passed and the matter was scheduled for court. I showed up to give my testimony and the Crown Prosecutor told me that he had received a letter from a law firm. Uh oh, I thought, what next? I'll likely have a lot of explaining to do. I was confused when the Crown said "Congratulations". He told me that I must have quite the gift for b··· gab. The firm sent a cheque to pay the fine and said there would be no contest. They had made an assumption that was a mistake. Further they said that the officer who served them was a credit and courteous.

I never told the Crown my bewildered secret. Don't match venom with venom, just keep your cool, be patient, and carry an invisible horseshoe. I left the courthouse without asking the Crown Prosecutor why the Romans once cried out "Kill All Lawyers". In retrospect I never did fully understand the reason, but I do think it is plausible that the Romans, like me, never knew what to expect when dealing with lawyers.

Lake Learnings

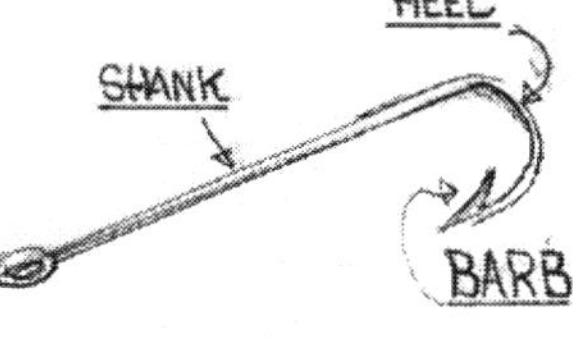

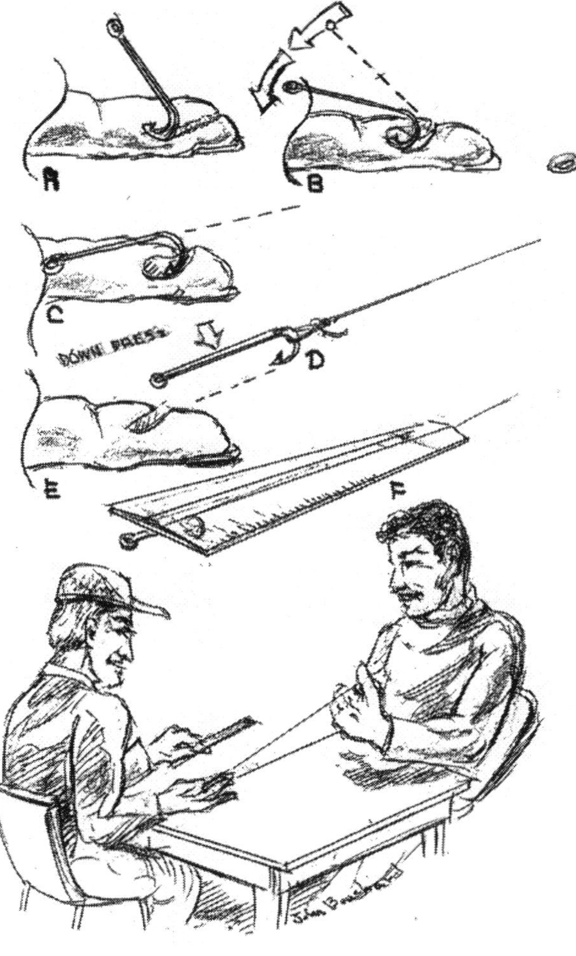

Reverse Hook Removal

A Hook Angle

B Hook Placement

C Pull Position

D Note: Mono-noose on heel of hook

E Angle of Trajectory Press down on Hook

F Ruler aligns and guides direction of pull in line with monofilament

The Biggest Lure I Ever Saw Was Stuck in a Child's Head

The more you looked the larger it got! Miles out on the lake the panic was etched on the faces of all involved. Anglers do have accidents. . .

Conservation officers learn early to expect the unexpected, and that their jobs are not only about checking angler licenses and writing tickets. There are situations when one shouldn't attempt anything more than a motorized trip to a waiting ambulance. Such was the case of the screaming child with a hook in his head. This was not a push-the-hook-through situation. It was gut wrenching, but not life threatening. Professional help was available less than an hour south at the end of the Gunflint Trail.

Little did I know that another incident on another day would make the victim my teacher. A late evening knock on the door at Saganaga Lake Lands and Forest Station, brought a man with a hook in his finger.

"I need your help, actually your assistance, in a way," he said. "Me and the kid paddled all day. Someone at the resort said to see you. We're not done fishing yet." In spite of discomfort, the man had a sense of humour. "No. I don't need a doctor," he continued. "I need someone with a steady hand and some nerve. I hear wardens are built that way. My son's too young yet."

I looked closely at the hook in his finger·

"Let me explain," he said· "I don't want the hook pushed through, I want it pulled back·"

"What? You mean pull it back against the barb?" I asked· "You're liable to pull your finger off·"

"Not if you do it right·"

He explained his theory· "The objective Officer is to render the barb on the hook useless by use of precise pressure and trajectory· Pressure on the shank will elongate the wound and free up the barb· The hook will be free of my finger like a happy divorce·"

I followed his instructions and learned a new technique; the hook came out neat and clean·

"Thanks, man," he said· "This means Sonny Boy and I can go fishing·"

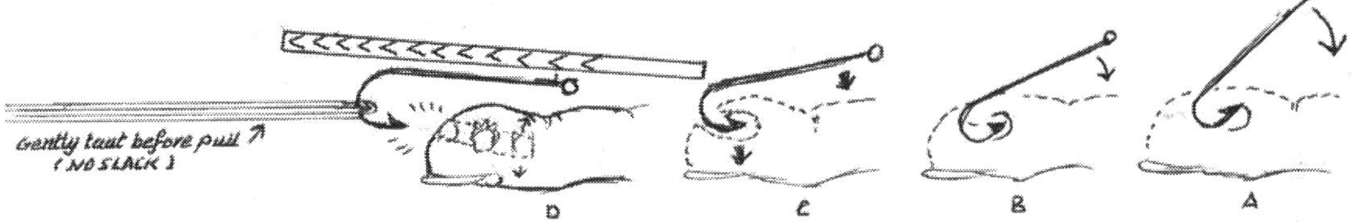

This reverse process is explained in reverse: Starting with A, the shank is lowered· This widens the entry wound· The barb is rendered useless by the time you get to C· A small ruler can be held over the shank to ensure proper trajectory removal· This also maintains that the entry wound channel stays wide to prevent the barb from grabbing· A monofilament loop gently extended without jerking is swiftly pulled back like a catapult·

In emergency wilderness situations, when one is miles from help of any kind, it may apply· I know it worked twice in my career in fleshy places such as this man's finger and after that in a calf muscle· This technique does not apply in every situation, such as hooks imbedded in a skull near an eye, throat, or any vital area· Obviously, arteries, throats, and membrane areas should not be risked·

Some Things are Learned the Hard Way

I learned many things over the years through observation. Many of the tragedies on the lake occurred as the result of a large male ego. After witnessing the aftermath of several drownings that occurred because the female person in the boat had no idea how to operate it. I made sure I taught Eve how to operate our boats and navigate the lake with confidence.

Unfortunately I became the victim of the macho-man syndrome myself. Caught between two lakes 22 miles from home, I had to get this motor across the portage. My mistake was doing it in wet weather. While crossing the portage I slipped on the wet rocks and hurtled forward, wrenching my knee. The motor was saved, but the rest of the summer I battled with a wounded knee.

Lake Travel

I was lucky to learn lessons of the wind from Jock. Things like: quarter the trough; learn to accelerate with the rhythm of the waves, slow down going down, a bit of speed going up to the crest; keep your motor in tune with the action, don't panic or bull you way through; use your head and work your throttle at the right time and you can have a swell time! Jock Richardson had a knack for getting his point across and it paid to listen. Displace some weight to the bow of your boat before a storm hits, lest the wind spin you like a top.

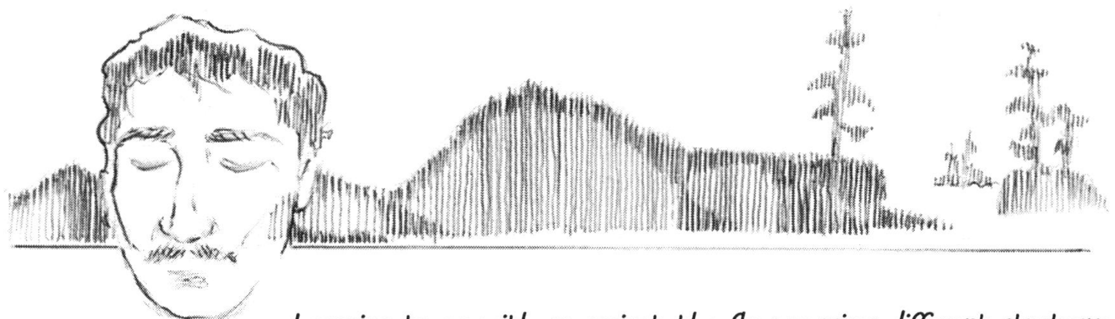

Learning to go with or against the flow requires different strategy.

I never relied on stars to navigate a night. The hills and shapes of my surroundings guided me. Night travel does unravel like a tape, except if you lose the sequence of the treeline shapes etched in the mind. Having to change fuel tanks in the dark can disrupt the sequence because the boat invariably turns during the process causing a loss of bearings and confusion. Night travel is easier with boat lights on behind your back, not bow lights on in front. Reefs, rocks, sandbars and deadheads also need memorizing. Night travel is dream-like; if you have the knowledge it can prevent a nightmare.

In dense fog my boat and I lost our equilibrium. The boat stood upright reaching for infinity.

The worst ride of my life was a night when there was a dense fog over the lake. Turning on my flashlight only reflected the white mist into my eyes. Fatigue and a loss of horizon led to a very real sensation that the bow of the boat was pointing straight up. Curiously I enjoyed the sensation although it took me 4 hours to travel a mere 3 miles home. Nothing was familiar in a landscape I knew like the back of my hand. The fog erased everything!

Dealing with the Spirit World

Experience taught me that it is better to check a morning hangover rather than a campsite full of drunks at night. Routine patrols, working alone, miles out on a lake are at best speculative. Drunk people tend be boisterous and offensive beyond sense or reason. "Wobbly-pop" alters normality, and can lead to irrational behavior in a heartbeat. The only thing predictable in certain situations is the unpredictability of the outcome. For officers it helps to have eyes in the back of their heads.

"One of you b--s charged my uncle last week!" one might holler.

Dealing with a dozen or more men in varying stages of stupor with others egging on, can cause problems that wouldn't normally exist. It can be a challenge, so much so that upon reflection I thought that the book about Jekyll and Hyde was inspired by liquor, as it turns ordinary people into unreasonable beasts. After a few incidents that involved pushing or having my tie pulled off, I found that when working unarmed and alone that it was far better to deal with drunks in the morning when they were hung over. Usually all aggression is gone in the early morning sunlight, while their headaches and stomachs are healing. I learned that people who don't understand their own limits usually don't hide their over limits well· It takes a clear head to count fish accurately·

At times I would use different tactics when other situations needed diffusing· Alone at night, I evened the odds by using the pretext that another officer was working with me in his own boat· I'd feign taking a radio call· Approaching a campsite I'd say, "Roger, over and out· See you in thirty minutes·" All calls made loud and clear were made to the wind, but usually had a desired effect· "Oh, you have a contact?" they'd wonder· Wisely, I did not reveal that my contact was only with the spirit world· So I'd say, "Yes, I have a contact·"

Very drunk, his swing pulled him face first into the snow and slush

Enforcement uses very real ruses: the mechanical moose ploy often netted poaching activities· Even the smallest tricks on bush roads are effective in slowing vehicles down, especially during hunting season when loaded firearms in vehicles are far too relevant and illegal· The element of surprise is needed before guns or firearms are unloaded· Officers play on the notion that humans love good fortune, especially when they think they've found a lost item in the middle of the road· Any useful item usually slows a vehicle down· Such distractions allow officers time for a quick response· A ruse need not be mechanical or material, it can often come simply from words·

"Sir, have you heard of any shooting or shots in the area?" This question has brought enforcement results, especially when posed to people who are being good sportsmen. They too have little use for poachers or people who want an edge during the hunting season. Public response is valuable.

Sometimes what one finds on wilderness roads does not always bring good luck. Some things that don't belong can lead to downfall; temptation and greed are part of the make-up of most poaching activities. Temptation is key to how well ruses succeed. Officers know that every time a mechanical moose is shot, perhaps a live moose has been saved. It's a bit like fighting fire with fire, even if it means playing by the poacher's rules, and if it leads a poacher into temptation, so be it.

I am reminded of the poet Dorothy Frances Gurney, who wrote: The Lord God planted a garden in the first white days of the world, and there he planted an Angel Warden in a garment of light unfurled. Gurney apparently recognized the need for some kind of warden to preserve the garden; the garment of light unfurled suggests wisdom. Her poem reminds us that nature has limits that must be preserved by all possible means.

Wildlife officers must innovate according to need. Recalling a curious phrase which I never understood in my youth, my mother often said, "Catch as catch can". I now believe that she was referring to the word ruse. It seems that ruses are as old as time. Helen of Troy used a wooden horse to win her battle. Was that not a ruse?

Today, certain animal parts are being sold for high profit. It seems that wildlife is likely in a war for survival. If our job is to protect wildlife, the best weapon against poaching is to "catch as catch can", and raise public awareness.

Are Lakes Less Hazardous Than Mountains?

The day had not gone well. I had managed to wrestle my snowmobile out of slush many times. It was nearing dark, the snow was waist deep and beneath it were globs of heavy slush. This meant that I needed more than my legs or back to clear it. It meant arm lifting to the extreme. I managed to muster up the extra strength. I remember the pain; the bicep on my left arm was hot and stinging. I looked at the bulge once I had made it home and hung up my Superman cape. I later learned that I had ruptured my bicep. There had to be an easier way. Next time I would be equipped.

Sunset at
Trafalger Bay '74

*I devised a plan_ to deal with **SLUSH***

EVELINE HELPED
THE WORD HAD
DUAL MEANING
YONNY_ be smart
YOU BE ABLE!
I couldn't argue
my bicep hurt and
and I wanted..
sweet x sour..
walleyes!

I modified an old car bumper jack that I had retrieved from a junk yard and reduced the jack to minimal parts with a hack saw.

On my next encounter with slush, I jacked my machine up with a simple screwdriver as my lever.

The snow could now be swept under the track. I cleared out the mush and then decided on an escape route. I used snowshoes to sweep snow and build a trail to allow the ice to refreeze. This took about ten minutes.

Gently I lowered my machine onto my new trail. You learn not to destroy new snow bridging by soft throttling, but by slowly building up speed running alongside your machine. I vaulted on when speed and time were right. This technique has never let me down. I learned that an ice chisel made a good anchor point if I wanted to use a come along. This worked in certain aggravating situations. The key is not to rush the process. Patience defeats slush. Do not panic. Slush is an inconvenience but preparation makes the difference! Being stuck is only temporary. I was confident, and thanks to this method, I always made it home for dinner. Travelling alone you must harness the elements that exist; cold, snow, and slush. I learned that the elements which once held my machine could also set it free. The jack and snowshoes became a part of my machine and I never left home without them.

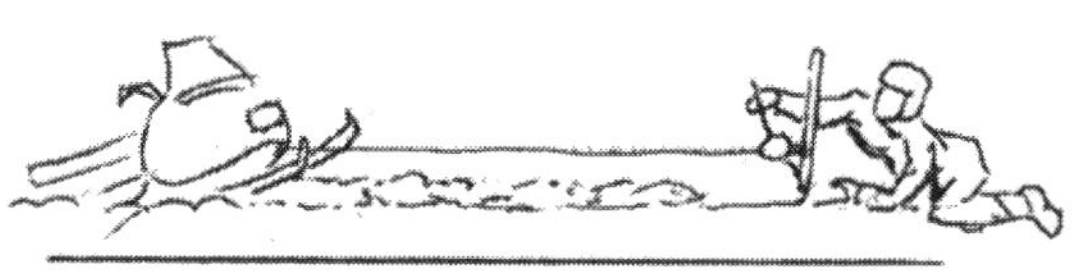

I knew I was in trouble so I chose words carefully, "If I make it – follow!"

My American cousins were visiting from Chicago. They never stood in deep slush before. The big crush happened at Mosquito Bay. The sandwich of ice, water, and ice had broken. Soon water filled boots and machines were sitting on the lower level of solid ice. The lake was a cold martini. I barked instructions, "Build a ramp of snow, let it set, ease your machines back on the top layer of ice, then get it up as far as you can." Then I added, "Take pictures as we go. You'll laugh later at home." That advice brought incredulous looks and a few questions. The looks that I got told me that they thought their Canadian cousin was disillusioned.

"What's that you're wearing?" one cousin asked.

"It's a life jacket," I said. "I always wear one on spring ice." I looked at what lay ahead. "I want you guys to wait, watch, and if I make it to the shadow areas, then follow me, one by one."

"What do you mean, '**If** I make it?"

"I mean if I make it to solid ice, the ice should be better in the cool shadow areas."

My plan worked for several miles. Morale was up and the open stretch gave pause to make choices. We could wait until dark and let the cool ice strengthen on our way, or we could hope that previous snowmobile trails were still sound.

My cousins decided that they were not going to be late for supper at Landry's cabin. Their mighty machines would make my day and theirs too! Finally the public landing at the resort could be seen in the distance. We still had four more unstable miles to go. It seemed that dinner was calling, and they could not wait. Rupp! Rupp!

One by one, powerful machines raced off. My 12.5 skidoo could not do more than follow. It was every man for himself. They disappeared like specks around an island while I puttered away with my light machine. Then I noticed that they had decided to abandon their machines and walk home. I wondered the reason as to why they had left the trail? Had they assumed a straight line would be a shorter distance to dinner?

Observing darker snow where vapors were rising, this was a place that needed to be avoided. It meant water under the snow. Near a reef abandoned machines were deep in slush. As before three specks were walking; but my smaller machine was the only one to take me home. A day or so later I learned that my cousins had spent countless hours chiselling solid ice to free up their machines because the slush had frozen.

A week later a letter came with thanks. They said they had blow-up photos of their race to supper, and that they were a hit amongst their friends in Chicago. They were the envy of many who never had the opportunity to snowmobile Canada's great white north. They had overcome hardships, taken pictures of the day which were now displayed on their walls. Eventually these memoires became points of laughter for themselves and friends who viewed them.

Sometimes It Pays to Be a Chicken On Ice

I spent many seasons as a trapper and officer travelling alone across the uncharted hazards of Ontario lakes. I was often stunned where weekends would go on high powered foolish machines. Off trail riders often didn't realize how lucky they had been riding in places where the ice was always dangerous and thin no matter how cold the winter had been. Thin areas where creeks, little falls or rapids entered the lake, or where strong currents exist present certain peril. If you were to go through the ice in one of those locations the current could pull you down under unbroken ice where only an otter, beaver or mink could escape and if you could escape what about the effects of hypothermia? How to broach the subject without insulting the snowmobilers?

I felt the easiest way to set the hook was to be obvious, especially on spring ice. I let them ask me why I carried a Jack, well displayed on my snowmobile, or why I was wearing a life jacket over my snowmobile suit. I knew questions would come to satisfy the curiosity they had.

Points to Consider
Ice can be thin near dark rocks

I told them of unwise things I had seen while patrolling Saganaga Lake and on Northern Light. I told them a cut green balsam or spruce set out on the ice at Windy point meant stay away, thin ice, and use the portage at Frustration Bay. I told them of foolish tracks that ran over thin ice at a beaver feed bed where ice can be paper thin no matter how thick the ice is elsewhere. I never showed them how a bicep could pop as you try to extricate a machine mired deep in snow and slush. Thereafter I carried my friend jack, and if the victims of my tirade were really interested I might explain that the snowmobiles are likely in better shape than they are!

I loved the punch line the best, showing my ice pick sticks, and water proof matches.

The biggest question would always be about the life jacket. I looked into their curious eyes and replied with confidence: "Sir, you see ice on the lake. I see nothing but frozen water." Those who were listening to what I *had to say often left looking around and down, or asked me where they could get a set of pick sticks for themselves.*

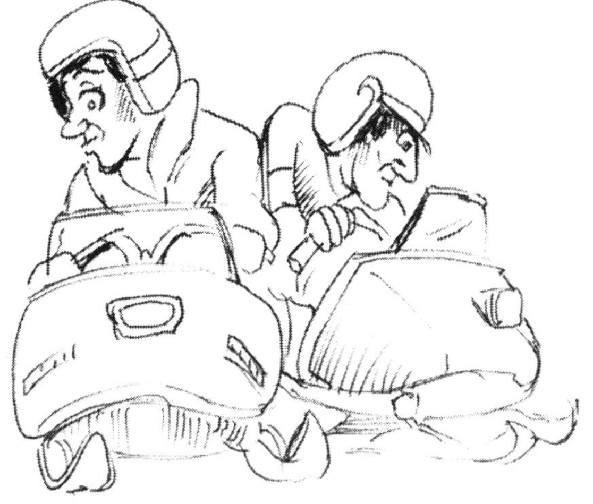

In time the MNR had me design a program to teach snowmobile and ATV safety courses to new employees throughout the district. My intent was not to fear-monger, but I told them the truth. I told them the stories of Saganaga Lake dwellers that devised ways of making the 7 mile trip for mail on spring ice. Before they got a hovercraft, they had a snowplane that resembled the fan driven machines of the Florida Everglades. Even before that Dicky Powell went for mail with 2 empty 45 gallon oil drums attached to his snowmobile in case he went through the ice. The lesson I wanted to get across was that lake people were not macho-riders, they are survivors!

The Long Night Ride Home

November 29th is a date that I remember.

It was the day for goodbyes at Saganaga Lake. It ended the first phase of trapping on open water.

Returning from Saganaga to Northern Light Lake, I knew what to expect on the lee side of the Northern Light portage. New hard ice would be formed as far as the eye could see. Usually about a mile or more... How thick was a dreaded thought. All things being equal, Jock's technique would get me home. The first good sign was that the ice under the boat broke as I loaded items to the back. The bow had to be elevated to allow the boat to slide up onto the ice. Lessons of old included that you never try to ram a straight line through fresh hard ice. Aluminum boats will not withstand straight line scraping. The ice could act like a can opener. The technique, when using a boat as an icebreaker is to drive the boat up onto the ice with each thrust of the motor. Then move your weight and a side to side rocking will do the rest; and so it was each fall.

I had twenty-two miles to reach home. The first task, all things being equal was to reach the open water, where wind and wave action slowed nature's process of freezing. The trip home in the dark is a dream state in spite of the cold. The sounds of summer are gone. Each empty campsite provides memories, mostly good and some dubious. As winter changes, so too do all who live in Border Lake country. Those who live on islands stay on islands, waiting for ice and snowmobile time. Winter produces its own metamorphosis. Most who dwell here in the winter months, aside from gathering firewood, trap.

I was alone on this trip. Eve and Gypsy were at Northern Lights, roughly twenty-two miles from the rail portage. I was heading home on a cold still night with beaver, packs, and a laden boat. The water was heavy and very cold. Ice formed on the boat.

The boat could barely plane when suddenly the 20 hp motor sputtered out. All the cranking in the world wouldn't thaw the motor or gas lines. With six miles to go, I knew what typically took twenty-five minutes would now take hours. It was now past 1:00 a.m. The bright moon was helpful as I pulled the 20 hp up to reduce a deadhead drag. My old 3 hp Johnson with a gravity feed tank would have to do. On a canoe, a full tank might get eight miles. I knew it could do about eight miles per hour, but this 16-foot boat with a heavy load would plow low and slowly.

I added what I had left of gasoline and gasoline antifreeze, and asked my adrenaline glands to slow down. On the second pull the motor started. I nosed on ridiculously slowly. My top speed was perhaps one and a half miles per hour. It took a lot of handle wagging to maintain direction. I knew I'd have some explaining to do to Eve.

A steel thermos and coffee helped, but more than anything else the fact that I moved at all was relaxing. I settled in for the long ride. I knew I'd get home. That was all that mattered.

The moon was full, the lake dreamlike. I felt as if I was traveling in Ryder's paintings. Usually his paintings depicted night scenes and a sense of mystery; a great yellow moon amongst dark clouds. I was looking at reality in the dark... Crystal masses of roaming ice masses, like sharp shards of glass, drifted by in the black waters of the lake and disappeared behind me.

Around 4:30 a.m., the lights of my boat hit the many mirrors on the back wall of our A-frame and shattered into a thousand lights. As I pulled up to the shore, I saw the beam of a flashlight bobbing up and down the steep incline.

"So late?" Eve's voice had an edge to it. "Where were you?"

I was home.

Nature has Beauty and a Downside

Nature produces its own unpredictability that we cannot manage or control: fire, ticks, disease, injury... There are no hospitals for animals in the bush.

When I was young, around seventeen, I splinted a seagull's broken leg with split willow and string. Thinking I had done a good deed, I set it back in the water. I made the mistake of looking back. The gull had a new problem; he could only swim in circles, and the circles eventually could only get tighter. For more than fifty years the memory lingers. Some things cannot be undone. The problem was not the gull's or mine. The problem was carelessness. Another example of carelessness is monofilament which is left behind. Over the years, I learned it happens more than we think.

For wildlife, surviving in nature is not like our survival. A beaver, slashed by a bear, tries to live life with his intestines inside out. It's a lot like city life, according to the news. We don't have to live with quills in our faces as a fisher might. I don't mean to convey or cause concern over animal cruelty or man's inhumanity to man. Churches and politicians do that better than I. It's best to stick to experience. Animals do not attend churches in order to learn better behavior. Animals have to deal with parasites. They are very taxing. I once saw a rabbit with so many lumps that he looked crazed. I saw a blind moose wandering in circles, unaware of human presence, and as I watched it took a few more faltering steps, crumpled to the ground and never got up again. He was a victim of brain worm.

What I'm saying is there aren't a lot of big things we can do when visiting in wilderness settings. However there are little things we can do that can help wildlife. Leave nothing, and when going home take only your memories.

The Cache Bay Pig List

Q – Is the pen mightier than the sword?

A – Yes… If you attach names, addresses, provinces, states and details on a public list. And so it was at a remote ranger station at the entrance to Quetico Park. Cache Bay Ranger Station was on the west end of Saganaga Lake and was a gateway into the parks interior. Thousands of canoeists visit and traverse this fragile and rugged land featuring ancient Indian rock paintings each year. Visitors from the USA, Canada, Europe, even Asia come. Some repeat this journey year after year. In the late 60's and early 70's the Park hired portage crews. Young men and women would travel great distances within the park by canoe, cleaning portages on established canoe routes. They were the eyes and ears of the government in the forest. Out on the lakes they welcomed their rendezvous at ranger stations. It didn't take words to tell what they were finding on their journeys. With every trip they would return, their canoes were piled higher and higher with Park issued *litter bags given to visitors with instructions on them to please carry garbage and litter out of the park. At the Ranger Station there was no place to get rid of the garbage either. Planes had to be brought in to remove the trash.*

Hence the cash Bay pig list was hatched and placed in view of the visiting public eye. As visitors arrived, soon we had a chorus of expletives' mixed with strong language in reaction. "Why that so-and-so lives down the street from me! He's going to get a phone call from me when I get back from this trip. What a turkey." We were now getting a symphony. As the weeks went on "Geez, she's from my state, town, province. He needs his ears wrung!" Once a man in a low tone asked, "It's been two years. When does my name come off the list?" He was told, when you come back on your way out, stop in with your garbage, then your name will be removed from the Cache Bay Pig List. He smiled and said "See you in a week."

It seemed that the Park now had more concerned volunteers from everywhere taking care of their own trash. Over time the problem waned. Who knows if it was the Pig List, growing public perception, or strong measures of enforcement on the US side. Can and bottle laws were brought in with the newly established Boundary Waters Canoe Area designation. Whatever the reason, the reduction of trash in the wilderness enhanced the experience for everyone.

I worked with and witnessed US wardens in action. We often patrolled together. They had a no nonsense policy. I do know that by the 1980s clean campsites existed as never before both sides of the international boundary I like to think that ripples on the water help both sides of Saganaga Lake. Such places are rare and should be remembered for their beauty.

Tragedy & Rescue

Two Dramas, One Hour - Northern Lights Lake

So much can happen in an hour, and in the space of five miles. The Judge, as he was known, was a popular man. Judge Hachey and his daughters hailed from St. Paul, Minnesota. He and his daughters, Judy and Deb, volunteered to stay and take care of the abandoned fire of a campsite. The fire was out of control and situated on a small island near Arrowhead Point. I went to the resort and used their radio phone to call the fire branch of the Department Lands and Forests. They loved the area and hoped to suppress the fire before it jumped to the red pine on a distant landmark. Arrowhead point was shaped as an arrowhead. They would fight the fire with minnow, or bailing buckets, and wet jackets the best they could.

I would get word to regular fire crew professionals with fire pumps by phone. The Fire Branch advised me they were on the way and also asked if I would wait to assist and ferry equipment and men to the fire site. They would arrive by truck roughly 45 minutes away. As luck had it, a crew was at Nolalu.

Before leaving the site at the resort, I was advised by a guest that her husband was out in the yard and needed assistance. I caught a glimpse of Jack handing an old octagon barreled rifle to a man looking up a giant red pine tree as another man slid down. He explained his long pole was stuck. Both men looked dejected. They had brought their family out on the past weekend, Jack explained, and the kids haven't stopped crying since.

"Our cat, Num Nums, went up and has been up for three days," the man sliding down the tree said. "We tried everything—begging, cat food. He just won't listen."

"We tried the snare," Jack said. "Almost caught him. Now the darned snare is also stuck. We can't take any more time off work. My buddy saw a movie once where branches were shot to get selected pine cones from a tree. He thought I should try that with the cat. I know he could get hurt in falling. Hopefully he'll cling hard to the branch on the way down and have some sort of protection." Filled with hope, they gave this method a try. The first shot split the hot still air and barely nicked the branch. The cat leapt to another branch above.

"Not bad," his friends encouraged. "I better shoot quick. If the cat goes any higher, I won't see him." Taking a deep breath, he released a thunder clap. The jolt didn't shatter the branch, but it jarred the cat loose. In a free fall, the cat descended. We were all surprised that he didn't land on his feet. Unfortunately, the cat would never get the chance to test anymore of his nine lives. He had taken a direct hit.

I can only guess what story went with these men home. They could say the cat was gone or lost when they came out to the resort this day, and all efforts to find poor Num Nums will remain a mystery unsolved.

As for me, I never knew what each day would bring. All I ever learned is that each day brought surprises, some good, some not so good. The day would end with the fire out and the Hacheys covered with black soot.

Some measure of success for a long day.

Lucky to be Alive

After a run-in with the Cut Throat Boat

1980s

Nine o'clock in the morning and the water was as smooth as glass. Filling tanks with outboard gas at the dock, I suddenly heard a boat roaring, a wild sound, and looked out to the reef approximately a half-mile southeast. I could see a boat. Around and around it went in tight circles, crashing and bobbing through its own waves. However, I couldn't see anyone driving the boat.

I got into my boat and headed in that direction. Other boaters began to head out in caution of the whirling dervish. Two men from Quebec, bush workers, raced in first and struck the boat with their bow, knocking the boat one or two times to change its course. We could see a man in the water desperately discarding his life jacket as though it was a red flag enraging a bull. As the boat came closer, the man ducked underwater to avoid a direct hit. The boat nicked him. He resurfaced. Off course, the boat again tightened its circle. The man again attempted to duck under, but the boat struck hard and fast, wild in its fury. This time the man did not resurface. We had to act fast. Where was he?

One of the bush workers caught a glimpse of the man beneath the thrashing waves, about two feet down and sinking. The men moved their boat closer and hauled him out. He had a hole in his throat.

From shore, Ida Richardson had called in ahead in anticipation. An ambulance was on its way. She had a chair waiting in place on the beach. She covered the man in blankets. He was conscious but unable to speak. His eyes were wide with shock. A swarm of onlookers circled around him. "Let him have air," Ida shouted.

The ambulance soon arrived and took the man to Thunder Bay, Ontario.

About three years later, an oil tanker truck pulled into my yard. "Where's your tank?" a smiling young man asked, extending his hand for a shake.

"Wow," I said. "Your company is heavy on public relations consumer confidence."

"You don't remember me, do you?" he asked. "We met a few years ago under unusual circumstance."

My mind was scrambling. After so many contacts over the years, I wondered if this was someone who had learned the error of his ways? Was it hunting, fishing, a fire violation...

"It's me. Ron."

I must have still looked puzzled. Chuckling, he supplied the essential clue by opening his collar. A scar ran down his throat.

"You!" I exclaimed, remembering. "Ha! I'm very glad you made it."

"Yes," he said. "Guess I'm lucky to be alive." He explained what happened that day on the lake. "I had surgery on my throttle hand and shoulder. The turn tension on the outboard motor was set very tight. I let go at full throttle and the boat torqued hard and threw me in the water. Luckily those Quebecers knew what to do." It wasn't luck that saved Ron. It was the Quebecers' quick action and thinking.

Barcelona Rock--Just beyond Silver Falls, Quetico Park

You won't find this place or name on any official map. I remember the name: Frank Barcelona. A priest, trying to hold the canoe steady from the bow when a boy fell out with a life jacket on. Frank Barcelona, the boy's father, without a life jacket and without hesitation, leapt into the raging torrent where a moose drowned just a few days before. Frank leapt in to save his son. Caught between raging torrents, the priest opted to land on a rock. The boy was swept to shore. The priest was on the rock and the boy at hand, but Frank was gone. His ten-year-old son kept asking, "Do you think my dad's okay? Could he make it? Could he be okay?"

The boy asked the hard question we could not answer

OPP and a chopper would be coming from Atikokan to assist and help rescue the priest, who was held captive on the rock. The roar of the torrent was so loud that words could not bridge the gap between us.

The large white pines in the area prevented the helicopter from getting close enough to affect a rescue. We would have to do something from shore. I suggested that a Swede saw could be the answer. If we could fell the large pine on our shore and could aim the angle of the fall to the right of the rock we

would create a bridge from the island to shore. Through sign language, the priest showed he agreed and understood. He covered his head with his hands. We worked on the opposite side on the trunk with only inches on each side of the saw blade. We heard the creak. The police officers had arrived. "What if the tree doesn't land where you intend? We don't want to do harm to the person we're trying to rescue," he said. This caused anxiety; nonetheless, we continued in silence. The creaking was followed by a rush. The tree fell true to target. The priest, with rope around his waist, straddled the log and climbed his way to safety. Except for badly swollen feet, the priest was okay. I remember clasping his hand and thinking, "They will never know. . ."

The tree landed precisely where we wanted

On a somber rainy day eleven days later, they found Frank in a quiet bay more than half a mile beyond the last rapids. With a canoe, we towed him to a point where the coroner and OPP had been designated to wait. As we quietly paddled along loons with mournful sounds cried. We saw a group of Boy Scouts passing by. With shock and awe they were heard to say, "It's a . . . it's a body.".

Conservation Officers roles are dictated by circumstances that often go far beyond enforcement. Each circumstance is part and parcel of duty. Naturally, this was not the last sad drowning circumstance.

Portage Ghosts Can Haunt You

My experiences include unfortunate incomprehensible errors in judgment. Here is a case in point.

Two fathers along with two sons embarked on a journey on the Falls Chain, a series of spectacular falls deep into Quetico Park. Carefully they negotiated the turbulence of high water. They made every portage competently, that is until the last falls. The boys decide to take pictures below the thundering cascade. There, "Fast Eddy" did his work, drawing them ever closer to tons of water overhead. Too late. The boys and their canoe disappeared. When the canoe appeared again, mangled, it bobbed up for an instant only to be pulled under by the current once more.

Fast Eddy often appears innocent on the surface. His treacherous work is done below most falls. Fast Eddy can provide terrible consequences for anyone, brave or innocent, who enters the water below waterfalls. He proved his point one sad day in the 1970s. These dads, unable to help their sons, made it out and returned home with a much heavier load, too difficult to explain.

Two Men without a Canoe

Spring traffic was slow, currents fast. Two men pulled their heavily loaded canoe as far onshore as they could. They were in a hurry as darkness approached, and they wanted to set up for the night on the far end of the portage. Each grabbed a heavy pack from the beached canoe and headed up the path. While away, buoyancy increased and the canoe decided to go it alone. It drifted out into the tumbling water. Like a bumper car, it bounced from rock to rock until it bent in half around a rock. Held by a current, it stayed out midway, while water poured in through a gaping hole. Its ribs broken, it could not escape.

The men returned, looked around, and with hearts beating fast, realized they were onshore miles from nowhere with a paddle but no canoe. In essence they were up a certain creek with ***only*** *a paddle. Not only was the canoe gone but their food pack as well.*

They walked some and picked a grassy spot away from the din and roar of the nearby falls, hoping they could be heard and possibly seen by passersby. The two men spent three days without food or bug repellent before travelling canoeists found them stranded. The Samaritans gave them food and use of their own canoes. This meant heavier loads all around. Two canoes now carried three men. Two other canoes out of the four increased their weight with supplies. Burdens increased for everyone. Now everyone had more to consider than just portages. They had to seek calm waters, being more aware of wind and waves.

One folly increases chances for another in remote circumstances.

Mishaps occur. Cool heads have to prevail. When choices are made, like running rapids, most people recognize the risk. Other times, simple mistakes can play havoc. Buoyancy, a breeze, being in too much of a hurry… These types of occurrences can send you on a canoe trip you never imagined. For these two men, three days waiting had been an ordeal. Six days or more could well have been a disaster. In this incident, success was a matter of timing, plus the excellent choice to reserve strength while waiting, in spite of stomachs growling.

The Man in the Blue Coveralls

I recall crossing the rail portage en route to Saganaga Lake when I saw, stationed on my left, a man and a boy fishing. The man was wearing much too large coveralls. Every so often, people get wet, and sometimes someone might find a note on a paper plate explaining their plight: Sorry, we broke into your cabins. We only did it to get dry clothes. That's all we took. Sorry.

This day, the man had a dry rental boat from Art Madsen's Lodge tied to the shore. I approached the man curiously and said, "Sir, I must get to the point." He had a valid license. I couldn't help but add, "I noticed your coveralls are awfully big."

"Yeah, they had to be really big all right. I borrowed them from Don. He's a big guy. Without these coveralls, I couldn't take my son fishing." He paused and looked closely at me. "What would you do if you were hit by lightning?"

I must have looked surprised and sympathetic. He continued. "We were sleeping in Art's #9 cabin. Last night, the cabin was hit by lightning. Thankfully, I had just gotten my son out of bed to take him to the outhouse. His bed was blown to pieces, splintered, and scorched· We're lucky to be alive· The bolt came down the wall along the floor, went up my feet where I was standing, burned my shorts off and blew seven shards of skin off my back right after I let go of my son's hand· I'm a veterinarian, just glad to be alive·"

He went on· "I'm concerned about what lightning may have done to my enzymes· I understand it can lead to premature aging· For now, I can't stand anything touching my skin· I promised my boy we'd go fishing· · · ·" I now understood· He had had a rough night, so I wished him luck and said goodbye·

Later, Art Madsen pointed to the crease in the cabin's floor down the wall from where lightning came· The etching was a fine line, bold and straight as a dye· Lightning can never tell you why, so it only leaves a signature·

Other people noticing the magic of lightning, Irv Benson at Saganaga has ample photos to show lightning's work· I recall how one piece of plywood ripped from one wall, curled itself like a buzz saw and imbedded itself into another wall· His photos deserve archrival consideration· I know of nothing on this earth that lives or acts in ways as mysterious as lightning·

I myself experienced it once· Eve and I had been visiting and staying with Greg Kemp· Around midnight, we all awoke, jolted by a cannon shot, but not rolling thunder· It was more like a loud cannon shot· We all began yelling at the same time· "Are you okay?"

A sleepy croak came from the other room, "Yeah, I'm okay, but my heart's in my throat·" Eve insisted we look around· "No one will go back to sleep unless we do·" We walked out into the night· To our surprise, dry leaves under the cabin had caught fire· The *fire wasn't much, thankfully, and the propane pipes in the immediate area held fast, for they had dropped loose from their mooring. Even though it was raining, we crept in the crawl space and poured water under the building. Metal water pipes ran under our heads, spanning two bedrooms. These metal pipes extended some thirty feet to the base of the radio tower. I'm not sure if Greg or I would have gone out immediately after the lightning struck. I did learn a lot that night. It's not always the strike but the aftermath of lightening that can pose dangers. The three of us had our hands wrapped around coffee mugs in the morning, listening to Eve laughing and saying, "I told you so! Go look! Go look!" We finally conceded that she did make us look outside, but, on reflection, it may be she had advantage over us.*

Eve was born in Indonesia. She lived half of her life on islands where rain, called monsoons, can pour for months. For me, old times Saganaga told me long ago that when a storm catches you on the lake, head your boat to the lowest, closest point of land, a swamp if possible, where trees are smallest. Avoid high ground, white and red pines, and mineral rock where tall trees grow.

Johnny on the Spot

They say that timing is everything… At the landing, near a portage, a lone vehicle caught my interest. I sauntered over with my camera in hand. Looking across a narrow passage of water, I observed a man getting ready to head out to a greater lake. He was located on the opposite shoreline. While trying to start his boat, I sensed that his motor was flooded, as short bursts of his starter were repeated. After another burst from the starter suddenly hell flames engulfed his fibreglass boat. I couldn't believe what I was seeing! I just happened to be, "Johnny on the Spot", watching a drama unfold!

He leapt from his boat into the water as black plumes rose with red flickering flames. Flames zigzagged on the carpeted floor. When it was prudent, he moved slowly away from the boat. I began yelling as he went back towards the boat, wading neck deep. He obviously was intending to beach the boat onto the muskeg and turfed grass humps on shore. I yelled louder. Eventually, he heard me above the noise of the rapids.

"Get away from the boat. The gas cans are going to go! Save Yourself!"

I don't know if he was worried about insurance, or what he was hoping to accomplish; by then, the boat was totally on fire. Whatever beauty it had, the boat would be no more.

"Move away! Let it go!"

No sense being killed when one of the gas cans could explode at any time. My thoughts were echoed by my shouts. Finally my message was understood and he swam towards the landing.

"I'll meet you there!" I yelled.

Relic boats, tethered nearby, would make retrieval possible. We paddled back to what was left of his boat. We knew that it was all over as we reviewed the scene. We heard a few POPs and sizzles. What was left was easily snuffed out. The remainder looked like a giant potato chip or a burnt rice cake. Resins melted into an abstract blob, and floatation in the hull held up. Fortunately, the fire did not ignite the shore.

He lamented his bad luck and loss.

"Don't," I said. "You're very lucky to be alive."

With the transom gone, the motor could later be retrieved from the river bottom. I wrote a brief account about what I had observed. He came away unscathed after nearly sacrificing himself. He obviously loved his boat very much. No one will ever know if he filled the tanks while they were in the boat, or if expansion from the hot sun caused gasoline to leak onto the floor. Undoubtedly, sparks from cranking his motor had caused the rest. Certainly his insurance company would have a few questions. He'd also likely be greeted by a few questions at home and from neighbors. "Where's your boat?" they might ask. "Did you lose it from your trailer? Did you bring any spare walleye home?"

With thanks he said goodbye, "I'll be back later to clean up the mess."

I looked at the mangled blob propped against the tree. I mused that others might wonder if a spacecraft had crash-landed. Others who viewed the spectacle would likely add their own ideas, never to really know what had taken place.

I must have been hungry because my last thoughts went from pancakes to pizza, maybe because his boat looked like a giant potato chip.

What was left of the boat was propped against a tree as a UFO. You Figure it Out!

Vigil Means around the Clock, not Eight Hours

Every officer who is given enough time in an area of wilderness gains a pulse for activities and potential occurrences, which is near instinctual in harmony with the season. The more time in an area, the more one seems to have success with law enforcement. This applies to night as well as daylight. It's like playing a tape; conditions make little difference. It's the knowledge stored in memories that matters.

Even after twenty years removed; particular roots, stepping stones at portages, and rocks in channels are easy to recall. Deadheads need assessing because they can move around. Ice and wind things considered. Water level can make a safe route hazardous. Many holidays have been ruined by simply following a map. Power boats can have a propeller sheared off, making for a long unwieldy paddle home. Worse yet, a rock can catapult a man foreword and, if the windshield doesn't stop him, more than bad luck can happen.

Here's an example: A bad rock slightly submerged at Windy Point almost ended one man's life on Saganaga Lake. He knew the lake well, but on this day the very windy conditions affected the boat's trajectory causing the propeller to fan the waves with each *rise and fall of white caps. The white rock was obscured in the wild wind. Then came the big crunch. Like a pilot ejected from a crippled jet, the man flew through the air, but not clearly. The boat stopped on the rock. No brakes could ever be more efficient. This incident was further hampered by the fact that the boat was run from the back. Steering cables had become disabled, and one factor lead to another. Flying without wings, the man's body hit the windshield. He was unconscious. How long the motor ground away at the rock is unknown. He was alone, but he eventually woke up, alive, albeit with nasty bruises. As he related the story to me, he said he was lucky.*

We both agreed that hitting the water with the howling winds could have been far worse. Years later, he assisted me in rescuing a girls' canoe group. They lost a canoe that trapped by rocks in rapids. I remembered his words to the group. "One thing you learn about rivers and lakes is they give and take!"

We teach from our own experience and learn from another's experiences. Lake travel is a precise skill, a bit like flying an aircraft. Equipment has to be maintained in a functional, ready state.

The Man in the Swamp

Mid 1980's

A serious report of a man in a swamp arrived at Government Island. "He's standing on shore waving a white rag and holding a pistol in the air. He came from nowhere, yelling, and looks rough. He's hard to understand." Everyone was afraid to approach him so we came here for help. Turi Benson from Canada Customs, Peter Johnson and I would go and investigate. Peter was married to long time resident Marilyn Powell, they owned and operated Saganaga Trading Post on an island adjacent to Government Island. Peter had just checked in with Customs and a load of supplies he was bringing in, when the reports arrived. He willing volunteered to assist.

We travelled to the location described and as reported the man stood on the shore, somewhat incoherent. We coaxed and reluctantly he entered the boat. He babbled that he had found villages but all the people were gone. Turi, a veteran himself said this man needs medical attention and other help as soon as possible. He has trench foot, he's likely of Belgian descent and likely has shell shock, possibly schizophrenic. Empty villages suggest he may have been in the French army when France was in Vietnam.

As darkness approached we knew that this meant a night run, some 30 miles to the landing at Northern Light Lake. We would have an ambulance meet us there around midnight. Having done the trip many times before I knew I could navigate the route by whatever moonlight was offered and the tree line shapes of the shore. One problem would be if I ran out of gas part way there. In the time that it takes to change tanks the boat can change direction and cause a break in that tree line sequence, very confusing. I would make sure my tanks were full before we left. A bigger concern was the erratic behaviour of our passenger. The unknown man would sit beside me in front, Big Pete and Turi would ride immediately behind him to handle any volatility. Pete carried a fish bat.

Nothing I know of quite matches a dream like a long night boat ride. Our passenger became very excitable and manageable as we roused the operators of the rail portage. He talked of a Russian General angry with him for refusing the General's daughter. I found humouring him helped settle him down. As we rounded Arrowhead Point the lights from Jock's Resort meant we were close to accomplishing our mission, only 4 miles to go.

Suddenly there were outbursts. He shouted "Are those Jock's lights? No violence! Don't go there! Communists are waiting! Jock's one of them". I said, "No, Jock's on your side". He seemed interested and calmed down a little. The poor man had endured days lost. It seems he was a transient worker, hired by Jock to run the rail portage. Somehow he strayed from his lone cabin post and got lost in the bush. His revolver was an air pistol; perhaps he went to hunt partridge and got lost. Jock surmised his new man caught a ride with a boater and beat it back to town. It happened before.

The ambulance provided sedation and a night ride to Thunder Bay for assessment and care. Pete's presence was appreciated. He already had put in a full day. Turi had to get back to Government Island, tourists would be arriving early.

Recognizing Impasse

From the dock, we watched canoeists rounding through Jock's Narrows. The July day had been still and hot. Suddenly there was a chill in the air. To the west, dark ominous clouds were preceded by smaller low scudding clouds. This always brings hellacious winds, blinding rain, and great swells.

Suddenly, like a cavalry charge before the main storm arrives, the fast low scudding clouds quickly brought screams and blinding rain to the backs of canoeists whose paddles could not match their speed. Flail as they would, two canoes swamped. Shrieks! I saw four girls in the water. One was quite large. It all happened so fast. There was no horizon or bright sky in the distance, only steady rain as Sam and I launched the patrol boat. Big swells forged through Jock's Narrows. Three girls managed to grasp and hold fast to their canoes. The larger girl wasn't able to catch up. The boat bobbed as we neared her to attempt a rescue, posing problems. Pushed by waves, she could be struck by an uppercut as we drifted towards her, because of the boat's up and down erratic motion.

Soon Sam and I each had an arm and were able to maintain her head above the

gunnels. Holding fast, we swayed as her motion was in sync with the bobbing and swells. Here we were stuck. We pulled for all our worth, but the boat would lift on the wind side, drifting sideways and causing her legs to thrust under the boat. We were in the precarious position of capsizing; if we did, our boat could be on top of her.

People on the dock were yelling support. There was nothing more that we could do in our position; nothing we did could change the impasse. We could not get her into the boat. It was as if she was clinging to a cliff. We were forced to make an unchivalrous decision. Sam would hold on, and I would drag the damsel in distress slowly to the dock. Sometimes in life you make hard decisions. There was no possibility of a grand rescue where we could make it to the dock holding her aloft, chest out of water and cradled nobly in our arms. Neither of us could lift her. We all understood this as we inched our way shoreward.

All in all she seemed grateful as she shivered in the warmth of Custom's office, comforted with blankets and warm tea. Her friends soon came. Everyone was okay.

We all marvelled at how suddenly the wind can come up on a hot July day. In the future, they all promised to keep eyes glued to the sky. They camped on Government Island for the night, singing songs for a while. In the morning, they paddled off, laughing and waving goodbye with their paddles. I suspect that some girls saw the event as the highlight of their canoe trip. I can only hope their account to friends would be relayed in a more romantic version of the rescue.

Oh, Saganaga Lake. Hardly a day with you is ever dull. Your islands lie like puppy dogs in the sun. All is great as long as you watch for clouds and sense the wind that pushes clouds to you. Nature provides signs; it's not all that surprising. The forces of nature that day wrapped the girl around the boat like a hooked magnet. Whatever the day was, it had all ended okay.

Freak Axe-ident

Tough Trip through the minnow ponds

I guess everyone would like to go through life without a stumble, but this is often not the case.

It was one of those days for Irv. He was on his way home and a few portages away in an area known as the Minnow Ponds, a series of ponds with pullover beaver dams north of Saganaga. Being a woodsman with thorough knowledge of all manner of elements and conditions necessary for his livelihood and survival, Irv navigated the Ponds easily. Working in the wilderness, one knows there is no such thing as on-the-job training; experience comes on the job. What you learn in the wilderness makes you more a teacher than a pupil.

Life is often a solitary world for woodsmen. So it was on this particular day that Irv faced a different test than normal endurance. Pond after pond he traversed, portaging first *his canoe and then packsack. He anticipated he'd make it home before dark. After the Ponds, he hit a stretch of trails that would lead to the spot where his motor boat was waiting to take him to his island home. All in all he was perhaps an hour away. The sun indicated that it was about 4:00 PM. He had more than enough daylight left.*

Irv was a Renaissance man: gunsmith, trapper, mechanical innovator, writer, photographer, and welder. His US Lancaster flight navigator uniform hung in his trap line cabin. He often mused that the war years were his most exciting.

Suddenly he stumbled. He knew very well how to walk with a sharpened axe in hand, but as he fell the axe flew from his hand, bounced off a rock and ricocheted, striking his hand and slicing through his mid-palm. His thumb laid back, the space between his palm and thumb bleeding, he folded the open flap of skin down as airtight as possible. Later he recalled, "The bleeding was pretty bad. By the time I reached the last trail, I had lost a lot of blood. Luckily, a creek ran parallel to the trails, and I tried to appease my blood loss by stopping to drink water many times along the trail. When I reached my boat I was weak. I could barely pull the starter rope. I thank my lucky stars that the motor did start. I sent word to the end of the trail. They called back on my CB radio that help was on the way." A realist, Irv added, "From the minute it happened, I knew it would be hours before I received help, so I took photos just in case, to help understanding you see."

He endured. In the hospital at Grand Marais, Minnesota, his lost blood was replaced and his gash stitched. After a few months, his hand healed with full use. Always the teacher he later quipped, "Never carry anything dangerous by its head." I'm not sure if he meant axe, cobra, or cougar. I only know he was a good mentor with sound advice based on experience.

Some might argue that advice is the cheapest commodity in the world. I say advice is invaluable when it comes from a woodsman on Lake Saganaga.

The Waters Boiled Near Cache Bay

In the early 70s Bill Douglas unloaded his cargo of lashed canoes and park enthusiasts at the Quetico Park Ranger Station. Marie issued park permits. Her husband and fellow ranger Jon Nelson was down the lake some nine miles away. The winds blew wild. Word came that canoes lashed at the bow were in trouble. One canoe with a motor was attempting to tow the other canoe. The waves took advantage, swamping the canoe being towed. The motored canoe made shore but those aboard could not assist their friends in the water.

Bill took off and after many attempts from his big blue boat he managed to rescue the stranded without crushing either man. Negotiating big waves was not easy. The water was cold, which meant that these men needed more than rescue. Hypothermia had to be dealt with. One man was much worse than the other. The ordeal was not over. They were brought into the ranger station past sympathetic onlookers near the warmth and glow of the fireplace. Marie Nelson took command.

Marie spoke well of the events. At some point, a tired but happy Marie said, "I drafted two men from the crowd to lie beside the two young men in order to provide warmth. One man, the worst of the two, suddenly and incoherently lunged towards the fireplace and had to be strongly restrained. We stripped him to his shorts and the tub was filled with lukewarm water. I'm happy to say it worked." She continued, "I recently read about hypothermia." Everybody listened attentively. "I'm a teacher, not a nurse. There are times when new knowledge has to be tested." She explained her actions, "There was no time to think, only to act. The young man was mumbling and losing consciousness. I thought, this man is in deep trouble. I knew we would have to work together. "You, fill the tub with lukewarm water. Not too warm, body temperature. Do it quickly. There's no time to waste!" And to the others, "You two, off with his clothes, down to his shorts. Now, everyone grab a limb. Keep them raised. Good! Keep his limbs high. Yes, his trunk should be the first to enter the water. Slowly, gently now. That's it. Keep his arms and legs above the water. We want the cold to move out of his trunk, not from his limbs to his trunk. I knew his arms and legs would more than likely send cold inwardly to his heart", she said. "The heat had left his

body. It likely remained in the greater mass. Therefore the cold had to be thrust outward", Maria reasoned. Whatever the theory, it worked. This man would be able to live life with family and friends.

As the years pass we still hold Marie accountable for saving a young man's life. It's not difficult to imagine that although Marie was a teacher by profession, somewhere along her path she may have wanted to be a nurse. Whatever it was, at times one has to factor in a woman's intuition.

In life you learn from other people. Dicky Powell once said, "Having been born a second generation on this beautiful lake you learn that Saganaga gives a lot, but it also takes."

I learned that all lakes can give or take in certain conditions. As for Marie she was our hero, a prominent figure in the memory I held of people I'd met. Even if 30 or more years have passed, I hold the view that she deserves a medal. I understand that Marie and Jon lived and taught school in canoe country, Atikokan, Ontario. Later they retired and now reside in Thunder Bay, the land of the sleeping giant, Nanabijou.

During the Vietnam War the big waters of Saganaga Lake had their share of canoeists, they arrived in droves. Joan Baez was popular, Kent State University was on the news, and more than a few of the arrivals wore Senator McCarthy pins on their headbands. Buffy St. Marie sang songs about the Eagles of war. Out beyond Jock's narrows, an invisible line separates the waters of the USA and Canada. South of the line, islands large and small dot the lake. It was there that I met Grand Marais Sherriff Light.

"To go or Not to go?"
that was the question in the 70's

Canoe, gear, packs, life jackets were awash and drifting toward shore. No people were found. Usually with time the waters give up what they hide. Every square inch would be patrolled slowly, searching; nooks, crannies, bays, the north and south shores for the next 2 weeks. Volunteers and family members were on the Lake with large boats searching with much concern. Day after day from dawn to sunset and nothing was ever found. Old timers like Jock explained, "Where the Lake is deep, water is very cold, nothing might come up or ever be revealed. Big Sag runs deep!"

Conjecture included other possibilities. His brother was back from Vietnam, they could have been picked up. A big boat was seen in the area amongst the islands. The rumours that ran rampant with the mystery included that they could be living in Canada somewhere. When there are no answers the tales live on.

Another time and another place was my new trap cabin in Petry Ontario. Purchased in 1962 for 700 dollars it was broad axe hewn with dovetail corners. Petry was a whistle stop hamlet, long since abandoned where our nearest neighbours were 11 miles away. I was the mayor of Petry, population 2 in the winter. In the fall Tony Romanchuk and Grandpa Paul Iwasenko, both retired railroaders, occupied an old railroad section house during mosse hunting season. Old world Ukrainians, they explained how the Chinese built the railroads through the Rocky mountains and how the Ukrainians did the same in North-Western Ontario. For awhile Petry had a population of 4. Grandpa Paul was a young 84, hard to match stride for stride. He showed me starting points, portages north to outpost trap shacks miles away, and locations identified with simply an X on a map. There was no snow for skidoos, trails in the early fall had to be walked. Out 15 miles NE, we found a shack in a black spruce bog and settled in for the night. It was not long before we were being chewed alive by red ants. The person who built that shack never peeled the logs, creating the perfect home for the ants. We quickly decided that a night under the stars was going to be the preferable accommodations. Carrying on the next day we were fortunate to find another shack near McCasland Lake. This shack looked much more liveable but strangely it included a well made root cellar and garden tools. It made no

sense since trap shacks are primarily designed as primitive overnight shelter. Twelve by fourteen foot log structures for rest and survival are the norm. This shack had pole roof structure, logs chinked with moss, small windows to keep bears out, 2 bunks and the root cellar.

Some time later back at Petry a story began to unfold. The story was of an uncle with 2 nephews in the 1940's. Back then there was talk in Canada of conscription to bolster its armed forces. Hitler's jack boots were about to stomp over Europe. A secret allied airbase was established at Graham Ontario, surrounded by miles of hard wilderness. Some investigation may have taken place to find the ghost men in the forest who stayed hidden for 4 years. Grandpa Paul remembers that nothing was ever found, only myths and stories persisted. Like the drowning at Saganaga, all I have is a Senator McCarthy pin and memories of a root cellar.

The Sad Trapper

The Siess Lake trapper had a bullet, belt high, behind every door of his remote trapline cabins. Somehow he forgot himself in the scheme of things.

One of four American hunters explained, "We found him with his knees up and hands over his stomach, lying in front of his cabin. The door was slightly opened. We immediately went to the police. He was a great guy once you knew him. We stop in every year when we come up, he treated us like friends. Last time he said vandals were breaking his stuff in his outlying cabins. He was upset that it kept repeating. Using a shack was one thing; smashing and trashing it, was another. It seems that he took one right in the buckle. It's a shame, too much frustration I guess."

Officer Elliot and I heard the story being described by the hunters. The police investigation was over. We too had known the solitary man. On rare fall occasions he offered us coffee. All the things he had were handmade; even his clothing was hand sewn. His furniture made from scraps of nature. He had forsaken city life for nature and the solitude north of Graham. It was a quiet area but there is never anyplace that cannot be reached by man and machines. Some people depreciate whatever they discover in the wilderness. These peculiar sports would never set foot in the woods without machines. They use quads, boats or snowmobiles to reach remote places then damage what they find there. Logging machines with windows or tires smashed, a machine set in motion unmanned, left to crash its way through woods and swamps with dire consequences. These are not idealists protesting on behalf of nature, they are vandals, sick thrill seekers running amok. These idiots are sometimes caught, sometimes not. There is no condoning what the Siess Lake trapper had done, unfortunately he paid the ultimate price.

The door on each trap shack had to be disarmed

Even though all outposts were disarmed it remains a disconcerting to enter such a cabin where test shots can be seen in the door. The traps were set by tying a string in such manner to allow a small opening of the door. If the door was opened all the way a bullet would fire. Conjecture was that this allowed you a small opportunity to change your mind. Did our trapper simply stumble at some point before disarming his trap or forget? No one can ever be sure. We only know the consequences were deadly and he was bothered no more by vandals. It could've been another story for vandals or innocents alike, had anyone else opened those doors. The trapper's friends from the states held certain views on who was at blame. They liked the man who lived his life in the north woods.

Conservation officers learn early that not all things are natural in nature or the woods. There are problems caused by human nature sometimes.

Tragedy on the Firesteel

Officer Steve and I waited at the landing. We could not see who was approaching but we heard a motor behind trees. Expecting to see some hunters who at times could have loaded firearms in boats, we decided to wait. We usually find dangerous practices during hunting season. As the boat approached we could see that the bow was heavy. We shouted over the engine, "What happened?"

They shouted back, "Thank God you're here. We need help!" The man in the bottom of the boat was a blue and white coloured. There was no need to check for a pulse. The way his knees were bent up indicated he could not respond; he could only be respected.

This was not a case of men being careless with firearms. The three men in the boat were made up of 2 brothers, one now deceased and a friend. The friend of the brothers was nearly incoherent. "What will his wife say? It was my idea for this trip. What could I ever tell his family? I may as well go off into the bush and get lost." Shaking and uncontrollable he showed signs of following through on his comments. Shock and hypothermia combined were adding to his grief.

The brother of the deceased had also endured the ordeal. Perhaps he knew he had done all he could trying to save his brother as they were all hustled down the chute clinging to the boat. He told us he tried to grab his brother who had been pitched from the boat, but the raging water pulled him under.

Something in this man was strong. We asked and posed a problem for him. "Your friend is in need of help. Can you help drive him to the resort? His hypothermia needs attention. When you get to the resort they have a radiophone. Here is the phone number for help." He agreed that he would be able to help. He realized that his friend was not out of the woods yet. Sometimes in life there is an opportunity for at least partial redemption.

We told him that when we got to the highway our radio would work and we could double check to see if the nurse or ambulance made it to the resort. This would save a lot of time for all concerned. We assured him that we would see to his brother, and that the Ontario provincial police would be in contact with him.

All accidents usually possess similar elements. The long drive to the police give us time to ponder what had happened out there. Was this a case of stalled motor, a faulty wire or frozen gas line? What we knew for certain was that the Firesteel Rapids was no place to ride. It had a steep down slope with many boulders. The water moved at incredible speed. It wasn't too difficult to recognize some of the factors in this ordeal. The Firesteel was formidable. Boats on the high side were meant to go upstream. Later we found out that initially their motor started and cranking furiously the boat was drawn into less calm water. Paddles were now futile as this watery escalator was wild and had full control. There was no stop button as they hurtled down the chute, twisting, turning, and bumping into submerged rocks. Everything in life was in the hands of fate and even if they had no time to think about consequences somehow they knew the results would not be good. It ended with one in the water and missing. He would be found later, too late for help. Regardless of their feelings or injuries, the other two would have to carry him out.

Perhaps years on the farm in Wisconsin, coupled with the desperation he felt made the task of carrying his brother over the portage possible. They had to reach the other boat moored there and get to their vehicle at the landing. Fuelled by desperation they made it to find Conservation officers waiting. The chance of such a meeting in miles of wilderness is infinitely remote.

As we entered the highway, Ivan's voice crackled over the radio. "Yes, ambulance was dispatched. Should be at the resort by now. Over and out." As we made our way in to Upsala we spotted the Ontario Provincial Police cruiser at the Cafe. The officer was just coming outside. "Hey, what brings you boys in green here so early in the day? Coffee and donuts?"

"No, we already put in a day. We brought work for you." The police man's smile said are you guys serious? It quickly changed to a frown when he realized we were. We began the process of dealing with the cargo in the back of our truck.

Where did it happen? What are the details? You mean the three went down the

Firesteel and two survived? Yeah, hard to believe. The police often do cross assist with conservation officers. This was an aftermath situation. In the fall it is not unusual for the public to see blue and green together. Drinking while fishing, using firearms and hunting with liquor are all risk factors that can lead to other stories. Today's event only involved nature's dark side. Fog and mist caused ice in the carburetor of the engine. All elements collided at a place where there was no room for error.

Moving Forwards - Backwards!

The Evening I Forgot to Bring My Bowman

I would like to say mistakes never happen, but that would not be true. This particular evening I was returning to Saganaga in falling darkness with heavy packs. I thought I would save time by not taking the portage and running the S-shaped rapids between Devils Elbow and Saganaga Lake. I had run these rapids before with Ted in the bow steering the canoe into the proper chute with his deep hooking paddle stroke. I was alone on this trip and with a heavy load in the bow I discovered I could not manage the sharp manoeuvres needed to avoid the wild grindstones on the way down. Midway down the rapids I found myself stranded on rocks with white water shooting by. It was a shaky predicament with no end in sight and no way of getting to shore, not a place that I wanted to spend the night. With no time for lengthy contemplating I put both hands on the gunnels and rocked the shuddering canoe from side to side. A moment later the canoe spun like it was launched by a catapult and I found myself careening down the rapids backward like I was riding a wild bronco.

Drifting in the calm water at the bottom of the rapids I felt a giddy moment of relief and a sense of lucky satisfaction. My aluminum canoe had a few bruises but was intact, and the load safe and dry. I wondered what Ted would have thought had he seen my solo attempt.

I finished the trip back to Government Island with darkness deepening. I decided not to tell my wife Eveline of my adventure when I saw her after 4 days alone in the bush. She had my favorite, sweet and sour walleyes waiting for me, and I wanted to enjoy my dinner. In her Dutch Indonesian accent she asked, "How was your trip Yonny?". Truthfully I answered her, "The trip was great!" She seemed puzzled when I told her that her locks looked nice with their S curves. I didn't mention anything about the S curved rapids.

A Sad Trip Home

It was an unusual sight and scene as 2 figures emerged from the woods. The man's face masked in pain was from more than his swollen bleeding feet. The wind buffeting trees was howling on the lake. The lone vehicle at the landing indicated New York State. OPP Constable Crow and I were on joint patrol and we had in tow their detachment's patrol boat. We asked "Sir, are you all right?"

"No Sir, I have a big problem", came the reply.

Chance and happenstance had collided at this remote lake and boat launch landing. In minutes we could have gone when we heard the sounds coming from the thick brush. This man was a Marine, on leave. "My 2 boys and I came north to go fishing", trembling, "We were having a great time in a quiet bay when we noticed a dark cloud in the distance. We decided to make it back to our island campsite. Suddenly the waves became wild and swamped the boat. We all ended up in the water. We had life jackets on but the wind forced us to the far end of the lake. We were in the water a long time. About 100 yards from shore my older son, nearly 13, called out. His head went down. I got my younger son on shore and I went back. I brought him out but he was limp. Nothing I tried worked. Mouth to mouth, nothing revived him. We had no choice, to get back here we had to walk the shore all the way around the lake. We were trying hard to make it before dark. We were wet when we started out, my soggy shoes fell off. We walked many miles to get here. I'm worried about a bear. My son is on shore. We hung a yellow raincoat to a tree above him. Do you think your boat could retrieve him? We'll wait here in the car till you get back."

Launching the boat was not easy. We pushed and poked our way out into the waves. Once we were satisfied that we were deep enough we started the motor. We took the waves and swells at a three-quarter angle, a circuitous route to where we were headed.

Navigating was slow but we made it to the far end of the lake. As described we passed a small island tent site. Eerily offshore, a small duckboat nearly on end was bobbing up and down like a button, synchronizing with the waves. The bizarre image told its own story.

Without prejudice this light aluminum duckboat was not designed for this big lake, especially in these conditions. Wearing life jackets help your chance of survival but there is no guarantee since there are always other factors in play.

We continued to scan the shore and eventually the bright yellow rain jacket came into view. Every drowning leaves an impression that remains throughout the years. This one was the white shoes that exaggerated the gangly stage of the 13 year old boy.

We retrieved the boy and brought him to the landing. The aftermath of the tragedy was not yet over. His Dad requested the nearest telephone. Enroute we stopped at the nearest logging camp. A telephone was on the hallway wall. We could hear the conversation, "We'll be coming home right away…me and Donny…we had an accident". "What do you mean?" A scream, "Jerry's not coming back!!?"

This man, who seemed so composed, so strong given the ordeal, perhaps also in shock, became broken in spirit and grief, wept. He said "I've to get back home, Thanks". He assured us he was able to drive.

I formed a personal opinion on that day. I decided that people under so much stress should have friends or others fly up and drive them home.

Lighter Moments

"Wow, an early morning Thumbs Up!"

Exclaimed Officer Bob

Nero Was Officer Dave's Hero

In my career, I often worked with Dave, and at times, with his dog, Nero. Officer Dave was a wildlife supervisor, who delighted in our being older than the other officers in the crew. We often volunteered to do the most out of the way canoe trips to the most inaccessible lakes. Fall hunting season spared no one. BJ Wall would assume a supervisory role in Dave's place so that we could make our trip.

"Our Officers always look sharp, then Nero and you guys walk in and look like you should have sunk with the Titanic"

Dave's favorite quip was, "We have whiskers". We patrolled remote locations by canoe, in places where hunters never thought they would see an officer. Many similar trips had been successful in terms of enforcement and some of the more serious violations were encountered, like illegal hunting before season. We always reasoned that those who play farthest away at remote fly in camps by now expected aircraft checks, but never in their wildest dreams would they expect enforcement via canoe. Once with Nero, we had success along the Quetico area of the

Boundary Waters. On that occasion we walked over land to a site where non-resident hunters had a moose down. They were definitely surprised.

"Canadian wardens, huh? Boy you guys really get around. Lucky we shot this moose on our side."

Soon a man came over, shook our hand, and departed. His duck boat sped away toward his group of hunters. Sounds from a boat carry well over water. Their words came clearly. "Those guys aren't lost. They're Canadian wardens. They came out of the bush, out of nowhere with a bloodhound. "

When violations take place, public relations have their place in enforcement. In my deputy years, I had a trap line cabin on Saganaga, a place where officers and their dogs could sleep in comfort.

One night, Dave told me about Nero. His police awards, how he tracked lost children, and how he tracked criminal elements successfully. Nero was a good ole boy. Although Dave didn't explain how he got so many wrinkles, I think I figured that out by myself. As Nero and I struggled over the bed, I thought, Darwin had his theories regarding evolution. Why should the world not have mine?

When it came time to sleep, Nero believed if he was on the bed first, the bed was his. Bracing my back against Nero with my feet on the wall, I hoped he might share, but he

wasn't about to give up any of the bed. I began to notice that with each push he did not budge; however, his hide did, like an old accordion. The more I pushed, the more wrinkled he became.

I wrote letters to the Smithsonian Institute, World Press and scientific community years ago explaining my findings as to why bloodhounds are so wrinkled. Dr. Suzuki never did respond. I even thought that perhaps I'd send a letter to Al Gore. Someone had to listen!

I recall telling Dave that long ago night, but he was already sleeping with a smile on his face. Nero as a friend was great, but he did have boundaries!

I have much to say about my life on the border. My friends are equal in numbers and in quality. Most letters I get are from the USA. As an average 50/50 is a great number. Distance and time has not changed our friendships of thirty or more years. Friendship has no borders, and memories are the reward.

Today as I reminisce about Nero, I can't help but wonder, had he met my dog Gypsy, would he have been my wonderful doggy-in-law?

Moon Over Madeline Lake

At times, my duty included transporting Junior Rangers. The ministry had a program involving camps in Ontario during summer holidays. Free room and board and a small wage allowed students to gain bush knowledge and wilderness experience. Madeline Lake held such a camp situated within one mile of Northern Light Lake. The students who attended were mostly high-spirited city kids. This day's duties involved a group outing to clean campsites and clear windblown portages. Five girls with litterbags would have a treat. They piled into the patrol boat, the girls mindful that this boat carried ministry emblems and thus they knew they would have to behave accordingly.

This day was glassy calm on Northern Light Lake. Heading southwest a mile or two beyond Arrowhead point, we were nearing a view of the ancient Indian rock painting. As we stopped, a large encampment of boys began hooting and hollering at the girls. Rather than resisting, my Rangerettes added their own response. The boys seemed perfectly choreographed, a dozen or more standing in ledge. Perhaps they thought if these girls liked rock paintings, they might appreciate some anatomy lessons. In unison a dozen did an about face, lowering their drawers to show with their backsides where the sun doesn't shine while the others cheered.

By day's end, the last of our campsites clean, the boat loaded with litterbags full, we left Wartells Lake, near the Falls, and headed back to camp. I'm sure that many stayed up late swapping adventures and experiences of the day's experiences well into the night, as the moon rose over Madeline Lake.

I can only assume that my particular group did eventually fall asleep with smiles on their faces.

The Hills Were Alive with the Sounds of Gypsy

Gypsy was no Pavarotti but she was a diva. Half hound, half opera singer, she would entertain visitors to Saganaga. I adopted her at an early age from the US Forest Service on the Gunflint Trail. Her greatest musical fans were the Boy Scouts of America and church groups. She hit notes unlike any other canine. She didn't have a great repertoire, but brought joy to the ears of many. Her magic came from her soul. The tilt of her head, her regal pose, and the grandeur of her notes, rose higher than Horsetail Falls and echoed amongst the hills. Her song "AH-Woooo" could melt the soul and bring tears to any aficionados of music.

She was a purist that would not sell her soul for money or even a dog biscuit. She would sing on cue as a welcome to Saganaga Lake. She could sing as she'd cling to a boat or *a skidoo with grace. Her world was her stage, and she was an inspiration all the way to Northern Light Lake. She sang "AH-Wooo" for all who came, regardless of creed, colour, religion, gender, social status or political affiliation. Eveline raised her that way, without a bone of prejudice in body, soul, or dog dish. Gypsy learned well from Eveline. They both were goodwill ambassadors!*

Gypsy was a great singer and a diplomat. You could say she was a dual citizen. Gypsy had a jolly youth. In defence of her young years, unsubstantiated gossip or rumours never resulted in court or conviction. Gypsy was never charged with stealing sandwiches from a person's backpack left on the dock at Government Island while that person was being processed by Customs. True, she was observed running and being chased around the island with a bag in her jaws. Witnesses claimed that the bag had holes, but when confronted even they could not identify shreds with any certainty. To cite a famous defense: "If the gloves don't fit you must acquit!" My defense of Gypsy was similar. "Shreds do not make a bag hole, whole; therefore, Gypsy must go free! If justice wanted to pursue matters, my jury selection would insist on a pool of church groups and Boy Scout canoeists. I would insist on a venue for court to be held directly beneath Horsetail Falls. When the jury would decide the verdict, it would be innocent. Otherwise, I would sue on the grounds of Gypsy's celebrity. NO! She would not be forced to testify in her own defense; because a burp is not evidence!

The Legend of Waffleback

Conservation officers often innovate and share techniques for catching poachers. One technique that we realized was very effective was patrolling in a group. A wary poacher might hide their activities as soon as they spot a single or couple of people approaching, but a small group rarely raised the alarm. The element of surprise was always an advantage. In preparation for a day of group enforcement a few officers arrived to use the guest house. I pulled out cots in our guest house but was short one mattress. It was late Friday night and Eveline had supper ready. For dessert Eve provided homemade Saki, a concoction made of rice, a powerful kind of punch popular in Indonesia and Japan. We drank it hot. Tired, some of the guys thought a second cup might help them sleep. Tomorrow would be a busy weekend. Some of the men looked exceptionally tired as they struggled up the hill to the guest house.

While officers are a hardy lot, they were fatigued from long hours and miles of driving. They literally crashed on cots covered with colorful blankets. Steve cussed me in the morning. He was stiff. With indignation he showed me his back which looked like a waffle. He had slept on the cot where I hadn't placed a mattress. He said, "My back feels broken". I said, "Have a coffee. You'll be fine." Some officers said his back looked like laminate. Another officer said, "Look at it this way Steve, you're probably the most decorated officer on the team." The officer ducked as a wet towel flew past his head.

Soon we were roaring down Northern Light Lake with snow machine throttles wide open. Some of us slowed as we encountered huge snow drifts. Machines were bouncing high. To our total surprise Steve revealed a new tactic. He decided to launch a missile. We saw a blur go by. It stood completely on end and upright sliding on a helmet. It destroyed a large

We learned,
Properly launched a Waffleback can destroy an angler's snowfort

drift. The missile was Steve himself. Knowing that Steve was all right we wondered, "Could we utilize this technique to smash a crooked angler's snow fort?" There was no need to deploy the waffle rocket. We handled a lot of violations that weekend. We decided that Steve's technique was something that should be sworn to secrecy in the event that poachers got worse in the future. For technical and security reasons, the officer's full name and technique cannot be revealed because NASA is negotiating with Steve, who goes by the code name Elliott. For security reasons, he was later transferred to Fur Management.

Down East Brass ...
Astutely recognized a man who could use his head

Under the Guise of a Fur Management Officer - S.E. became
SECRET AGENT S.E. WAFFLEBACK

Secret Agent S·E·

Officer S·E· cannot be named for fear of retaliation·

We crossed paths early one morning on the steps of the courthouse; I was coming, he was leaving· While on the steps of the courthouse he appeared tired and flushed· He had spent most of the night cleaning up road killed moose· With little sleep he drove to Thunder Bay to testify; a duty that requires proper and prompt attendance· He managed to get to court on time; 9:00a·m sharp·

"Steve", I asked, "how did things go?" "The pits", he replied· I immediately assumed my most pitiful and sympathetic look· "What happened?" I asked· Steve replied, "Instead of addressing Justice Don as Your Worship during the swearing in, I called him YOUR MAJESTY!"

Nearly convulsing, my sympathy restrained me· Quickly I consoled him· "Steve, what did The Justice say?" "Well, he looked at me with a quizzical look from his lofty perch·

At first he seemed very stern and was nodding his head· Then he smiled and said, "To err is human"· "Steve, Steve, it's not as though you were deliberately perjurous, it could have been far worse· Your address was not demeaning, imagine if you had called him "Your Holy Eminence"· I'll never know why my attempts did not work· Perhaps laughing with empathy does not work··· I heard his truck door shut and saw him

"Do you swear to tell the truth?"
"Yes, Your Majesty"

It may be the only time in his career he will be a Majesty

heading west.

The most I can say about Steve is from vague recollection. He came from Eastern Ontario; Elliot Lake, Haley Berry or possibly the townships of Kincardine or Minden. I do recall that his wife baked great pies, and that he had attended Aylmer Police College. We worked together ninety miles northwest on Highway 11, during the 80s. He never shot ducks while they were swimming, and today loves fishing in the French River areas.

Now it was my turn to attend court. The courtroom was crowded with activity. Some were smiling with tears in their eyes. I didn't ask why, because I knew that court that day had been a royal occasion.

In the docket, the judge allowed me to refresh my memories from my field notebooks. Disjointed jottings came out like this (some thought on purpose). I knew that delivering testimony is serious business. Officer credibility is at stake. My account of events nearly caused an outburst. "From my notes, Officer Elliot and I, well after midnight, opened the gate to the Upsula dumpsite. With flashlights, we approached lights out, to the dump proper. After several moments we heard a noise, "and our attention was drawn to a tree. We were surprised to find Mr. Raven up a tree." The courtroom, police, and others erupted into laughter. Struggling to maintain a solemn composure I blurted out, "Mr. Daniel Raven, Your Worship!" He gave me a knowing look, and a faint smile on his face implied "continue Officer". We asked Mr. Raven why he was up a tree with a flashlight, and a powerful loaded rifle so late at night. We reminded him that No Hunting signs were displayed. He explained that he wasn't really hunting; he carried his gun for protection, and claimed he had walked in at daylight to dispose of garbage. While there, a skunk came by and forced him to seek refuge up a tree. "With a flashlight?", asked The Justice, obviously reaching the same conclusion which Steve and I had.

The charges; hunting at night, hunting within 400 metres of a dump, having a loaded and uncased firearm after sunset, all stuck. Mr. Raven was found to be in violation on all counts. He was not allowed to "crow" about his clandestine hunting efforts. Besides he never passed the sniff test and we didn't find any evidence to corroborate the evidence that a skunk had made him do it! The gate was locked when he entered the dump, and there was no reason to have a firearm to enter the dump. There were fair warning signs posted: No Hunting signs were all around, including at the site itself. A rifle with a flashlight was the best evidence of all. "If you carried it in during daylight there had to be a reason!", said The Judge.

"Your Honor,
We found
Mr. Raven night hunting from a tree"

The case concluded with Mr. Raven's wallet echoing. I noticed a lot of smiles and nodding heads as I left the courtroom. After court some policemen asked me, "John, do you always render your notes and dispositions to the courts that way?" "Not always", I replied. "My objective was to tell the truth, and in this case I did it my way."

Later at Upsula, Steve and I recounted the day's events, and that our day in court had been a day for royalty and ravens.

The Tribunal of Red

There was much talk around the water cooler. Red had been seen in the district manager's office many times lately. Conjecture was growing amongst the office staff. I decided to put my spin on things…

Deep in the belly of Natural Resources, the district managers wanted answers.

"How did your bike get smashed in the middle of a railroad track?" they glared on a in a need-to-know no-nonsense basis. It was a harrowing experience as they stared boldly with pads and pencils. It was as scary as any job interview. This was more like a dual in the sun.

Red wondered, "Maybe if I tell them a joke they'll lighten up?"

Nah. Their faces were frozen.

"Well?" asked the manager.

"Well?" was a good beginning. "Thanks for asking. I feel fine actually, fit as a fiddle, raring to go catch bad coyotes." Feeling hopeful he asked, "Can I go now?"

"NO! Answer the question. Explain how a bike, YOUR bike, got smashed in the middle of the railroad tracks."

Red wondered why they were so rigid and tenacious. They didn't look like clones, and the answers they sought were inevitably simple. "A train is much more capable to smash a bike; the sheer mass and weight of a train is in its favor, add speed and logic and anyone can imagine what would happen."

"Never mind the —. We want a simple answer. How did the bike wind up on the tracks?"

"It didn't wind up on the tracks. It's impossible, right? Didn't we all agree that it was smashed? Would it not be seen as unreasonable that having been smashed it could never wind up again, if it was nothing more than twisted metal, broken glass, loose nuts and bolts, and wee bitty pieces? Who then can describe the truth better than I? I'll tell you what happened. On patrol I was all alone without a telephone. Near a railroad trestle, where there was a peat moss bog below, I parked my bike well away from the tracks on a cut bank. My attention was drawn to an unusual trail of huge footprints which led away from the trestle. Sometimes things happen so fast. I heard the roar of a train thundering through the hills. To my dismay, with the earth trembling, I watched my bike tumble as the cut bank gave way, causing my bike to land in the middle of the tracks. While looking at a huge footprint, I heard a blood-curdling scream from somewhere below. For a fleeting moment I saw a hairy creature running down a hill and a girl's arms waving frantically. I knew I had to make a hasty decision. I could save my bike or save the

girl. It was a tough decision... I plunged into the dark abyss not knowing what to expect. My feet barely touching the ground, I flew into Bigfoot's midriff. As he lay panting on the ground, I turned my attention to the girl. In the mean time Bigfoot escaped. I would have pursued him, but my pen was gone. I knew I would be unable to write him up."

"Give this man a box of pens!" exclaimed the manager.

Red continued, "My attention returned to the girl. She was frightened, but not hurt. I wanted to get her back to family and friends. Once we reached the truck she said that she was hungry. I reached into my emergency supplies and handed her the last of my twizzlers. As luck would have it, my truck wouldn't start. Within moments, a long haul trucker stopped; I presumed to render assistance... To my surprise, the girl jumped in and they headed west. There went my witness."

By now sympathetic, all three managers voiced a delicate question, "Where then is your proof?"

"Here's your proof. I managed to retrieve my pen."

Red plunked it on the table, and there in the clasp were three long strands of hair along with a clump of peat moss. All managers agreed to replace not only his twizzlers, but also to get him a brand new truck and quad.

Red had won the day!

Ayatollah Morning

The day started much the same as any other day. Morning crowds on the dock were receiving clearance, customs was glued to Government Island, and Officer Turi was very busy. (Turi, pronounced Turee, came from a long line of ancestors, the Bengstones, from the land of the Vikings). Often I would do dock and aircraft checks for illegal game fish. In the summer, crowds and pressure usually diminished around noon. I would then patrol the rest of the day by boat. I had more of a Huckleberry existence than was the situation of a Canadian customs officer tied to his station.

Living on an island, serving different functions, we officers naturally supported each other. At Saganaga Lake, we worked together more than with our respective fellow officers. We were all the law there was. We represented Canada and the Province of Ontario; with Customs officials wearing white and black and I wearing my new army green uniform. Sometimes our work allowed for public relations, bantering and mingling with the crowd, sharing information and listening to fish stories from anglers and tourists.

On this day, Turi was processing a young couple while I was engaged with a guide. At some point, a dark haired girl stared at me, seeming to want anonymity on the far side of the dock. A tall young man seemed to be consoling her, but was glancing towards me in a curious way. It was with some apprehension that I looked downward. My new and latest uniform seemed right. My brass buttons shined, my boots were polished and all things were zipped up just right. I wondered and dismissed any notion that either one of us had ever met before; but still she seemed to cower. She had an accent and he had a drawl, but they were both definitely American. UW on his sweater caused me to think the initials were from a university. Perhaps Wisconsin? Hurriedly, they left by canoe.

Whatever I wondered would have to wait. Turi, at customs was swamped with processing, but after a half-hour or so, during a lull moment, the smiling, laughing customs officer piqued my interest in the couple even more. "I know you're dying to know what went on with that couple", chuckled Turi. "She was scared of you and your uniform. She saw you and had glimpses of Ayatollah! She didn't see you come down the dock, and when she did she was startled and had a moment of panic. She's studying in the US but comes from Iran. She's even afraid in the States because of the US hostage crisis going on in Iran. You reminded her vividly of police or military in Ayatollah's regime, and she was stunned to see Iranian officers on the Canadian border."

While I had no doubt that Turi was not giving a fictional account, I also knew from the look on his face that he enjoyed telling it. While we enjoyed the humour of it all, for the girl from Iran there was no humour at all. Her reality was from a different experience and perspective.

Did Ayatollah visit Saganaga Lake on the US/Canada border?

Maybe not but his fear did!

Customs chided, "We don't have that problem with our image because of the color of our uniforms!"

Windy City Air

One day in 1973 I was working the dock with Officer Greg at Customs on Government Island, Saganaga Lake. The morning rush was nearly over, a few live bait infractions, no drug seizures, when out of the blue a vintage aircraft came for clearance to enter Canada. It was definitely not Airforce One. A young boisterous crew popped out of the hatch onto the wing and onto the dock. They were in a fun mood, clowning for attention, waving at departing canoeists, smiling and then the theatrics began. "This place reminds me of a dock in Mexico". "Yeah, man, did we get turned around" "Yahoo!" "O Whee!" The banter went on. "Say are we in Mexico?" Haw ha. "We wanna go fishin', are you guys Mexican?" "How long is this gonna take?"

Greg responded: "Si gringo. Long enough for you to completely unload everything from the plane onto the dock"

"Shoot man, we were only kidding, we know that, all the stuff on the dock?"

"Yes sir, all the stuff on the dock, really, no kidding, no kidding" The small audience paddled off into the sun laughing and cheering.

I think if Ed Sullivan would have been there he would have said it was a really good Sheew, or was that show? In the end even Gypsy wagged her tail.

Waltzes with Dogs

No one ever said that enforcement had to be quick or easy.

"I am the land, forests and lakes! I am the King of the north!" the monarch proclaimed vociferously. He'd had more than enough to drink. Built like a tank his friends clung to him. Leering, laughing and lurching he demanded respect. Bumping, grinding, and mood swings went from outbursts to grinning and more proclamations. Northerners understand patience. Time would abate the storm. There was no need to allow any carnage; the man was simply overly drunk, strong as a bull and hard to control. This village had neither doctors nor police. Folks dealt with things their own way, knowing that tomorrow would be different. Entertainment was often each other's shenanigans. These became things to talk about on long winter *nights; the wilder the tales the better. Whatever went on was theirs, not for outsiders, as outsiders had their own sense of social interaction. They did try to preserve each other whatever might transpire. "What happens here belongs here, nowhere else!" I suppose in part it was much like a tribe. In ritual a leader could be possessed or in a trance brought on by an unknown quantity of spirits.*

Did their leader while possessed not appear godlike? A king of northern lakes, land, and streams? Did visions of him not manifest from the supernatural world? Where then to anyone's doubt did the weaving power of the dance come from? Does such spontaneous outbursts not prove that here too the village of the north has some remnants of the lost tribes of mankind. "What luck brought me to witness this?" I thought, as the crowd shouted in cadence, "Easy! Stop! Hold the devil from himself!" The chant from the villagers went on. "Cool it man! Stop!" A curious calm followed as though dark storm clouds had departed.

I recall a precise moment when a great dark blur came out of nowhere. "Ouch! Yow! Wow!" yelled the King. A great shepherd had entered the fray, who nipped and clung to the rear of his blue jeans. I was amazed to see the effects when man's nature and the forces of nature collide. It seems that many aspects of ritual, even in modern times, carries the need for some kind of sacrifice. The King accordingly did all he could to sacrifice himself in front of his people. In the end, what I admire about the King of Graham North, is that unlike other kings of ancient times, his end goal was noble, albeit sore. He did nothing to sacrifice his subjects; he did not utilize slaves nor throw people or goats off cliffs.

In hindsight, I must say that the King gave of himself and his blue jeans. No deed can be nobler than that, especially when one considers the price of blue jeans today. Not only was sacrifice ultimate, it was also humbling.

Suddenly he stopped, came over and shook my hand. The jig was up!

Some Events Had Humour

On a joint patrol with Ted Chisholm, also known as Red Fox, without a canoe, we walked over portages, our silhouettes dark on the shoreline holding the last light of day. Long days and five o'clock shadows no doubt matched the shadow of No Name Lake. Truth was, we were worse for wear. Forced to identify ourselves to two fishermen in a rental canoe, from shoreline we showed our badges and requested they come to us. Most often there would be a response. No, these fishermen simply stared in our direction. Without movement, quiet and still lines lay in the water. No action from either of us. No one moved. More like a stunned silence. Maintaining our composure, we became much more vociferous and shouted, "Ontario Conservation Officers!" We knew "Don't make us come to you" wouldn't work. We had no means, save for Ted, who was a good swimmer.

"Suspicious?" "Yup! Something's wrong", he whispered.

Eventually compliance came. Our American cousins paddled over and produced licenses, explaining that they didn't understand the term Conservation Officer. They were familiar with Warden. We asked, "Why did you take so long to respond and come to us, especially due to the fact that you had done everything right, license and all?" We eventually got the most unexpected answer. It seems that the woods had caused it all. The wide-eyed young men asked, "Have you ever seen the movie Deliverance?"

Mystery solved.

Later I shaved and Ted trimmed his beard.

Duty calls.

True Tales of Quetico

It is not unusual for city kids to find nature strange and mysterious· · ·

A young couple heard mournful calls for help all night long while camped in their tent on an island· I recalled loons long calling that seemed to coincide with their story· I never dismissed things offhand· Last night had been hot and still at Northern Light Lake, and many loons had been observed gathering·

Today I was at Cache Bay, Quetico Park visiting the park rangers· The border boundary zigzags west along very narrow waters towards Ottertrack Lake, a popular route for canoeists· As I was about to say goodbye to Terry, his wife, and pet rabbits (all manning the ranger station), six girls came paddling furiously· They were near hyperventilating and wide-eyed· Their orange life vests were stencilled with L & F; Lands and Forest· They were Junior Rangers· They had been out cleaning campsites and brushing out portages· They were 17 years old, and often experiencing life in the woods for the first time· Most came from large eastern cities· I suspected they had encountered a bear, the monster Ogee-Pogi, or the lynx-serpent which natives call Mishipijou—maybe even a Sasquatch. Red rock pictographs of painted creatures are seen along the vast area of Quetico and beyond.

Calming down, the leader began to explain with interruptions coming from her younger charges. She said, "It's my second year as a Junior Ranger. We never would have believed it had we not seen it—and we all saw it." All eyes were locked on hers, their faces flushed like tomatoes as they nodded. It became apparent that surely what they had seen was real and traumatic, perhaps even unbelievable. One girl looked away. She was trembling and at times her body was heaving.

"Easy. Easy. It's okay."

I knew that whatever had happened had to be handled with sensitivity and patience. Slowly she turned, removing hands from her face. We were shocked to find her incoherent yet laughing. What they had seen was too indescribable for words alone.

What the girls had seen on a portage marked with bronze boundary markers, were a man and a woman, each wearing boots, a hat, holster with gun on waists. They wore nothing else. No one spoke.

We could only surmise they had come from the west, perhaps even the Wild West. Being a common portage, and with nothing in the Fish and Game Act, a small tent on the US side was out of jurisdiction. Terry and I agreed: There was nothing to pursue. Besides those strangers seemed straightforward with nothing to hide.

At least the girls had a tale to tell of their adventures in the northwoods.

Uniforms

I could have replied, "Of course you idiot, it's my uniform. Who else is wearing it?" Instead I elected to be collected, knowing in time he would stop laughing.

My earliest uniforms were worn with pride no matter how they fit. Such hand me downs, chopped down for short or stouter men may have been years ahead for inspiring trends today. The years 1967 to 1970 did have moments when I pondered what disgraces I could inflict on my uniform. Here I was on duty on the high profile international boundary. I had just handed a man a ticket when he convulsed into laughter.

"Sir, do you think getting a ticket is funny?" I queried.

"Ah. No. No. It's not the ticket," he said. "It's your uniform!" After the man in the boat left, my wife said with her little Dutch accent, "What's the matter Yonny?" She too burst out laughing. "Don't feel bad Yonny, you made someone laugh and be happy today." Lucky for him I holstered my pen..

In Canada, a deputy has no right to" bare" arms, save for on hot days; then, they may roll up their sleeves. The truth of the matter is that unlike the United States Constitution, the right to bear arms is not entrenched. Only policemen and those under special permit are allowed to carry handguns. Deputy conservation officers rely on their wits and pens to enforce the regulations.

Public Relations Is a Skill That Must Be Honed

Today was a bit unusual, not a normal patrol. The big brass was coming.

Ontario Natural Resources is comprised of many services. Today the lands branch was coming by aircraft. "Your boss wants you to assist," I was told. I realized then and there that while I lived on an island, no man was an island. One of the most powerful ingredients a young warden must possess is curiosity and wanderlust.

My day was dashed by a message. No chasing bad guys today. Why is life so cruel? Ahh, well. Maybe this boss will give my boss a good report. A public relations day.

We loaded up after the plane arrived and sped off to a splendid cabin and island location. Andrew and Dorothy owned their paradise in Ontario. They lived in Chicago, an affable couple that were the epitome of how opposites attract and it showed immediately. Andy had a big smile and shook and shook his hand. He was top notch, as a salesman, now retired. Dorothy was a fair lady, actually a proper southern belle. She had distinct charm, a Dixie sound that garnered respect and attention. At home she tolerated being called Dot. In formal settings, she expected Dorothy.

It has been said that Canadians are reputed to be polite. If so, I thought, Dorothy *was the teacher. At the dock, I introduced Boss first to Andrew, his hand extended. Should I introduce ladies first to each other then Boss to Dorothy, or, to make everyone feel at home, use Dot to break the ice?*

A strange sound emitted from my head. It wasn't loud but it might just as well have come from a bullhorn. "Boss, I'd like you to meet Dort." Then, still air filled the room. I wanted desperately to reach out and pull Dorothy's eyebrows down. Paralyzed, Andrew saved me with his great roar of laughter. He gave a wink and provided damage control. He provided a road for salvation and said, "John, heard you had a long day last night. Must be rough?"

My peripheral vision saw Dorothy's brow normal. I put on my best Garfield cat look. "Only two hours sleep!" I said. My throat was parched, and I said next, "Unh, un, ha!"

I knew I was okay when Dorothy said, rushing from her fridge, "Boy, ah think you need some of my homemade lemonade."

I sensed even Boss was nodding loud approval. My PR must have been working because eighteen years later I was able to gain a full-time position. Conservation Officer 1985 was official, but to me I was a warden much longer than that. I was able to backpack my prior years. In the end, I was credited with 29 years. Success can come early or it can come late. Self worth and values are decided when you live and work. Anything else is bonus! In the end, you praise life and circumstance for all opportunities.

Eveline and I forged great friendships. This couple were endearing friends longer than my career. I'm happy that I never had to imitate Garfield again, but then when I think back, no one had concerns about identify theft. Time changes all things. Now, a world of computers and credit cards that are meant to enhance our lives present new threats. They may save us some time, but come with the need for financial paranoia or else your identity can metamorphosis into someone else's identity and wealth.

More and more we become enslaved by merchants of convenience. Obviously merchants have great skills in selling the masses their ideas, which causes another wonder: Did anyone ever really own his identity? Junk mail companies make me suspicious but also grateful that more than 60% of my life had freedom. Not bad in my estimation. I grew up in a time when credit was something to be ashamed of. I love phone calls that warn me "Your credit is currently okay." I thank them profusely for knowing and caring so much.

I don't hang up as an ingrate. I simply accept such calls are likely Big Brother worrying about my wellbeing. Whoever coined the phrase Knowledge Is Power is an SOB, especially when knowledge is being distributed so insidiously.

You can say what you want when you retire. That's my new PR policy. Buzz off!

Ghost Whispers – La Verendrye Park

Situated along the US-Canada border is an area established as La Verendrye Park, honouring the French explorer and voyageurs of the past. Tom Logan and I decided we should do some joint patrol along this historic canoe route in search of fish and game violations. We found more than a few and with our findings came some unusual events. If someone should ask "Who are these men?", we fancied that some ghost whisperers would answer:
Shhh... they are known as the "La Verendrye Brothers"!

They travel the woods with big black books, they seem to come from nowhere, hand out tickets and disappear.

Frank Nummikoski volunteered to haul canoe gear and us to our embarkment area, North Lake, after we stashed our patrol truck in a remote area, miles away, from where we planned our eventual return. I knew as soon as we loaded the canoe Tom travelled first class. He was not a bologna sandwich traveler. As in previous trips we had taken, he brought everything. His fresh garden veggies, fruit, stove, and air mattress. In my view, enough to survive an eternity. Since I usually patrolled alone, although sometimes accompanied by my adopted American forest service dog Gypsy, I travelled as light as possible. There would be no room for Gypsy on this trip.

I was grateful for calm water as we started our journey down the long North Lake, with high bluffs, and on into Rose Lake. When we reached Gunflint Lake we got busy. Anglers with no licenses, anglers with too many lines, nothing unusual or unexpected. Sometimes criss-crossing, sometimes even backtracking our load was near equal. After several days our food supply was lighter but the weight of seized equipment compensated. By the fourth day we decided to head on to our waiting truck. We decided to check out a portage near small noisy rapids. The devil is in the detail of what we saw so it is illustrated modestly. The situation was serious and we had no means to obtain backup!

We found a poor young couple. We knew they were poor because they had hardly any clothes. Indications were that they were cold because they were embracing. They seemed delirious because they ignored all our attempts to get their attention by throwing rocks into the water near them. We had come too far to ignore the sight of fishing rods nearby. Our clomping boots and loud whistling finally got their attention. A blanket and towel provided them some modesty. We approached, ensuring a large rock was between us.

To break the ice, sometimes words just tumble out, we asked "Sir, are you having any bear problems?" I never saw such a strange quizzical look as he stared at me over the rock. He provided a fishing license for our inspection and we parted.

We left in grim silence, understanding the perils of enforcement. You never know what you'll encounter in the woods. Sometimes it takes a while to get over the shock, but you do, as the next portage awaits.

Whitefish Landing- The Day I Stopped Doubting Thomas

Canadian conservation officers are also peace officers, meaning they have a duty to perform beyond their mandate. It hurts me even to this day that I witnessed an officer ignore his duty. It wasn't the officer's hands in the air that was inexcusable. He was tying a canoe high up on the rack of his truck. I was tossing him rope and loading gear in the truck. I couldn't act on what I could not see. It would not have held up in court and would have lacked credibility. I would have been clobbered in court by some lawyer yelling, "Your Honor, it's all hearsay." The courts would be tied up all day.

I could say in court that I saw fellow officer Tom Logan's eyes bug out and stare at me with a frown on his face. It was nearly dark at Whitefish Landing. He said something

about flashing at him. I could not render what I thought beyond what I had witnessed. Tom was the essential main witness of whatever was going on behind my back. I wondered if we were in mortal danger. I watched him turn his head away. He did nothing. We jumped in the truck and sped away.

Tom said, "Okay, all right, enough. I'll explain what I saw and why I didn't act. I know you're disappointed in me. It's hard for me to say it. What I saw was wrong, certainly illegal. To be honest, I just didn't know how to deal with it in a highly charged moment." Tom blurted out what every officer dreads to hear. "Don't tell my wife. I panicked and chickened out."

I began to gain empathy for him. I recalled how he looked past me, almost in a hypnotic state, sort of a shell-shocked look. I had heard of such things as breaking points. Law enforcement is not an easy game. A few days rest can do wonders.

Tom was driving with hours and miles to go in the night. I decided not to ask questions, and instead I decided to whistle a happy tune, Passing shadows in the night, with his eye on the steering wheel in case the moon shone through the windshield, he concentrated on his driving. As we climbed Sandstone Hill, Tom was smiling. He said, "I think I can talk about it now. Remember how crowded the campground was at Whitefish?"

"Yeah," I said.

"Everyone partying?" said Tom.

"Yes."

"Well, I happened to look out while tying up the canoe," he said, voice rising. "I didn't say something's *flashing*. You need a hearing aid. I said someone *flashed* me." He looked over at me. "No, there was no mosquito in my eye," he said, and continued. "I observed the subject carefully as she pulled her tank top up. I realized her crime was omission, not deliberate, so I simply used officer discretion."

Now I appeared in shock. I had failed to offer assistance. You can call me chicken all you want. I never doubted Thomas again. It seemed the lady had tugged too hard at her halter top. At last the truth came out.

The Subpoena

Deep in the forest it was time for some surveillance, the wildlife needed protection. T.C. chose a position on the top of a knoll and hunched down about as low as a man could get. It was a deliberate tactic chosen so that he could increase his speed and add an element of surprise in response to an infraction. As he waited for his quarry he wondered, would it be hunters or poachers? He knew from both his Police College training and practical experience that it would more likely be hunters, yet he waited; patient, prepared and vigilant. He maintained his attack mode position, it was the perfect set up. As he waited patiently, he heard a door slam, then voices from down below. Shots were fired. He felt many sharp stings on his legs and saw small pellets rolling down his pant legs. He let a war whoop and said "Stop Shooting!" In broken English one of the men replied "We so sorry. We don't mean to shoot you". "Officer we no break the law, we have license." Ted grudgingly realized that the hunters met all the legal requirements. They were not being careless, they held valid licenses, they had offered assistance, there was not much Ted could do. He decided it was time to head home, he needed to lick his wounds.

Soon the story reached the courthouse. An unknown officer reported to the Justice of the Peace that Ted had been struck in the pant leg by bird shot. The JP said "I don't want to hear this second hand; I want that man to come in and tell me what happened. I'm going to issue him a subpoena".

Not long afterward, Ted checked his mail and thought "what's this?" He racked his brains thinking I haven't been speeding nor doing anything illegal, what could this be for? He read: T. Chisholm is to appear in court on the date indicated and answer to the judge personally to the following grievous charges. To wit: Did by clucking and cooing like a partridge cause certain hunters of foreign origin to incite and excite them to shoot partridge.

T.C. was left to wonder all his days – who told the judge about the story. The mystery remains.

Skull Gull Duggery

"Nesting gulls are disturbing people," Supervisor BJ Wall advised.

Attending business in downtown Thunder Bay, Officer Willy, who was dressed for a trip to Toronto, had an hour to spare before his flight. Complaints were non-stop, as the gulls were causing issues. Officer Willy and I were selected to answer the calls.

Coordinator of Wildlife, Berny advised, "Hold a shovel over your head. They strike the highest point when they attack."

For a while the battle went well. "Clang! Clang!" The shovel sounded like a dead bell. The gulls however brought reinforcement. One was unorthodox. He whopped Willy on top of his head, lacerating his skull. Time was running out. He needed to get to the airport. There was no time for first aid He dabbed the blood on his head with a Kleenex. Maybe the airport had an aspirin?

I told him to ask the stewardess for an aspirin once he was up high. "And when she asks what happened to your head, tell her you just got hit in the head by a seagull. I'm sure you'll get a reaction." The stewardess was obviously confused. There were no apparent holes in the airplane.

Back in the office, I relayed the events to Berny. An accident report was to be expected. "Next time you go on this type of call make sure you take a shovel, and wear a hard hat or skidoo helmet!" Berny exclaimed.

I thought, "Maybe complete hockey gear might be a better option?"

As I drove home to my station on Northern Lights Lake, I wondered about how Willy's flight went.

Holy Crow

Conservation Officers who live in high moose density areas, aside from developing cat-like chameleon eyes, often drive in sunrise, sunset conditions, times when wildlife collisions are more likely to occur. In collisions between moose and 18 wheeler trucks, neither party are undamaged, but with smaller vehicles the odds shift in favor of the moose. Moose are as big as they are hard to see, especially at night. Warning signs were increased in size to emphasize the danger. Officers stationed in such areas were called on to attend to accidents any hour, night or day. Enforcement vehicles were equipped with special winches, extra heavy grills, even extra lights were retrofitted to help the situation.

Today I had to travel from Upsula to attend court at 9 am in Thunder Bay. Driving into the morning sunrise along the Trans-Canada highway I waited for one of the strategically placed passing lanes to get around a large pulp truck. As I was pulling past the rig I noticed some low flying crows pass by. I was thinking that I was glad it was not a moose. I was making good time. I would have time to stop at the Ministry of Natural Resources Fish and Wildlife office located at mini Queens Park before heading to court.

I had barely parked the truck when I noticed one of the timber guys fast approaching. He asked "Did you do your circle check this morning before starting out?"

"Yes I did. Why?"

Smiling, he said he had never seen anything like it. "You guys really know how to promote wildlife".

"What do you mean?" I asked.

Smart as a whip he nodded toward the front of the truck and said "I think you better circle check your vehicle again".

I was thinking "Holy Crow" when I got out and had a look at the front of my truck. I was stunned by the sight of a crow caught beneath my front grill with wings spread larger than an eagle. The image grew larger as I envisioned all the traffic I had passed on my way in to the city. The large crow dangled there and was never more hastily removed than on that day. I'm sure it never felt a thing.

I was actually surprised that the timber guy had managed to keep such a straight face when talking to me. I didn't want to ask him to keep this a secret. I simply thanked him. Pushing the envelope could have had me eating crow for a long time.

The smiles at the office seemed genuine as opposed to knowing. Everyone said goodbye, have a safe drive home and watch for moose on your way to Upsala.

Vive, Quebec! Libre!

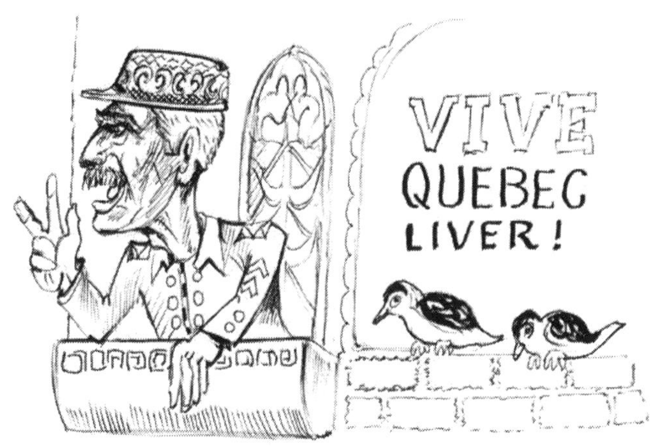

When I first arrived at Saganaga Lake, Canada was in political duress and upheaval over remarks made to Quebecers. A reporter mistakenly thought that a visiting president was inciting people in Quebec to separate from the rest of Canada. Charles de Gauile, liberator of France, was said to have uttered the words in French, "Vive, Quebec!" and "Vive, Quebec! Libre!' which means, loosely translated, "Free yourselves! Grab your yoke of independence. Secede from Canada!"

I happen to know what Charles de Gauile said and meant that fateful day. His remarks were taken out of context. Charles de Gauile really said," Liver, Quebec! Liver!" and "Merci à vous, and onions, too!"

Some reporters seek sensationalism.

Saganaga Lake, aside from its endless beauty, is no stranger to celebrities. NHL hockey players visited to fish, Grizzly Adam types did shoots with Kodiak bears for Hams Breweries commercials, and so on. One could get tidbits at the docks where people exchanged news on the lake. As a young deputy, I was sometimes agape with such. Once I overheard a discussion between a Customs Officer and a tall well-regarded man whose name I learned was Judge Hachey. Seeing his gesturing and hearing the name Charles set my heart thumping. Over the drone of the outboard motors and wind I heard, "Officer, Charles is at my place and I definitely want him out!"

Seeing me, the customs officer said, "Maybe the new deputy can assist you."

At last I thought, a chance to meet and have rapport with a well-respected judge who had a cabin on the Canadian side of Lake Meronash.

We shook hands and he began a tale of intrigue. "I have two young and sensitive daughters," he said. "This lake is their second home. They've spent half of their lives here." He continued. "I also have an unwanted house guest that they encouraged to stay."

He had my attention.

"He makes a mess all over the place," he said. I don't know where he's from, the US or Canada. His name is Charles."

He peered at me closely. "You will handle this with sensitivity but firmness?"

"Yes," I said. "I will."

We devised a plan.

"I'll pay you a surprise visit," I said. "As soon as you all gather for supper the issue will be handled with utmost discretion. My source will not be revealed

One Last Time
where is Charles?

for fear of any future retaliation." The judge was satisfied.

"I hope you understand," I said. "I'll be dealing with Charles. It could get messy. There could be tears in the aftermath."

Later that evening, buttons polished, I played good guy/bad guy in front of two astonished girls.

"Give him up, girls," I said. "I know you're hiding him."

Judy, the eldest girl, piped up. "Are you saying Charles de Gull has to go back to Seagull Island for life?"

"Yes, for life," I said.

Debby, the younger daughter, nodded sadly. "For life. Otherwise Daddy says we have to go!"

After some hesitation the dam broke. Slowly, one of the girls edged towards the bedroom door, opened it and Charles was revealed. This story is stretched a bit, but it's otherwise true. Every time I see a gull I wonder . . . Is it Charles?

The Glory Games Of Minnesota

On a beach in northwest Minnesota, a small island contains the remains of a wildlife officer competition; know as the Glory Games. Back then, officers from both sides of the border competed in a rappelling event. Gone are the footsteps washed away in the passage of time that brought glory or the sadness of defeat. What does remain is the depression of a man. An officer known as Shebandowan Red, from Ontario, Canada, left his mark in the sand, while achieving victory against all odds. A crater exists on a beach at Hiedy's Hideaway; an island in the border waters canoe area. It was not caused by an asteroid. It's very configuration bears only the resemblance of Shebandowan Red.

In the late eighties, USA officer Al watched as officers gathered from both sides of the border; enticed to the rappelling event. Each man stood high on a cliff. All on the brink of glory at Hiedy's Hideaway. Every man stood poised at the ready, knowing not who would win the event. For all the endless hours of practice had reached the moment of truth.

Officer Al surveyed the event through his binoculars. Tension was great, but he had reasons to have confidence, as his oculars spotted the frame of big Ollie Gunderson. He exuded confidence. Al felt great; his man Ollie had won last year's event; not only won but had shattered every record with ease. He observed Gunderson convulsing with laughter, while looking at his opponents. All were tethering safety lines to trees. Suddenly his binoculars began to shake. A lump was in his throat. Immediately to Gunderson's left stood Shebandowan Red, from Ontario, Canada. "What...What's this?"

Red's tying his safety line to a tiny evergreen sprout." Al watched as the starter pistol was held high. One of his officers blared through a loud speaker, "Ladies and Gentlemen, welcome to Minnesota's Glory Games! Please remember, whoever gets down to the bottom fastest wins." Al set his stopwatch as tension was building. Gunderson was flexing his knees. Red seemed perky standing on the precipice. The starter pistol went up, then down and the tension became unbearable after three false starts. The cause was a distant haul truck labouring in the hills of Minnesota. It was backfiring under a heavy load. Suddenly, the loud unmistakable sound of a bang split the still air and reverberated in echoes around the lake. Al's eyes were near tears as he spotted a silhouette of dread. Arcing through the air was the unmistakable form of Red. He had back somersaulted down the face of the cliff, trailed by a tether line and a sprig of evergreen. Al heard a wailing yodel from the canyon floor. He knew the games were over before they had hardly begun. Red had shattered Gunderson's old record. Trees on the way down had broken his fall but Red still left a great crater on the beach below. Red stood up, unscathed. The crowd surged forward. Even Gunderson wanted his autograph. Al felt there was only one thing left to do; shake the hand of the man who had won the Glory Games.

I watched proudly as my fellow officer climbed the podium to receive his awards. I confess I was proud and envious. He received a bouquet of flowers from a beautiful young lady. Minnesota's Department of Natural Resources presented Red with two vacations. One being a cruise off the coast of Italy, on the Costa Concordia, and if that didn't work, he could enjoy a one way trip to Juarez, Mexico. The *true keepsake prize was "The Glory Stone", which now rests on Ted's front porch. Wildlife officers believe in great sportsmanship.*

A few weeks later, I encountered Shebandowan Red. He was packing his suitcases. "You lucky dog," I said. "Yeah, not bad, I guess I earned it." I asked, "To what do you attribute your success?" "Two things J.B., research and my mantra." "What mantra?" I asked. He explained, "My belief system inspires me to do super things. For example, Captain Marvel used SHAZAM, and the Lone Ranger liked HIGH OH SILVER AWAY! At the games I heard the loudspeaker say, "Whoever gets to the bottom first, that sounded like a good mantra. I use those magic words on a daily basis, when I patrol or investigate wildlife violations. It spurs me into action! I like getting to the bottom of things." "Wow! How did you apply research toward winning the rappelling event?" Red replied, "Well the rules were clear. I knew I had to use a safety line, or I could have been even faster. The lines had to be attached to a tree. So I dreamed up a hair trigger advantage. My safety line was secured to a sprig of evergreen, because I knew a sapling was a tree." "Man, Red you're a genius! You factored in a quick start advantage, the sprig went with you!" "Yessir!" "You knew that big a tree would momentarily slow you down." "You got it J.B."

Before we said, "Hasta La Vista," Red said, "Gotta to go! Sand beaches, coconuts, warm breezes, tequila, and Muchachas are waiting for me. I'll send you a postcard."

As we parted, I realized that success is not just plain old luck. It's something deeper than that. Perhaps it lies in the spirits of all men. Whatever can be said, Shebandowan Red will forever be remembered, for the indelible depression he made in the sands of Hiedy's Hideaway. He truly had made an impact on all who had attended Minnesota's Glory Games. Shebandowan Red is undeniably an asteroid of a man. He earned what he got. A courageous man can never be forgotten.

Personally, I will never forget his fantastic feat, as he yodelled down the canyon to obtain victory. Many men spend lifetimes to achieve success. Red did it in 3.5 seconds.

A Sea Gull Yelled

When I first started as a Conservation Officer I learned the hazards of the job. This particular day I headed north of Graham on a maze of log haul roads in my blue unmarked pickup truck to meet Steve and TC. It was the day before moose season opened. A large number of hunters were already in the area, setting up camp. Unarmed, my role would be to scout the area and report any suspicious activity or early hunting by radio to TC and Steve who had regular patrol trucks hidden nearby. This area was unfamiliar to me so I had to rely on maps and radio directed guidance from the others. The radio crackled at regular intervals; I heard J.B., go north to kilometer 44, watch for a rusty barrel and a road on the right. Follow it east for about 9 kilometers. Take care on the bridge, walk over it, once there take the left fork in the road. We heard there is activity in the area. Steve and I will catch up. Roger, confirm that. I'm on my way.

The area looked like a moonscape, but was really the remains of a slash cut logging operation. With a map and the instructions I was given, I found the bridge. I stopped the truck and crossed the bridge cautiously, on foot as instructed. My eye caught the movement of blaze orange, a man with a rifle. He ignored my call "Conservation Officers", and instead he turned his back to me and headed away with a swift walk. It was time to catch up! The man with the hood had some explaining to do, considering he was carrying a rifle before hunting season opened. Just as I finally caught up and yelled "Halt!" he turned to head off the road and into a moose maple thicket. My hands were reaching for the blaze orange jacket when he suddenly turned and said "Not bad JB, but your Halt! Stop!" sounds like a high pitched sea gull!

"Where's Steve?" I asked, panting as we made our way back to the bridge, laughing. Ted mimicked high pitched Halt sounds. "Over there, Over there" voice rising.

It was then that I heard my little blue truck start up and speed away, heading over the hill out of sight. As I hiked down the road hoping to find my truck again I realized T.C. and Steve were providing me with some on the job training, as I had yet to attend the Aylmer Ontario Police College. Up over a hill, about half a mile away, there was Steve, sitting in his truck grinning at me.

I was greeted with sea gull mimics the rest of the fall, winter, and summer after that. The season resulted in successful apprehensions but Steve and TC never let me forget that I'd been had.

Sagantics

This Beaver was mischievously dropping mud bombs on a confused muskrat.

Neighbours

In any remote community, where stores are hours away, neighbours come to rely on one another. Irv and Art were two such neighbours on Saganaga Lake. They had been fellow lake residents long enough to know how to get under one another's skin as well.

As winter inevitably turns to spring, Irv was preparing for the change of season by working on his outboard motor. He knew the importance of maintaining his equipment. One night he had disassembled his motor on the kitchen floor. He realized he needed some lower unit parts. Irv knew Art would be listening to his favorite baseball game and would probably be irritated to be interrupted. In Irv's mind, it would be the perfect time to call Lonewolf on the CB radio.

"How's the game going? What period are the Vikings in?" Irv asked.

"You don't know a thing about baseball!" Art roared. "What do you want?"

"I need lower end parts for a 20 hp Evinrude."

"Okay, but not tonight. I'll send some over in the morning. Use what you need and send back what you don't use" was Art's reply.

The next morning Irv looked out the back door. He saw a pile of green pine boughs that were placed to hide the late winter yellow snow and a huge jar marked lower end parts. Close scrutiny revealed pickled crow's feet. Art, true to his *word had delivered lower unit parts!*

This was certainly not an unusual exchange between these two. Winters on the trap line, being a creature of habit, Art liked to have an afternoon nap on most days. Irv was aware of this habit and decided to take advantage of it one afternoon in a blizzard. Art bolted upright from his daily slumber to find himself surrounded by a pack of yowling, barking huskies. He wondered is this a dream or a nightmare, then he saw pesky Irv's nose on the window pane. Irv had decided to let his dog team serve as an alarm clock. Irv watched the fun just to see what would happen.

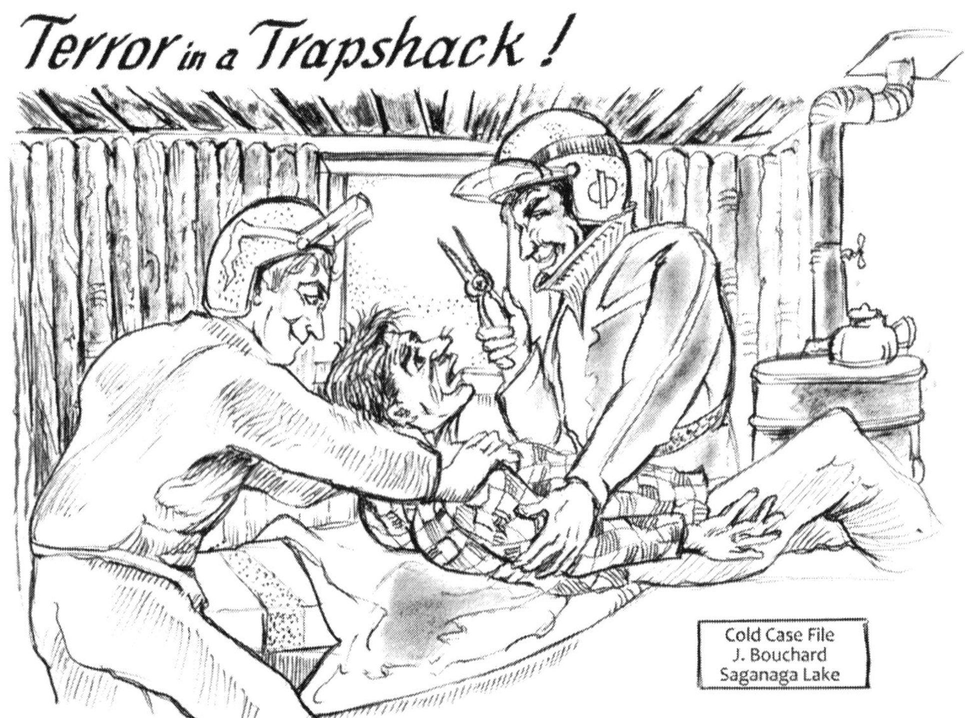

I have always marvelled over rock solid intuition. The Scandia Bay group knew little, yet it was they who offered pliers! Nordic mysticism with innocence? Curiously I had never mentioned which evidence was being sought.

From the cold case files at Government Island, Saganaga Lake, a tale of terror remains unsolved. Certain characters believed to be from Grand Marais had hidden in the dark limits of a low ceiling pole structured trap-shack at Saganagons Lake, Ontario. The trapper Irv, returning from a long cold winters run, didn't have a chance for his eyes to adjust as he fumbled for his matches to light his propane light. Some time earlier the villains had poured in like panthers in the dim light. Irv saw shadows from in front and behind, at some point he was held down and thought he saw a pair of long nosed pliers descending. The impact of being hurled onto the bed loosened the pepper which he had sprinkled on the bed to keep mice away. It was in his eyes. He fought the urge to sneeze as a hideous laugh followed pliers to his face. He was held in a viselike grip. A calmness of inevitable unknown invaded his thoughts. He had survived the war as a pilot/navigator in Lancaster Bombers! Proof: his old uniform hung on his trap-shack wall. Be still he thought, knowing well that his wallet would be of no gain. He didn't carry cash on the trap line. He knew that no matter whatever torture was intended there would be no gain! He braced and stiffened his resolve thinking, "My endorphins will see me through." He closed his eyes and thought about life's true rewards, Ritz crackers and tea.

Another hideous laugh . . .cold steel resting on his nose. "Be still," he thought. Warnings came. "We wanted to do this for a long time," one of the intruders said. "Before what?", thought Irv. A small burning sensation came. He knew only that a part of his total being was changed somehow forever. Two unique long hairs which protruded like tentacles from the top of his nose had been plucked to be lost forever. Then came a flash of light, the thunder of a slammed door, a quick "Rup-rup" and the two dark figures entered the woods and vanished on high powered snow machines. Gone were the two bandits.

Reports came within days via moccasin telegraph. As the news spread, I knew that I had to prevent fear and panic amongst the lake inhabitants. Most folks put on a brave front by laughing. Investigation, however extensive, was exhausted at Scandia Bay with cold tracks. The perpetrators tracks disappeared amongst multiple other tracks in an area of high activity and revelry. I talked to many of the cabin owners at Scandia Bay with no luck.

I tried a phone in one of the toilets, only to reach another outhouse. Service was only local and had no connection to the US authorities along the Gunflint Trail. I had cooperation though. Upon arrival, I'm not certain if consternation was apparent on my face. Whatever it was, it was quickly allayed by Doc Sandy, Karl, Olaf and Leif, who explained that the presentation of tools was a Scandinavian custom when welcoming strangers. Nothing more than a ritual... The presentation of the pliers was a symbolic gesture of the highest honor. Meaning: we will do anything to help you. The crowd at Scandia Bay willingly allowed inspection of all pliers. They were anxious to prove that their group was totally innocent. Some were visibly opinionated, saying that if they heard of anything at Grand Marais they would voluntarily send word back. Others concerned would drop a big bucket of ice cream at the trap-shack, to help alleviate hair loss endured by the trapper in such a diabolical manner.

The case remains in the Cold Case files; but it is never to be forgotten. Even now, retired, I wait in hope that someone will come in with the smoking gun pliers... I'll never forget the empathy shown for Irv and my investigation.

Irvinator

The question was: Could we stop the diabolic Irvinator before he struck again?

Strange things were happening at Saganaga Lake· Customs and I decided to talk to neighbours· Finally we got a break· Art Madsen described a man which he referred to as a "pesk"· The man described seemed to fit the profile obtained by the Royal Canadian Mounted Police and the FBI·

"Look for someone with tentacles," he said·

We thought we knew someone · · · Did our perpetrator feel cheated or angry? Who knows?

Irv was regarded like a national treasure· Did he change after vandals plucked two long hairs protruding from the tip of his nose?

Long into the night by a coal oil lamp, citizens lived in fear of what the morning would bring· For Customs and I it was hard to sleep· Someone devious was out to get us· We were under siege and we knew it· We had suspects· One looked particularly diabolical· He had bags under his eyes that suggested he stayed up late at night, long after the moon came out and the last motor boat was heard· We never knew who, or why· But we knew for certain someone was out on the dock in the dark, as the last wake waves slapped the rocky shoreline·

Customs Officer Sam the Man Holford was particularly worried· Having rounded a corner to enter a narrows en route to Pine Island, Sam's boat veered off and lurched to a bobbing stop· With knuckles white and eyes bulging, he saw a

"Your guess is as good as mine"

huge black mine with spikes sticking up all around, directly in line with the path he needed to take through the narrow rock strewn channel. Being a veteran, he recognized it as a type of mine used to sink ships in World War II. Hair up on the back of his neck and sweat pouring into his shoes, his mind said, "Turn back! Go slowly and carefully. Think of your family and kids. Get out and get back to the safety of Government Island." Curiosity overcame fear and Sam allowed his boat to drift ever closer to the mine. Just as he timidly touched the mine, Irv, hiding in the bush nearby and watching, fired off a 12 gauge shotgun. It seemed as though the mine exploded, Sam's confidence that day definitely had. Sam decided that a retreat to the safety of Government Island was in order.

Back at Government Island, we decided to do another profile. Our think tanks decided that whoever the perpetrator was, he had issues with all aspects of authority figures. On Saganaga Lake, such a profile could be anyone!

We did come up with one person of special interest, a man I called Irvine.

Rumours had it that last winter, an officer from Shebandowan , for no particular reason other than a friendly visit, arrived at Irv's door around 10 AM. He pounded on the door, and was surprised when Irv answered and immediately demanded a dollar.

Looking around the deep wilderness setting and quick on his feet, the officer said, "This don't make sense. What do you need a dollar for?"

"The dollar is for waking me up!" Irv replied.

The best Customs and I could do was upgrade Irv from person of special interest to devious suspect. The mine in the channel was a meticulous fake. Even his friend Art Madsen agreed that Irvine could be a "pesk". That's how the law works at Saganaga Lake.

Over the years, other officers agreed that Irv seemed to look suspicious and innocent all at the same time. The most anyone could ever prove was that of all people on Saganaga Lake his light was the last to be turned off at night. I learned that when you solve a case, you destroy a mystery! Unfortunately for Customs and I, what occurs in the summer expires in the winter at Saganaga Lake.

Another incident that got added to the suspect's profile occurred one night as Eve and I were about to leave Irv's. Because Irv lived on an island we were leaving by boat. As I gave the motor the first pull of the starter cord the night lit up. The cowl of the motor turned white hot, with loud popping and sounds of small explosions filling the night mixed with Eve's piercing screams and a cackling from the bush. Upon inspection I discovered that

a series of firecrackers had been tied to a spark plug lead. The spark then ignited the fuse.

Over the years we logged many incidents; a bomb in the channel, honey on the toilet seat, a Carnation milk can welded into a strange configuration to replace a carburetor on a government snowmobile which was abandoned and waiting repair, a fiendish spike with a note, a railroad spike protruding from the Custom's office door . . . The perpetrator had cut the spike, drilled the end, and using a small pin made it appear as if it had been pounded through the door. This wicked fakery almost caused the Customs Officer to have a nervous breakdown. It was never our failure that this mystery remains unsolved. Customs and I never had enough time.

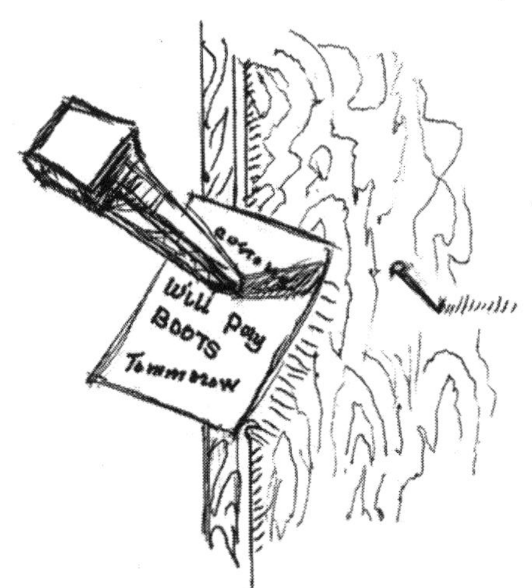

Both stations on Government Island closed down in the 1980s. End of story.

A Taste of His Own Medicine

Irv was known as a prankster on Saganaga. After years of enduring the creative but annoying pranks that Irv pulled for many it was time to get even. A great conspiracy took place. It was well know that Irv was a meticulous welder. Kramer drew up some blueprints for a "rock deflector" that he needed for his polished rock shop in Grand Marais and asked Irv to weld it for him.

Irv did a masterful job, creating the odd angled device out of stainless steel. Days later he delivered the device to the Kramer's and was invited for dinner as a thank you for all his hard work.

Phase two of the operation was planned and put into action. A dinner of fried chicken skin and Ritz crackers was prepared, Irv's favorites. While Irv was enjoying the dinner, under the cover of darkness the Kramer boys snuck past the window with the device and retrofitted it to the bottom of Irv's boat.

As Irv tried to leave late that night, across the lake Irv's voice carried. "I know the way to go home Tempest, but the boat will only go in circles".

Irv was a little sore about the whole thing. When he threatened to get even we asked him how he was going to get even with himself since he was the one who built the device.

Shadows on the Wall

Eveline had a dance that even her shadows could barely emulate. They followed the dazzle of her candles like arcing comets. She danced for Saganaga Lake residents and visitors and no one ever tired of her candle dance. Even people who were world travellers said they had never seen a candle dance before.

Eveline loved to share her Indonesian heritage with the people of Saganaga through dance. The Ojibwa girls on the small Canadian island adored Eveline and gave her star-status. Eveline was a little like them, an island girl who came from Indonesia. Some girls were intrigued by candle dancing; they thought candle dancing was intricate but difficult. They asked Eve if she could show them how to hula.

"We want to learn how to wiggle our hips," the Ojibwa girls said.

"Come tomorrow. I will teach you how to make skirts. Island dancers need hula skirts," Eveline said.

The girls' parents were enthusiastic about Ojibwa Hawaiian dancers.

The Saganaga residents shared in the culture exchanged. In the morning five girls arrived. On cue, Eve lined up the girls.

"You wanted to know how to wiggle your hips so fast?" Eveline asked. "Remember it starts with your feet!"

"Yes," the girls giggled.

Practice had gone well and the girls had skirts.

The next day Hawaiian music resounded over the lake. The last straggling tourist anglers came to receive Customs clearance. They were baffled to see young hula dancers in Canada.

"Ojibwa Hawaiian girls," one local resident piped up proudly.

Three worlds merged on the water: Indonesia, Canada, and Ojibwa. There were now three ways to say thanks.

A year later, another version of the day's events would come by way of Cyril the guide. He was in charge of a group of young canoeists forging their way north from End Of The Trail. They had travelled many miles from their cities and then motored the last 60 miles from Grand Marais on the Gunflint Trail. They came with maps and compasses, bearing north by canoes through a maze of islands; objective Canada. At last in view a red and white flag was

waving. As they drew closer to the big dock something else was swaying. Was it a mirage caused from a hard paddle? The compass read true north, but all of their senses indicated a vision of the South Seas. Cyril continued recanting events from the summer before to his young charges. "There were bodies swaying, hands waving, fingers flutterring... Five young dark haired girls dancing with a dark haired Indonesian. "Who would'a believed it?" he asked. "Sometimes real and confusion go together, and the unbelievable makes things true," explained Cyril. "Tired as we were we raced to the scene, some twenty paddles flashing. No wonder voyageurs travelled Big Saganaga Lake, signed up for years with little pay, ate pemmican, and fought for the Hudson Bay or the North West Trading Company." Unnoticed, the youngsters raised eyebrows. Cyril went on, "You never know what surprises you will find in nature."

By now the tired group were yawning, and with mosquitoes biting, the last embers faded as bedrolls came out for another starlit night.

A youth in the group, yawning, was heard to utter, "Cyril the guide must have run out of ghost stories and wants us to sleep. Tonight he's telling us real whoppers!"

"Yup, hard to believe!"

Merci beaucoup, trimakasi, megwich...

Unconfirmed reports have it that Cyril, well known for his gift of gab entered politics.

This Mermaid Said Go

Enforcement is not always easy.

One day Sam the customs man and I were on patrol, we were doing the north shore of Saganaga, changing routine was a good thing. Rounding Windy Point heading west, a flash caught our attention in the dark water between the north shore and Brown's Island. The high cliffs and shadowed shadows turned the blue to ink. It was a lonely spot on the lake, off the beaten path. We nosed the bow of the boat that way and roared the motor toward the Narrows some half mile away. We knew it was no loon skipping along for gradual takeoff, something bigger was in the water, perhaps a moose. Sam had his camera in hand as we slowed on approach. Hugging the shadows we saw a canoe onshore and a lone figure out quite far. Was she in distress splashing along in a dog paddle? Her mouth was open but sound was lost above the motor. No lifejacket as far as we could see. She was pointing, but what did it mean? Inching closer her eyes became wider than bow lights as we drew near at idle speed. We recognized her face. A girl from Grand Marais, well known in the area since her family had a business there. We circled as she seem to breathless and at times incoherent.

"Go, go away! Don't come near! I don't want to be rescued." Her behavior was not the same as when she came to Government Island. Perhaps the cold dark water caused the personality change. "Go! Go away," she repeated. I decided best we retreat. Lurching the Johnson outboard into reverse it stalled. We had to be certain she was okay.

"Can't we take you to shore?"

"No, please, I'm fine the way I am. Just don't come closer." We took the moment of lull looking for clues and determined she was fine. In fact she was competent and also clever. She had the good sense to hang her bikini in a tree branch to prevent disorientation. She had a huge plastic ball to assist flotation if she tired.

We decided she merely wanted solitude, a chance to be at one with nature. She wasn't meaning to be rude and for a moment her spell was broken by us. Sam said, "She really is a friendly cordial person. Yeah, I heard whole family is great. Maybe she thought, we thought, she was incompetent." Well for sure we do know she's no greenhorn. She really has bush knowledge.

"Yes, I'd say she's on the ball. She planned her day carefully, leaving nothing to chance. She left her bikini high enough to be easily spotted if the waves got choppy. Flapping in the wind, she would have no problem returning from where she started. You can't blaze a trail in the water". Sam and I made it back to base with one cylinder on my Johnson outboard. The last question asked: Could she have brought two bikinis? We never got answered.

Sunset Years

Remember, If you look for trouble you'll likely find it. If you don't see problems they don't exist.

Job Hiccups

As a deputy in 1967, enforcement was primarily self taught via a pocket edition of the Game and Fish Act. It was touch and go, officers trying to present an image and not make mistakes and learning legal issues, court processes, and procedures. There were a few rumbles on the way, like explaining to the judge how my dog, Gypsy, ate half of my walleye evidence.

The charge was six over the limit. In court, I only had three and a half pieces of walleyes to show. It appeared as as though an animal chewed it. This evidence might have impaired court credibility, but I suppose the courts could have done some sort of forensics on Gypsy's stomach to remove all doubt. You learn whatever happens, happens, however foolish, however long a career in enforcement will last.

It makes no difference how many poachers are caught. Catching is only half the battle; court is the serious part that makes success or failure possible. Image means you strive at all times to be better than that which you think you are capable. Trust is the highest honor of achievement. Respect cannot be ordered; it has to be earned.

The Fine Line

The fine line between perception and deception becomes ever more blurred, lost in the haze of bigger fires and smoke· Looking back from my perspective, I'm not so sure that all fires are good for forests, and that they're simply nature's way of renewing itself· Red pine is unique along the border of Minnesota and Ontario· This area became one of tourism's high density areas· Thousands of people visit the area each year· Forest values cannot be measured simply as timber losses measured by hectares burned and assessed on a map at some faraway office·

If we don't do anything about the growing number of fires, the red pine will be back only in time for your great, great, great grandchildren to enjoy· Mark my words, we will fight these bigger fires from the land, the sky and the water· Are we ready? We don't need manned patrols with pumps as before, and if fires become bigger, we will build bigger bombers· The wind proves to be the problem, but who knows when we might see another DaVinci who might one day harnass the wind to fight really big fires· I envision DaVinci designing large portable jet-driven wind machines, powerful enough to blow fire back on to itself, equipped with optional water cannons· This design could also retrofit to flat cars or trucks, forming a train on any terrain· Additionally, during slack times these whirling devices might also blow smog away from cities· In closing, I cannot resist saying, that the answer my friend to

DaVinci Smiles

putting out large fires, is blowing in the wind.

Personally, I think field officers on the ground or in the water with fire pumps, in high value areas were a good proactive measure. Many fires were nipped in the bud. Careless campers were often given the option to return and douse their fires, while others received fines. On a daily basis, patrol officers once carried a terry pump and fire hose, and at times used innovative measures.

Here's one example from many experiences: "Boys, fires burn deep in this country. Pine needles, dry humus, and twigs are similar to a mattress fire. They can come up to haunt you. Dump the water from your canoe directly onto the fire. All together now, tip your load, another load of water should do it. Fill your canoe only with as much as you can comfortably carry."

I believe the old ways worked. They allowed a proactive approach, people dealing with people. Today there is less pulse, therefore we rely more on reaction. I sense that smaller fires will be bigger in the future, and while the closure of ranger stations and Customs may have been cost effective, did anyone factor in loss at the grassroot level? If fire is only measured in hectares, more than red pine will be lost!

Words can be the tools of the trade. The detective who was speaking at the endorsement seminar was admonishing, "Flies are attracted to honey, not vinegar." Centralization was a fact. Outposts were closing; operations and manpower would work from the city. What this transition accomplished was to replace old school strategies (proactive) with new wave (reactive) measures. Chief rangers, generals in the field who had close contact with people and intimate hands-on knowledge regarding areas of responsibility, were eventually retired. They became history. Instead of an advance to wilderness, we saw retreat. As a result, we are less knowledgeable of the lakes, portages or the pulse of night or day, including contacts vital for sound enforcement. Maps provide locations, but intimate knowledge is learned by living in an area. Violations are reasonably predictable when officers are established as part of the landscape. Learned skills include night and day navigational abilities, knowledge of rocks in the lakes, and hidden trails, all essential to good enforcement and safety rescue. These things are never found in books.

For me, investigation became an alternative response, but the best response to violations is finding a violator committing an offense. The courts value what an officer says much more than what he thinks. Investigations include witness support statements and at times confessions due to evidence found. Connecting is direct, the shortest route to conviction.

Investigations are usually right after the fact, depending how long fruit can wither on the vine. When troops are withdrawn from the battlefield, it's hard to imagine any vision of victory for wildlife. It was easy to see that much more reliance on investigations would follow.

Old Days - Found Committing (Pro-Active)

1234

The era of reactive measure was upon us. The new warden will be called upon to be a super cop, investigating wildlife incidents miles in every direction away from his office space in the city. For example: 8 AM: load truck, gas, boat, ATV, equipment; 10 AM: commence drive; 12 noon: reach location; 1PM: look for evidence and try to make it back to town by 5 PM...

Today's Enforcement (Reactive)

Today, medical benefits are better. In yesteryear, the rewards of the job were greater. In the old days, we were proactive.

Man: "Officer, I underwent therapy on both shoulders."

Officer: "Oh I see. All the extra lines are doctor ordered. Go tell it to the judge!"

Today's reinforcement:

Officer: "Sir, did you say you were out on the lake with all these lines baited at the same time? Would you care to explain?"

Man: "Sure Officer. No problem. Each line was used one at a time. Never were lines used together in the water. I have luck—I use a different rod for every cast. Never once would I have more than one line in the water!"

It could be said that the officer missed the boat on this one. Mere suspicion is not enough. One rule learned early in all situations, was that volatile or cooperative, one had to listen, even if the pot was boiling. Turning the heat down, not up, usually worked best. Venting is reaction. Often fear mixed with anger subsides; patience can even lead to cooperation. Some things only fan the flames of anger. The word **liar** was not in my vocabulary when dealing with suspects. Firm but fair is part of the job.

It works or likely I wouldn't be here!

Strange Encounter at Muskox Bay

The snow was deep in the winter of 1985. Russ and Bob waited up the steep hill in a 4X4 truck. Eve and I had a bucketful of suitcases loaded in "Murgatroid", my yellow crawler tractor. Once up the hill, we would not see our home for the next ten years. We were off to the north, Nakina, Ontario. I had no idea what the vast northern region would bring, only that my deputy and trapping days were over. I was now a full-fledged conservation officer. My twenty years recognized that life on the boarder lakes was like a dream... the best years of my life. The problem with any dream is that in time you eventually wake up. Once you wake up you have to compromise, and you do. You leave the familiar and head into the unknown. We didn't know then what the great beyond offered, other than the north was a place of great vastness. As we entered our new home at Nakina, Eve noticed lights in the ceiling and at the flick of a switch we both knew that life in the further north meant that both of us had a lot of adapting to do. Laughing, because previously, for twenty years our propane lights hung from our wall. This land of vastness opened new vistas *for me. As a wildlife officer travel here was less by boat and more by truck, ATV or aircraft. I saw many rivers, as far north as the great Albany, from Ogoki to Fort Hope. I saw aboriginal people walk out of nowhere with moccasins on their feet, tents with boughs to sleep on, homemade children's toys, and in this modern world, to see the past "Still alive?", seemed to me that this was also a voyage. I had maneuvered through the past, to see the present and the past connected.*

Busy as things were ten years passed. Retired, we returned home, to the place where life with lands and forests had all began. Here old memories of times as a deputy floated back, allowing for reminiscence. I recalled the good old days, how the fishing was great, and remembering when I told officers that I had found happiness here. I recall their comments back in 1967. "JB, you have the best area of all!" True, I loved water. My patrol was by boat, nothing could beat that! But the best frost licking feature had to be that I worked alone from the office, and I had trust.

This is not a contest to describe the best place there is in the north-west. I leave it to the reader to decide…because I remain biased. Natural beauty has no bounds.

To the west of the trail portage there is a bay at Northern Light Lake which I call Muskox Bay. A conservation officer may never know what he or she would encounter on any given day. I roared around the lake swerving around rocks. To the shock of my life, a group of girls were in the water, minus all attire. They were like maidens in paradise, laughing and splashing like porpoises. Having blundered into privacy, I struggled to avert my eyes away. They were scrambling up the shore uncovered. Nothing in the Fish and Game Act said I had to check this out. I waved goodbye with prudence foremost on my mind, my curiosity being tested. I swear I only took one glance back, but it was more than I expected. I'm not sure if it was mischief or what it was. The girls were beckoning me to come to their campsite. I managed again to miss the pile of rocks as I approached. They were laughing as only a group of girls can. "Hi officer, is this against the law? Skinny dipping, we mean. Is it okay in Canada?"

I stifled the thought, "Oh, contraire, skinny dipping is the law in Ontario." Instead I said, "It's all right as long as it doesn't offend anyone!" With no more than towels surrounding them, they rounded in a tight circle like happy muskox, I thought.

The girls asked questions about availability of campsites and which routes had less traffic.

They wanted solitude away from power boats and anglers. I understood and gave advice. "Take the south route, via Wantelto Lake. Cross Bay has smooth rocky campsites. You won't find any boats there once you make the short portage around Northern Light Falls."

"Thank you," they said.

"It was a pleasure seeing—I mean meeting—you. Have a good trip."

Then I left. Duty called. I never ever knew what might be encountered around the next corner. Northern Light is an amazing maze of bays and islands, much like a giant jig saw puzzle. In time, I could navigate the puzzle in the dark.

So many youth today will never see or understand a world less contrived than the world they live in. Oh well, progress has the advantage of gadgetry. To each his own, is okay with me.

As in the song, "Life Can be a Dream": " Barroom, barroom, barroom, lalalalalala, barroom."

Muskox Bay does not have official status on a map; by luck I discovered it twenty years ago. In the interest of the public its location is vaguely described in order to avoid boat overcrowding... Because there are so many hazards and strange experiences on the job, I thought it prudent not to tell my wife.

Career Summary

I had an early start on the belief that everything we gain in life is borrowed. My early gunshot accident instilled that notion. Saganaga became my reward for value and reason. To have been able to see the value and live it while young and healthy was a bonus! Blessed is the lead in my head which helped me to see.

There is more to our world and life than what is advertised on TV. For me the notion of freedom was to be the smallest cog in an unnatural man-made system. In nature it's one way to achieve a small measure of actual success. My ambition was not to serve another man's ambition or any assembly line. That's not life; it's capitulation. Watching otters play or fish spawn is much more natural, in nature that's life! You can feel the power of creation. It belongs to no particular denomination.

For me the rewards of life are in memories. In wilderness I found independence, perhaps that alone is the essence of freedom. At what price do you give up convenience? Answer: nothing lasts forever. Do what you will while you can. Health may not wait until retirement. It was not a morbid reflection due to my accident, but more one of resolve with enthusiasm that whatever I did in life would have to have a worthwhile and meaningful aspect. Nature and conservation met the criteria. It was a vocation, a chance to be better than self. The second question is: If life should cease tomorrow, are you doing what you want to do? I had my own motto: No man my master, none my slave. My lobes registered a resounding yes! That enthusiasm remained every time I canoed or patrolled in a boat or by skidoo. My career niche on earth accumulated 29 ½ years. It's one thing how you stumble at the starting gate when young, often a fool's gamble along the track. I suppose luck and trust had a lot to do with reaching the finishing line. Looking back, I know I did my best. For me that's what matters. I can still see golden eyes beneath the Kashabowie River, hear moose crashing towards a call in the fall, and see bears munching green shoots of grass along roads while waiting for fish to spawn in the spring. There's more to life than drugs and video games. Hopefully other kids will discover life at its best. Some youth came to the lake for the right reasons. Others came with synthetics, perhaps to escape a synthetic world.

It would be great to say that my world on two lakes continued to be pristine. In the 70s we were surprised to find youths with drugs on the lakes. Our prism of the world came with some shock. We were making up to eighteen busts a month. These youths sought escape for the wrong reasons, likely a result that back then the war on drugs was waged mostly in the cities. Today my view is less that anyone lost the war on drugs, but more that we gave up. A terrible consequence of losing will is that apathy followed. In the cities, random senseless shootings are common place. Hitler would have given his eye teeth for videos produced today, as a means of molding his four year olds into the master race. While the symbioses between drugs, violence, and guns are recognized, the gun becomes the culprit and cause. In 1995 Bill C-68 was passed. Canada enacted a new law whereby all citizens (except criminals) must register firearms, shotguns and long rifles used by sportsmen, trappers and farmers; hitherto in our history these did not require registration. The effect of legislation was to potentially criminalize non-criminal people should they fail to comply. At enormous cost overruns the public bore the cost. The bickering between political parties never ends. A wonderful red herring issue continues to exist. In droves city dwellers voted in favour, while out-numbered country folks were like chaff in the wind. Such

polarized democracy usually works. All calls for a referendum were denied; to the greater number goes the spoils. City dwellers, beset with violence and drug related crimes fail to understand that the guns of choice most prized by the criminal element continue to be smuggled guns of a clandestine variety; deadly killing types, such as Saturday Night Specials and AK-47s, including the most coveted of all, the Kalashnikov. The obvious question remains: Was registration really a panacea for all that ails us? What happened to the good old laws governing illegal firearms? We Canucks always seem to enjoy a pastoral view. Picture a marvellous sunset with a lot of men in easy repose, sitting on fences appearing to be looking south. One might ask, "Are they sitting on fences watching our American cousins build nuclear detecting devices, beefing up border patrols, building great barriers to thwart illegal border activity; or is it none of the above?" It's all in one's interpretation; perhaps we simply love our sunsets. Is our tactic simply to wait for drugs and guns to arrive and then try to deal with it? As our war on drugs is waged in the cities, can we really win such a war? We would do well to remember the battles of Stalingrad. I see similarities on our streets.

In closing, if the odious seems obvious, I worry that gun registration may well posthumously include trappers, voyageurs and pioneers who built this great land. Guns don't kill people, people do.

To maintain balance with seriousness life needs a sprig of humour if not in the moment, in the aftermath. If a career ends with a lot of memories easy to recall, it can only mean life was lived well. I have a lot of memories with very few regrets and, given similar circumstances, I would do my life all over again the same way although next time I'd start earlier, first and foremost with my wife Eveline, who made all things possible. The best partner a game officer ever has is his partner. It takes a special kind of woman, one who enjoys nature and the wilderness. She is a rare find in modest terms.

About the Author

John Bouchard was born in 1934, in Falcon Bridge, Ontario. From an early age, John displayed artistic ability. As a young child, he drew detailed pictures, displaying talent far beyond his age. As an older child he began to paint pictures which caught the attention of many. In 1957, he attended The Southern Alberta College of Fine Arts, in Calgary, Alberta, where he studied graphic art and design. Upon completion, he worked as a sign designer, creating signs for various businesses. John had always had a penchant for the outdoors. He left his sign design job, pursuing his love for the wilderness. He bought a trap line near Petrie, Ontario. He enjoyed trapping, being his own boss, and working in the wilderness. That summer, he worked for the Department of Lands and Forests as a "tower man" at the Loch Erne fire tower near Shebandowan Lake. In 1967, his work with Lands and Forests led him to a summer job as Ranger at the Cache Bay Quetico Park Ranger Station. During the winter of 1968, John accepted a position with a toy manufacturer in Chanhassen, Minnesota, where he designed stuffed toys. Once again, John was not content with an indoor job. In the spring of 1968, John acquired a seasonal job as Deputy Conservation Officer at Saganaga Lake. During the winters, he trapped in the same area. In 1985, John was promoted to Conservation Officer and was posted in Nakina, Ontario. A few years later, he was transferred to Upsala, Ontario. John retired in 1994 and currently lives in Thunder Bay Ontario.

38203344R00200

Made in the USA
Lexington, KY
27 December 2014